THE ETHIOPIAN
THE LOST PROPHET OF THE BIBLE

WHAT THEY NEVER TOLD YOU ABOUT THE BIBLE

GREATER THAN ABRAHAM
HOLIER THAN MOSES

A MAJOR KEY TO THE THE AFRICAN ORIGINS OF HEBREWISM JUDAISM AND CHRISTIANITY

A&B PUBLISHERS GROUP

1000 ATLANTIC AVENUE

BROOKLYN. NEW YORK

11238

COVER DESIGN: *A & B PUBLISHERS GROUP*
COVER ILLUSTRATION: *CHRIS ACEMANDESE HALL*

Library of Congress Cataloging-in-Publication Data

Cush, Indus Khamit
    Enoch the Ethiopian: Lost prophet of the Bible: greater than Abraham, holier than
Moses / by Indus Khamit Cush
    p. cm.
Includes bibliographical references and index.
ISBN 1-886433-02-X (cloth: alk paper) — ISBN 1-886433-03-8 (pbk.: alk. paper)
1. Enoch (Biblical figure)   2. Blacks inthe Bible. I. Title.

BS580.E6 C87 2000
221.9'2—dc21   00-033135

Published
by

A&B PUBLISHERS GROUP
1000 Atlantic Avenue
Brooklyn, New York,
11238
(718) 783-7808

00 01 02 03 04   6 5 4 3 2 1

Manufactured and Printed in the Canada

ENOCH
THE ETHIOPIAN

THE LOST PROPHET OF THE BIBLE

Greater than Abraham
Holier than Moses

A&B Publishers Group
Brooklyn, New York
11238

Contents

4

INTRODUCTION

THE BIBLE (from the Greek biblia, books) IS FOR ALL CHRISTIANS the most sacred of books, the source of truth, the revelation of God's word. No other book has been so lovingly reproduced. Yet precisely because it is held so sacred, the Bible has been the subject of unending debate.

> The World's Great Religions, Henry R. Luce, ed., New York: Time Inc., 1957, p. 157

The first written languages used for the Bible were the ancient African languages of Egyptian, Gecez, Amharic, Aramaic, Phoenician-Hebrew says Carl C. Nichols in his Short History of the English Bible.

The logical extension is that the Bible must have originated in Africa along with practically everything else such as the human race, the first civilizations, the first religions, the arts, the sciences, and, as one European scholar put it, "even the use of the spoken word." All of which we will document in later chapters in this book.

According to The World's Great Religions:

> The Bible was written during some 1,400 years (1300 B.C. - 100 A.D.). Few of its many authors have been identified. No original manuscripts are known to exist - only copies of copies...

However, in 1952, manuscripts pertaining to Enoch were found among the Dead Sea Scrolls in Jordan at Qumran Cave 4 which added to our knowledge of this Ethiopian. In fact, one of the books discovered is from a larger work called 1 Enoch or Ethiopic Enoch. Since the discovery of the Dead Sea Scrolls, a great deal of controversy has followed because no one has been able to see them for over 40 years, except for a small circle of chosen —so-called white experts, mostly Jews.

One wonders if Enoch's Ethiopian connection was not playing some small role in the overall secrecy and limited access that has plagued the Dead Sea Scrolls manuscripts. There seems to be an ominous cloud hanging over certain religious circles in the world as if some unexpected revelation was about to unfold.

Perhaps those who guard them are painfully aware of the effects the Dead Sea Scrolls will have on the early history of Christianity. Geza Vermes, a Reader in Jewish Studies and Professorial Fellow of Wolfson College at the University of Oxford, asks in his book *The Dead Sea Scrolls*: "Can Qumran then be the parent of Christianity?"

One could also ask: What part does Africa play in this drama of Christian origins? These Scrolls experts certainly know something that the rest of the world does not. That is, the African origins of the Bible had another link to forge on the chain of Truth as to the real beginnings of Christianity and Scripture among the African Race.

How appropriate it is that some of this is found in the very book called Genesis which means "The Beginning" in "In the beginning God created..." (Gen. 1:1).

It is in Genesis that the man whom we call Enoch the Ethiopian is validated by Moses the lawgiver. It is Moses who refers to Enoch as a Patriarch (a head of a family) and Adam's 7th Seed (Gen 5:18). In addition, Enoch's lineage is detailed in Genesis Chapter 5 verses 18-32, and ironically this book written by Moses is the "genesis" of Enoch's mantle of greatness in Biblical history.

Special Note:

1) The word Negro is only used for historical accuracy when quoted. However, we believe the word is pejorative and degrading. Therefore we have substituted in brackets the word [Black] or [African] or [Edenic]. These are the better names that command more respect and self-determination.

2) For greater historical accuracy we have also done the same for the word Jew which is someone of European descent and Hebrew which is someone of African descent, i.e. the word Jew is dated after 538 B.C. and the word [biblical] Hebrew is dated 1665 B.C. to 538 B.C. Furthermore, the term Eden is an English translation for Africa which comes from the word Alkebu-lan. [see Carl C. Nichols lecture series *"The Bible in Africa."*]

3) There are two Enochs in the Bible. The evil one, the son of Cain is not discussed in this book. The line of Cain was destroyed according to the Bible.

CHAPTER I

ENOCH THE ETHIOPIAN, PATRIARCH-PROPHET AND THE STOLEN LEGACY OF THE BIBLE

THE GREATEST REVELATION AND BIBLICAL MYSTERY SINCE THE discovery of the Dead Sea Scrolls is Enoch the Patriarch (Gen. 5:18), the hidden Prophet, the First Ascender and Immortal (Gen. 5: 24).

Enoch the Ethiopian, Patriarch-Prophet is the **FIRST PERFECT HUMAN BEING** in the Bible and the **FIRST IMMORTAL MAN** according to Moses the lawgiver (Gen. 5:18, 22, 24). And yet, he has been kept a virtual secret for over 1000 years.

This prophetic man, an outstanding spiritual leader before the Biblical flood was the Seventh Seed of Adam (Gen. 5:18) from "the godly line of Sethite, the great grandfather of Noah, the father of Methuselah and the son of Jared. Enoch the Ethiopian is the first and greatest Patriarch-Prophet and has been described as the second most powerful man in the Bible.

According to the Bible, he was the FIRST MAN to have "walked with God" (Gen. 5:22, 24), and his great grandson Noah was the second.

The Bible also states that only three men ever ascended, body and soul, into heaven. Again, Enoch was the first, then Elijah and finally Jesus Christ. Enoch, however, is unique in that he was *the first* to have both "walked with God" and to have ascended into heaven without having experienced death.

He has been referred to as "an omniscient sage" and described as having assumed astonishing "superhuman traits" and "superhuman knowledge." Enoch lived so righteously that he did *not* die, but ascended into heaven, body and soul, THE FIRST IMMORTAL

MAN in Biblical history. The first among men to enter paradise (heaven) in an earthly form.

In Genesis (5:24), it is written that "God took him" which has been universally accepted to mean "into heaven." Meaning God took him up body and soul. He did not know death like other mortal men because he never died.

Enoch is the first Immortal Patriarch in the Bible and the first Immortal Prophet.

Enoch the Ethiopian was *greater* than Abraham and *holier* than Moses. Enoch was **THE FIRST** Patriarch and Prophet. Not even Abraham could make this claim.

> The Bible shows that Abraham was not a prophet. "...he did not make predictions about the future or in the name of God publicly call upon anyone to repent, as later prophets did..."

ABC's of the Bible, New York: Reader's Digest Association, Inc., 1991, p. 39

However, Enoch was also a prophet because it is said that he predicted, among other things, Noah's flood and the coming of the "Son of Man."

Moreover, he wrote the story of Creation centuries *before* Moses wrote his story. In fact, Enoch came 400 years before Abraham. Enoch, therefore, becomes the 1st Prophet in the Old Testament. An example of Enoch pre-eminence lies in the fact that Enoch comes 21 generations *before* Abraham. Obviously, Moses comes even later; he was the 50th generation from Adam.

If we compare Enoch to Abraham we will see that he is Adam's 7th Seed while Abraham is only Adam's 28th Seed. This makes Enoch 4 times older by generations than Abraham.

The same Abraham who is hailed as the "Father of the Faithful" by Christians; some know him as the "Father of Nations" and the "pattern of believers." Moreover, there are other Muslims who claimed their faith to be "a revival of the Abrahamic faith and worship". But even Abraham must bow to the greatness of this Ethiopian called Enoch.

Abraham was said to have "walked *before* God" (Gen. 17:1), but Enoch [is] said to have "walked *with* God" (Gen 5:22, 24; Gen. 6:9). In addition, it is recorded that "only two earthly men were made angels: Enoch who became Metatron and Elijah who became Sandalfon."

Furthermore, in another ancient writing it is said that "When Moses was shown Metatron-Enoch, he desired to go down on earth, i.e. to enter earthly life, in order to be able to rise to the height of Metatron-Enoch." *(The Hebrew Book of Enoch).*

In the Christian world, Jesus Christ is believed to be God modeling Himself as man whereas Enoch was a man modeling himself on divine, god-like levels. Thus, Enoch becomes the closest human example to Jesus Christ in Scripture. They both point to examples of what righteous living can do for those who seek to realize the profound gifts of the Creator.

Though Jesus Christ as the Son of God is more significant in the Bible, Enoch is Christ-like in that he conquered both death and sin.

"Ephraem of Syria (fourth century) stresses that Enoch, like Jesus, in conquering sin and death and in regaining paradise in spirit as well as body, is the antipode of Adam."

The Encyclopedia of Religion, Vol. 5, Mircea Eliade, ed., New York: Macmillan Publishing Co., 1987, p. 117

Enoch gains paradise and is elevated through divine knowledge whereas Adam suffered death and lost paradise by attempting to gain divinely forbidden knowledge.

"Enoch is given that heavenly knowledge and the tradition in which he stands, as we shall see, believed that such knowledge conferred angelic status and made one, in effect, like God."

The Lost Prophet, (The Book of Enoch and its influence on Christianity), Margaret Barker, Great Britain: SPCK, 1988, p. 24

Death had no hold over Enoch. According to the *Anchor Dictionary of the Bible* Enoch was "the first to forego death." Therefore, he was the first man to triumph over death. His was the first ascent into heaven without the stain of death on his earthly body.

"In the New Testament, Luke, in tracing Jesus' ancestry, repeats this succession of Jared-Enoch-Methuseleh (Luke 3:37). 'Enoch walked with God. Then he vanished because God took him' (Genesis 5:24). Was he assumed into heaven without dying? Ecclesiastics suggests this: 'No one else has ever been created on earth to equal Enoch, for he was taken up from earth' (Ecclesiasticus 49:14). This is reinforced in the Epistle to the Hebrews: 'It was because of his faith that Enoch was taken up and did not have to experience death; he was not to be found because God had taken him.' " (Hebrews 11:5).

Modern Catholic Dictionary, John A. Hardon, New York: Doubleday & Co., Inc., 1980, p. 188

"Enoch was also said to officiate in paradise at the sanctuary before God. Elsewhere, certain religious laws are said to have originated with Enoch and his books. In some later parts of this literature, Enoch himself becomes a divine figure who dwells in heaven and executes justice...Thus, Enoch combines the functions of prophet, priest, scribe, lawgiver, sage and judge."

The Encyclopedia of Religion, Vol. 5, Mircea Eliade, ed., New York: Macmillan Publishing Co., 1987, p. 117

Enoch is the first to enter paradise in a mortal shell and thus becomes an Immortal in the process. His is the first earthly body to see and experience heavenly paradise according to the Bible.

In addition, Enoch lived a perfect life. Thus he majestically soars above the weaknesses of this world. In fact, only two Biblical figures are reputed to have lived perfectly; Enoch was the first, and Jesus Christ as the Son of God was the other.

Every prophet of God had a flaw in their character except Enoch who was the perfect saint. Enoch was also the first "spotless lamb" because he lived a life without stain or blemish, without a defect in his "godly character" according to the Scripture.

As The Encyclopedia of Religion stated:

"The Wisdom of Solomon (first century BCE) explains that God prematurely terminated Enoch's life on earth so that wickedness would not infect his perfect saintliness." (p. 117)

Like Christ, Enoch lived a "God-focused" life. Thus he becomes "The Chosen One" chosen to be the first to walk the path perfectly and ascend bodily into paradise in "perfect fellowship" with the One Above All, The Most High.

Moses Nahmanides (Moses ben Nahman), for instance, speaks of "those who abandon the affairs of this world and pay no regard to this world at all, as though they were not corporeal beings, but all their intent and purpose is fixed on their creator alone, as in the case of Elijah and Enoch, who lived on forever in body and soul, often having attained communion of their souls with the Great Name." (in Levi 18:4)

The Messianic Idea of Judaism, Gershom Scholem, New York: Schocken Books, 1971, p. 204

The Hebrew Book of Enoch informs us that Enoch was taken from this world because of his perfect righteousness and in his capacity as the perfect witness. Thus it states that:

"Enoch [was] removed from earth qua Perfect Righteous or qua Witness. The occasion of Enoch's translation to heaven was...on account of the sins of contemporary humanity. Enoch [was] being removed...in his character of the only perfect saint of his time...

Hugo Odeberg, ed., New York: KTAV Publishing House, Inc., 1973, p. 80

Enoch is the first "anointed one."

Nowhere in the Bible is the word "anointed" given its fullest human expression as in the life of Enoch. He was the first to consecrate his life in perfect harmony with God. He was set apart in service of the Most High as the "perfect" witness and heavenly scribe.

No patriarch or prophet in the Bible could equal his position as "God's anointed" which is why he is the only one mentioned in the Bible to have both "walked with God" and to be taken straight to Heaven without dying as well as being shown the very "secrets of creation."

A.R.C. Leavey, a former Professor of Christian Theology at the University of Nottingham, states that in the work 2 Enoch "Enoch is taken up into heaven and has revealed to him [the] secrets of the creator and [the] order of the universe..."

The Jewish & Christian World, Cambridge University Press, New York, 1989, p. 163

Furthermore, so high was his heart and spirit that he was God's companion and lived a completely " blameless" life.

The Concise Bible Dictionary provides this brief definition of Enoch bearing witness to his perfect way of living:

A pre-flood patriarch who lived a godly life and was translated to heaven at the age of 365 years (Gen. 5:18-24; Heb. 11:5)

R.K. Harrison, ed., Chicago: Moody Press, 1994, p. 69

In the Apocrypha Wisdom 4:10-14 also treats Enoch as the outstanding example of the righteous man's hope of eternal life.

The Illustrated Bible Dictionary, J.D. Douglas, ed., England: Tyndale House, Publishers, 1982, p. 458.

To which Professor James VanderKam of Notre Dame University added:

[Enoch] "enjoyed angelic company during some of his 365 years."

Enoch and the Growth of An Apocalyptic Tradition, Washington, D.C.: The Catholic Biblical Association of America, 1984, p. 88.

The Winston's Original African Heritage Study Bible Encyclopedia makes a similar reference concerning Enoch:

Sirach praises Enoch in the eulogy of the ancestors as a person who pleased the Lord and was taken up, an example for the conversion of all generations (Sir. 44:16, see 49:14). The epistle to the Hebrews upholds him as an example of faith: "By faith of Enoch was taken away without dying" (Heb. 11:5).

Concordance, James W. Peebles, Tenn.: James C. Winston Publishing Company, Inc., 1996, p. 212.

In intertestamental writings, Ben Sirach includes his name in the list of Hebrew ancestors (Sir. 44:16), adding that Enoch was an "example for the conversion [JB; Gk. 'example of repentance,' so KJV, RSV: Heb. 'understanding,' i.e. of the mysteries of the universe of all generations.']. Similarly, in the Wisdom of Solomon he is portrayed as a righteous man who was 'carried off' so that evil might not warp his understanding nor treachery seduce his soul. (Wis. 4:11)

The Eerdmans Bible Dictionary, Allen C. Meyers ed., 1987, p. 336.

According to the Bible, only two men ever attained the spiritual level of perfection to have warranted the title of the "Spotless Lamb." Enoch was the first, and Jesus Christ, of course, was the second.

Likewise, Enoch possessed perfect knowledge.

"He is the great observer and recorder of all things in heaven and earth, of which God grants him perfect knowledge. The great learner, he is also the great teacher. Enoch the Initiator into the higher mysteries of the faith and the secrets of the universe."

Enoch the Prophet, Hugh Nibley, Salt Lake City, Utah: Deseret Book Company, 1986, p. 21.

Moreover, Enoch was the possessor of perfect wisdom.

Raphel Patai, a visiting professor at the University of Pennsylvania, recorded these words of Metatron (Enoch) who declared that:

"The Holy One, blessed be He, from that time on revealed to me...all the secrets of the perfect wisdom, and all the thoughts of the hearts of the creatures; and all the mysteries of the world, and all the orders of creation are revealed before me as they are revealed before the Creator. And I expected to behold deep secrets and wonderful mysteries."

Gates To The Old City, Detroit: Wayne State University Press, 1981, p. 387

Similarly, The Cambridge History of Judaism, indicates that:

"Ben Sira, writing about 190 B.C.E., bears witness to an analogous tradition about Enoch, calling him 'a sign of knowledge and wisdom' (Jub. 4:17)."

Enoch is also the first perfected human being.

According to the *Smith Bible Dictionary* Enoch is identified as:

"The son of Jared, and father of Methuselah Gen. 5:21 ff; Luke 3:37 (BC 3337 - 3013).

In the Epistle of Jude 14, he is described as 'the seventh from Adam,' and the number is probably noticed as conveying the idea of divine completion and rest, while Enoch was himself a type of perfected humanity.

The phrase 'walked with God' is elsewhere only used of Noah, Gen 6:9; cf. Gen. 17:1 etc., and is to be explained of a prophetic life spent in immediate converse with the spiritual world. Like Elijah he was translated without seeing death." (William Smith, ed., Mass.: Hendrickson Publishers, p. 174)

In a similar vein, Professor Emeritus at the University of Bristol, John Metford depicts Enoch this way:

"the father of 'Methuselah' (Gen 5:21), described as 'the seventh from Adam' (Jude 5:24).

As seven is symbolic of perfection this may imply that he represented a perfect man. Enoch 'walked with God: and he was not; for God took him' (Gen 6:24).

This was understood to mean that he did not die but was taken up to Heaven like Elijah.

Enoch and Elijah are thus regarded as 'the two witnesses' who will appear at the 'End of the World...' (Rev. 11:3).

Dictionary of Christian Legend, London: Thames and Hudson, 1983, p. 94.

Both Latin and Greek fathers of the church hailed Enoch as a historic witness "to the possibility of a resurrection of the body and a true human existence in glory. Rev. 11:3" (*Smith Bible Dictionary*, p. 174).

They saw in his example the blessedness of such a life; and his translation was an evidence of the truth of his prophecy concerning the hereafter, with its award of joy and glory and immortal life to the obedient...

Patriarchs and Prophets, Ellen G. White, California: Pacific Press Publishing Association, 1958, p. 88.

Indeed, Enoch remains the premier figure in Biblical tradition, as we know it, outside of Jesus Christ.

"The notice which invests the figure of Enoch with its peculiar significance is found in 5^{24}. 'Enoch walked with God; and he was not, for God took him.'

The idea here suggested - that because of his perfect fellowship with God this patriarch was 'translated' to heaven without tasting death (cf. Sir $44^{16}49^{16}$, 11^{15}) - appears to have exerted a certain influence on the Old Testament doctrine of immortality (see Ps 49^{14} 73^{24}) - A much fuller tradition presupposed by the remarkable development of the Enoch legend in the Apocalyptic literature, where Enoch appears as a preacher of repentance, a prophet of future events, and the recipient of supernatural knowledge of the secrets of heaven and earth etc."

Dictionary of the Bible, James Hastings ed., New York: Charles Scribner's, & Sons, 1963, p. 260.

Enoch was the original "friend of God."

The Bible points directly to Enoch's perfection in that it says two specific things about him. One is that he 'walked with God' and notice that in the whole Bible only Noah is given this type of "holy familiarity" with God.

For not everyone obviously is accorded that privilege unless under the most unique of circumstances. It is so rare that only two men in the entire Bible are credited with this kind of special relationship with God.

The other biblical reference points to the fact that in order to preserve Enoch's perfection "God took him up into heaven..."

Illustrated Encyclopedia of Bible Facts, J. T. Parker, Merrill C. Tenney, William White, Jr., Nashville: Thomas Nelson Publishers, 1995, p. 33.

The Bible's brief depiction of Enoch mentions no imperfections or weaknesses in him. Therefore the statement that Enoch "walked with God and he was not for God took him," (Gen. 5:22, 24) confirms his perfection and affirms, along with other biblical writings, his "godly character and life."

The author of the book *Personalities Around Jesus* in his other work *Everyone in the Bible*, William P. Barker describes Enoch in these words:

A son of Jared and a descendant of Adam through Seth, this Enoch was the father of Methuseleh, and one of two men in the Old Testament who did not taste death (Elijah was the other) because they were such godly humble men. GENESIS 5; I CHRONICLES 1:3; LUKE 3:37; HEBREWS 11:5; JUDE 14.

Fleming H. Revell Company, Westwood: New Jersey, p. 98.

Enoch was the first to accomplish this level of perfection, something neither Abraham, who threw Hagar and his son Ishmael out into the desert, nor Moses, who sinned by hitting the rock twice, could do.

Because Enoch lived such a perfect life he stands as a precursor of the Messianic figure in Scripture. He is the holiest man in the Bible.

According to the book *Enoch the Prophet*: "..a Catholic writer suggests, Enoch is 'next to God, but not God,'... In 1 Enoch 37:71, 'Enoch has become the eschatological Savior himself, the ideal of the pious community,' officially designated as the 'Son of Man.' "

Hugh Nibley, Salt Lake City, Utah: Deseret Book Company, 1986. p. 39.

The Similitudes offer some of the most interesting material in 1 Enoch for the study of the New Testament, especially the Gospels. The titles "Son of man," "Elect One," and "the Anointed," appear to be used almost interchangeably. Associated

17

with this figure are his people, spoken of as elect ones, holy ones and righteous ones.

Backgrounds of Early Christianity, Everett Ferguson, Grand Rapids, Michigan: William B. Ferdmans Publishing Co., 1987, p. 361.

Having conquered death and sin, Enoch is a logical messianic forerunner of Jesus Christ. In the Christian tradition, this can easily be seen when one considers the characteristic of a messianic figure.

The church fathers exhibit considerable interest in Enoch's transcendence of death as a paradigm for Jesus and the Christian elect.

The Encyclopedia of Religion, Vol. 5, Mircea Eliade, ed., New York: Macmillan Publishing Co., 1987, p. 117.

Enoch is the perfect leader and ruler.

He is the wise and obedient servant, the friend and helper of all, hence the perfect leader and ruler...

Enoch the Prophet, Hugh Nibley, Salt Lake City, Utah: Deseret Book Company, 1986, p. 30

Patriarchs and Prophets states that:

he walked with God three hundred years. During these earlier years Enoch had loved and feared God and had kept His commandments. He was one of the holy line, the preservers of the true faith, the progenitors of the promised seed.

Ellen G. White, California: Pacific Press Publishing Association, 1958, p. 84

Enoch was the first man to enter God's presence in Heaven without death as a former companion, and so he became the first man to achieve true human existence in resurrected glory where the earthly body has not been touched by death.

Nevertheless, many of us have only dim recollections or no recollection at all of Enoch even though he is the most towering Biblical character in history. His flawless credentials and heavenly achievements are recounted by Moses himself.

Here, in the Bible, we have a **LEGENDARY HERO**, almost completely overlooked by everyone. Why? That's the Mystery. Somehow a veritable *Superman* of early Christian history has gone practically unnoticed in the Biblical world.

Some have attempted to steal the Bible from its original source, and to steal by omission its greatest Patriarch, Enoch the Ethiopian. Both are African Legacies from Antiquity when properly understood.

It is unfortunate that some choose to use the Bible as an instrument of mental enslavement instead of liberation.

Take Enoch the Ethiopian as an example. Here is a man who was shown, with God's permission, the secrets of creation.

He was taught all wisdom and knowledge by the Angel of wisdom. In fact, Enoch visited heaven more than once and at various levels.

The International Standard Bible Encyclopedia revealed that:

the Angel of Wisdom at God's command, had instructed him in all wisdom and knowledge (compare ib. xxii, 11, 12 and xxiii.) and had imparted to him all the mysteries of creation, of heaven and earth, of past and future things, and of the world to come (compare ib. xxiv-xxxiii 2).

Grand Rapids, Michigan: William Eerdman Publishing Co., 1982, p. 677

Likewise, the book *Understanding the Bible* by Stephen L. Harris remarked that:

In 2 Enoch we learn of "Enoch's ascension to the tenth heaven, where he beholds the face of God, and is taught all knowledge; his thirty-day return to earth to transmit this wisdom and his permanent return to heaven." (London: Mayfield Publishing Co., 1980, p. 230)

Enoch is the supreme sage.

Enoch appears preeminently as the supreme sage whose wisdom knows no bound and whose messages rest on unfailing divine revelation.

Enoch and the Growth of An Apocalyptic Tradition, Washington, D.C.: The Catholic Biblical Association of America, 1984, p. 177

At the same time, he is known "as the 'Sign of science.' "

The Books of Enoch, Aramaic Fragments of Qumran Cave 4, J. T. Milik, ed., Oxford: Oxford University Press, 1976, p. 11

He was the first man to defeat death and conquer mortality. Enoch was given immortality by God Himself above all others of his time and before, as it is written in the Bible, "and He took him." (Gen. 5:24) He is the greatest biblical pillar in the architecture of patriarchs and prophets.

Enoch, the translated antediluvian patriarch, is the original "Lost Legend of the Bible" who was perfect enough to "walk with God."

Enoch the Ethiopian, the prophetic Patriarch, should stand as the tallest and the most revered figure in the halls of ancient Biblical heroes. Yet, we know so little of him and his matchless heavenly achievements.

Enoch is in "THE BOOK," and it is the Bible that bears witness to his unbelievable greatness. Therefore, let us now begin this journey into the seldom charted yet miraculous world of Enoch the Ethiopian as we trumpet the triumphant return of this little heralded Patriarch-Prophet.

CHAPTER II

THE ATTRIBUTES OF ENOCH THE ETHIOPIAN, PATRIARCH-PROPHET

ENOCH, THE PATRIARCH

ENOCH APPEARS IN THE BIBLE AS A PATRIARCH WHO "WALKED with God" (Gen. 5:22, 24).

Collier's Encyclopedia, P. F. Collier, L.P. NYC., 1995, p. 253

Enoch, the seventh patriarch in the book of Genesis, was the subject of abundant apocrypha literature, especially during the Hellenistic period of Judaism (3rd century BC to 3rd century AD).

New Encyclopedia Brittanica, Vol. 4 Chicago, 1995, p. 506

According to the world renowned writer, Isaac Asimov:

"The descendants of Adam, through Seth, are then listed through eight generations...As a group, these are the antediluvian patriarchs."

Asimov's Guide to the Bible, Vol. 1, Doubleday & Co., Inc., Garden City, NY, p. 36

A patriarch is the head of a tribe and by "antediluvian" is meant "before the Flood."

Professor James VanderKam of Notre Dame University in writing about the work known as *1 Enoch* stated that:

The chapters in this book offer a detailed study of the origins, development, and functions of the earliest Jewish traditions about Enoch, the legendary seventh antediluvian patriarch.

Enoch and the Growth of An Apocalyptic Tradition, Washington, D.C.: The Catholic Biblical Association of America, 1984, p. 1

The Oxford Dictionary of the Christian Church identifies Enoch thusly:

Enoch, Old Testament patriarch...In Jewish tradition many legends became attached to him and in the New Testament his translation is referred to at Heb. 11:5.

F.L. Cross and E.A. Livingstone, eds., New York: The Oxford University Press, 1974, p. 459

Enoch is mentioned in Genesis, in the list of long-lived patriarchal figures connecting Adam and Noah. He is described as the son of Jared and the father of Methuselah (Genesis 5:18,24).

Encyclopedia Americana, Int'l Edition, Vol.10, Danbury, CT.: Grolier Inc., p. 472

Enoch (Henoch) masculine name from the Hebrew meaning consecrated, dedicated, teacher...The seventh from Adam, and the father of Methuselah. Eminent as a patriarch who walked with God. He lived for 365 years then walked away and was seen no more, thus a sun hero was translated without seeing death.

Dictionary of Mythology Folklore and Symbols, Gertrude Jober, The Scarecrow Press, Inc., 1962, p. 512

Funk & Wagnalls describes him this way:

[The] "patriarch who moved in celestial realms, learning astronomical facts and observing punishments and rewards meted out to men and angels."

New Standard Encyclopedia of Universal Knowledge, Vol. X, Funk & Wagnalls Co., 193, p. 491

Enoch, seventh patriarch from creation in Gen. 5:18-24; he was the son of Jared and the father of Methuselah.

Harper's Bible Dictionary, Paul J. Achtemeier, ed., San Francisco: Harper & Row Publishing, 1971, p. 530

ENOCH, THE PROPHET

Describing the many roles attributed to Enoch, Notre Dame University's Professor J. VanderKam writes:

The ancient patriarch wears the mantle of both prophet and wise man as he looks to the day of judgment.

Enoch and the Growth of An Apocalyptic Tradition, James VanderKam, Washington, D.C.: The Catholic Biblical Association of America, 1984, p. 172

According to the Book of Enoch, Enoch was a prophet and was taken up to heaven and shown the mysteries of nature and the Messianic future...

The Universal Jewish Encyclopedia, Vol. 4, Isaac Landman, ed., N.Y., 1941, p. 131

Similarly, the author of *The Lost Prophet* stated that:

Enoch the Prophet is quoted at Jude 14, and the theme of Enoch is taken up in 2 Peter 2.

(The Book of Enoch and its influence on Christianity), Margaret Barker, Great Britain: SPCK, 1988, p. 16

In commenting on the work known as *The Secrets of Enoch* H.P. Blavatsky speaks to "Enoch's Commissioning as a Prophet of Judgment (Chaps. 12-16). In a kind of commentary on chaps. 6-11, this section describes Enoch's ascent to the heavenly throne room as a prophetic commissioning in the tradition of Ezekiel 1-2."

The Secret Doctrine, Vol. 11, London: Anthropogenesis, The Theosophical Publishing Co., 1888, p. 510

By the same token, George W. Nickelburg in his *The Bible Rewritten and Expanded* talks about "Enoch's ascent to heaven (cf. Gen. 5:24), where he is commissioned as a prophet of judgment and a scribe of esoteric traditions about the structure of the universe... (p. 22)

From a similar viewpoint, Lecturer in the History of Christian Thought at the University of Manchester, Professor R.J. Bauckham writes:

In the earlier tradition his scientific wisdom is prominent, acquired on journeys through the heavens with angelic guides and including astronomical, cosmographical and meteorological lore, as well as the solar calendar used at Qumran. He was also God's prophet against the fallen angels. Later tradition (2nd century BC) emphasizes his ethical teaching and especially his apocalyptic revelations of the course of world history down to the last judgment.

The Illustrated Bible Dictionary, J.D. Douglas, ed., England: Tyndale House, Publishers, 1982, p. 458

Collier's Encyclopedia says that in the First Book of Enoch (1 Enoch): "An impressive portion of the book is the Apocalypse of Weeks, in which the history of the world, seen prophetically by Enoch, is divided into ten periods." (P. F. Collier, L.P. NYC, 1995, p. 253)

Another prophetic example is provided by the book *Christianity, A Social and Cultural History* when it mentions that fact that:

One part of the literature (the Similitudes of Enoch) dates from about the time of the birth of Jesus and speaks of "that son of man" who will be God's agent to defeat the powers of evil and to establish the New Age. It was inevitably picked up by the early Christians and linked with the role of Jesus.

H. Kee, E. Hanawalt, C. Lindberg, J. Seban, M. Noll, New York: Macmillan Publishing Co., 1991, p. 116

"It has been stated that Ethiopic Enoch also speaks of the suffering of the Son of Man". (see Sjoberg & Mowinckjel SEA V 1940)

Israelite Religion, Helmer Ringgren trans. E Green, University Press of America, Inc., U.S.A., 1966.

In briefly outlining prophetic parts of Enoch's book, the *Encyclopedia Americana* indicates that:

The first depicts the Flood as a first judgment. The second (85 to 90) outlines the history of the world by eras, until the Messianic Age. (Int'l Edition, Vol. 10, Danbury, CT.: Grolier Inc., p. 473)

In discussing some of the prophetic revelations of Enoch, Professor Shiffman, editor of the planned Oxford Encyclopedia of the Dead Sea Scrolls, asserts that:

The resulting oracle explains the coming of the Flood (cf. 1 Enoch 6-7) and the role of Noah in saving the world from destruction. Accordingly, he is told to call his son "Noah" (rest), "for he shall be your rest...from the corruption of the earth." Enoch also foretells the decline that would again ensue after the Flood.

Reclaiming the Dead Sea Scrolls, Lawrence H. Schiffman, Philadelphia: The Jewish Publication Society, 1984, p. 184

Adds Professor VanderKam:

He [Enoch] discovers, moreover, greater detail about the future in that he hears of the fact that evil will continue to exist in the world until the final judgment...

Enoch and the Growth of An Apocalyptic Tradition, James VanderKam, Washington, D.C.: The Catholic Biblical Association of America, 1984, p. 131

Professor Milik works with the fascinating hypothesis that Enoch had prepared an account of the creation and the law of God that naturally predates Moses' account in Genesis...

Enoch the Prophet, Hugh Nibley, Salt Lake City, Utah: Deseret Book Company, 1986, p. 276

Says the author M. Barker:

Compare this ancient picture of creation with that in Genesis; Enoch's is probably the older picture.

The Lost Prophet:, (The Book of Enoch and its influence on Christianity), Great Britain: SPCK, 1988, p. 86

Recalling one of the better known books found in Enoch's works *The International Standard Bible Encyclopedia* explains that:

The book is called Jubilees because of its way of calculating time. History is divided into a series of forty-nine Jubilees of forty-nine years each. It has also been called the "Little Genesis," not because of its size but because it tells the story found in Genesis in much greater detail.

Vol. 1, Grand Rapids, Michigan: William B. Ferdmans Publishing Co., 1982, p. 156

Professor J. VanderKam cites the respected scholar H. Ludin Jansen's observations of the First Book of Enoch:

He [Jansen] found that when Enoch was depicted as a human agent he functioned as a prophet and wise man, similar in some respects to Old Testament models but a unique combination nevertheless. As prophet, Enoch declares judgment (1-5:92-94-105) and salvation (cf. 90:29-30; 93; 91:12-17; 92:3-5), focuses attention on the final judgment, receives revelations from an angel who has derived some of the disclosed information from heavenly tablets, and delivers his message, which serves as a means of salvation...

Enoch and the Growth of An Apocalyptic Tradition, James VanderKam, Washington, D.C.: The Catholic Biblical Association of America, 1984, p. 13

According to the author of the book *Islam*:

The *Quran* mentions only the twenty-five most prominent [prophets] by name after Adam. Enoch is the second name listed.

Ghulam Sarivar, London: The Muslim Educational Trust, 1989, p. 27

In like manner, New York University Professor Lawrence H. Schiffman points to "Enoch's ascent to heaven, where he becomes a prophet and scribe."

Reclaiming the Dead Sea Scrolls, Philadelphia: The Jewish Publication Society, 1994, p. 182

ENOCH, THE ASCENDER

Genesis, in listing the descendants of Adam until Noah and his sons, mentions Enoch, the seventh, in ways distinct from the others: Enoch walked with God...at the end of his life he "was no more, for God took him" (Gen. 5:21-24).

The Encyclopedia of Religion, Vol. 5, Mircea Eliade, ed., New York: Macmillan Publishing Co., 1987, p. 116-7

In using a verb to "take" it has a special significance and context which connotes a heavenly ascent as when:

Psalm 73:24 uses the same word in a similar context...In Genesis 5:24 the same word is applied to Enoch. "And he was not, for God took him," this obviously means that he was carried off. II Kings 2:9 ff. uses this verb in the same meaning to describe the ascension of Elijah.

Israelite Religion, Helmer Ringgren trans. E Green, U.S.A.: University Press of America, Inc., 1966, p. 246

In Gen. 5, Enoch is said to have lived 365 years and walked with God, after which he was no more, "for God took him," a phrase that has been understood to mean he was "translated," or carried bodily to heaven.

Funk & Wagnalls, New Standard Encyclopedia of Universal Knowledge, Vol. X, Funk & Wagnalls Co., 1931, p. 491

Explains the famous writer, Isaac Asimov:

What is meant by saying that Enoch walked with God and was not is uncertain, but later traditions made it clear that the usual interpretation was that he was taken up alive into heaven as a reward for unusual piety.

Asimov's Guide to the Bible, Vol. 1, Garden City, New York: Doubleday & Co., Inc., p. 37

The Septuagint (the Greek translation of the Bible, c. 250 BCE), Ben Sira (c. 190 BCE), the Jewish Antiquities by Josephus Flavius (37/8-c.100 CE) all state that Enoch was taken by or returned to the deity.

The Encyclopedia of Religion, Vol. 5, Mircea Eliade, ed., New York: Macmillan Publishing Co., 1987, p. 117

An identification of Enoch is given by The New International Dictionary of the Bible:

Son of Jared (Gen 5:18) and father of Methuselah (Gen 5:21-22, Luke 3:37). Abram walked "before God" (Gen 17:1), but of

Enoch and Noah alone it is written that they walked "with God" (Gen. 5:24; 6:9).

Walking with God is a relic of the first paradise when men walked and talked with God in holy familiarity, and it anticipates a new paradise (Rev.24:3; 22:3-4).

The secret of Enoch's walk with God was faith - the ground of his pleasing God, and this was the ground of his being "taken from this life, so that he did not experience death" (Heb 11:5-6).

After the monotonous repetition of the patriarchs who "lived...begat...and died" (Gen. 5 KJV), the account of Enoch's walk with God and translation without death stands forth in bright relief.

J.D. Douglas & Merrill Tenney, Editors, Regency Reference Library, Grand Rapids, Michigan: Zondervan Publishing House, 1987, p. 313

Methuselah, the son of Enoch, lived 969 years, "the longest of any person in the Bible."

In 2 Enoch: "Enoch ascends to heaven (14:8) and is brought near the door of the divine throne room itself (14:25). Second, not only does he ascend to heaven but he does so without angelic accompaniment. ("Apocalyptic and Merkavah Mysticism," Gruenwald, p. 36)

Enoch and the Growth of An Apocalyptic Tradition, James VanderKam, Washington, D.C.: The Catholic Biblical Association of America, 1984, p. 135

Encyclopedia Judaica calls the Ethiopic book of Enoch "one of the most important of the apocalyptic works, dating from the period of the Second Temple. It is named after the Biblical Enoch, son of Jared, about whom it is stated in Genesis 5:24 that he "walked with God then he was no more, for God took him" which was understood to mean that he ascended to heaven during his lifetime...(Keter Publishing House, L.T. D, David Flusser, ed., Jerusalem, Israel, 1971, p. 796)

Referring to the manuscripts known as the Dead Sea Scrolls Professor of Middle East Religious Studies, Robert H. Eisenman and Assistant Professor of Aramaic in the Department of Near Eastern Languages and Civilization at the University of Chicago, Michael Wise, wrote the following:

> The preserved portions of these two fragments appear to contain information about Enoch similar to the Book of Jubilees 4:17-24. A good deal of the interest centering around Enoch, as we have noted, was connected with his assumption alive into Heaven and the mysterious allusion in Genesis to 'walking with God'.

The Dead Sea Scrolls Uncovered, New York: Barnes & Noble Books, 1992

The world renowned Dead Sea Scrolls scholar J.T. Milik in a similar fashion refers to "...the Assumption of Enoch..." (*The Books of Enoch, Aramaic Fragments of Qumran Cave 4*, Oxford University Press, 1976, p. 113)

Associate Professor of Armenian Studies at the Hebrew University of Jerusalem, Michael E. Stone, shares a similar observation:

> Chapter 71 tells of Enoch's assumption to heaven and transformation into the Son of Man.

Jewish Writings of the Second Temple Period, Van Gorcum, ed., Philadelphia: Assen Fortress Press, 1984, p. 403

Likewise, the author of *Enoch and the Growth of An Apocalyptic Tradition* states that with "...Enoch's ultimate assumption by God. He is removed from human company, is with the angels (106:7), and dwells at the ends of the earth (106:8)."

James VanderKam, Washington, D.C.: The Catholic Biblical Association of America, 1984, p. 174

The Book of Sirach (Ecclesiasticus), in the Apocrypha, says that Enoch "pleased the Lord, and was taken up. " (44:16).

Encyclopedia Americana, Int'l Edition, Vol. 10, Danbury, CT.: Grolier Inc., p. 472

Matthew Black, a professor of Biblical Criticism at the University of St. Andrews, Scotland, describes Enoch's heavenly ascent from the book *The Slavonic Enoch* (2 Enoch) in this fashion:

"Enoch ascends through seven heavens, each with its own special secrets...

Enoch is confronted by the Lord himself in the seventh heaven and is shown the secrets of creation and human history down to his own time...Enoch returns to earth to brief his posterity before ascending again to the heavenly world."

> *The Oxford Companion to the Bible*, Bruce Metzger & Michael Coogan, eds., Oxford: Oxford University Press, 1993, p. 185

Says Barker:

there is no book of the prophet Enoch in the Old Testament. Until recently, all that we knew of Enoch was in Genesis 5, 18-24. He was the son of Jared and the father of Methuselah; he walked with God and he was not, for God took him.

> *The Lost Prophet*, (The Book of Enoch and its influence on Christianity), Great Britain: SPCK, 1988, p. 5

A prophet named Idris is mentioned in the Koran in Suras 19:57-58 and 21:85. The commentators identify him with Enoch, whom God "took" (Gen 5:22-25), namely, that he did not die.

> *Encyclopedia Judaica*, David Flusser, ed., Jerusalem, Israel: Keter Publishing House, 1971, p. 797

The author of the best selling book *A History of God* lists the legendary figures in which great "secret" knowledge has been passed through, namely: "Idris in the Koran or Enoch in the Bible; in the Greek world it had been transmitted through Plato and Pythagoras..." (Karen Armstrong, New York: Ballantine Books, 1993, p. 65)

> The Arabians called Enoch Edris, and say that Edris was the same as Elijah, who did not die. And the Arabians and the Jews also had a tradition, that Phinehas, the son of Eleazar, revived in Elijah (See Hottinger de Mohamedis Genealoia). Thus the Jewish and Arabian traditions unite Enoch and Elijah.

Anacalypsis, 2 vols., Godfrey Higgins, New York: University Books, rep. A & B Books, Brooklyn, New York, p. 198

...some biblical Apocrypha as the Book of Enoch...individuals... through the mechanics of a visionary revelation whereby the suspect is carried to the highest heaven where the mysteries of creation are revealed, [on the parallel experience credited to Muhammad by the Islamic tradition see G. Widengren, Muhammad, *the Apostle of God, and His Ascension* (Uppala, 1955)]

Children of Abraham, F.E. Peters, Princeton: Princeton University Press, 1982, p. 143

Professor Lawrence H. Schiffman who was featured in the PBS Nova series, "Secrets of the Dead Sea Scrolls," also, talks about "...the figure of Enoch, Adam's descendant who, according to Genesis 5:24, "was no more, for God took him." That...Biblical statement led to the belief that Enoch was translated alive into heaven, where he saw apocalyptic visions.

Reclaiming the Dead Sea Scrolls, Philadelphia: The Jewish Publication Society, 1994, p. 182

By saying that God would eventually "receive" them after their deaths the psalmists boldly reuse the vocabulary traditionally associated with figures like Enoch...[God] "bodily assumed [him] into heaven"...(Psalm 49)

Heaven, A History, Colleen McDonnell & Bernard Long, New Haven: Yale University Press, 1995, p. 15

ENOCH, THE IMMORTAL

He lived in such close relationship to God that he was transferred to heaven without having died.

Baker Encyclopedia of the Bible, Vol. 1, Walter Ewell, ed., Baker Book House, 1988, p. 702

Professor of Near Eastern Languages at New York University, F.E. Peters, reflects the same view:

"Enoch it appears from Genesis 5:24 did not die...but was taken up by God."

Judaism, Christianity and Islam, Vol.3, Princeton: Princeton University Press, New Jersey, 1990, p. 191

Enoch (Heb. Hanokh):

Father of Methuselah (Gen 5:18-24). The Biblical account ("And Enoch walked with God, and he was not; for God took him") was traditionally interpreted to mean that he did not die naturally but was transported to heaven in his life time on account of his righteousness...the early Christians utilized the accepted view on Enoch to expound the immortality of Jesus...

The New Standard Jewish Encyclopedia, Seventh Edition, Geoffrey Wigoder, ed., New York: FACTS ON FILE, 1984, p. 307

As Hyam Maccoby, a specialist in the study of Judeo-Christian relations, notes:

The belief that Jesus had been resurrected was indeed the mark of the movement after Jesus' death...Jesus was still alive and would soon return to continue his mission like...Enoch...he had entered Paradise while alive... (*The Myth-Maker*, San Francisco: Harper, 1986, p. 190)

"Enoch walked with God." He typifies the saints living at Christ's coming who will be removed from mortality to immortality without passing through death (1 Cor 15:51-52). His translation out of a wicked world was an appropriate testimony to the truth ascribed to him in Jude 14-15, "See, the Lord is coming...to judge everyone."

The New International Dictionary of the Bible, J.D. Douglas & Merrill Tenney, Editors, Regency Reference Library, Grand Rapids, Michigan: Zondervan Publishing House, 1987, p. 313

Following his son's birth it is said (Gen 5:22-24) that Enoch "walked with God these hundred years...and he was not for God took him." As a reward for his sanctity he was transported into heaven without dying, and thus the doctrine of immortality was plainly taught under the old dispensation.

The Unger's Bible Dictionary, R.K. Harrison ed. Chicago: Moody Press, 1984

He is said to have "walked with God" so that God "took" or translated him (Gen. 5:24, 6:9). The author of Hebrews sees faith as the key (11:5). He is mentioned by Jude (vs.24) along with a quoted testimony of warning as to the lord's coming in judgment.

The New Smith's Bible Dictionary, William Smith, rev. Reuel G. Lemmons, New York: Doubleday & Company, Inc., 1966, p. 97

He is the only one of the line of Seth who is not mentioned as having died: "Henoch walked with God; and he was seen no more because God took him" (Gen. 5, 24). He was translated so as not to see death (Heb. 11, 5; Sir. 44, 16; cf. Antiq., 1,3,4; 9,2,2). Henoch was translated into Paradise (Sir. 44, 16 Vulg.), or the Garden of Eden (apocryphal Book of Jubilees 4, 23...)

A New Catholic Commentary on Holy Scripture, Rev. Reginald Fuller, Gen. ed., Catholic Biblical Association, Thomas Nelson and Sons Ltd., London, 1969, p. 457

A son of Jared and the father of Methuselah (Gen. 5:18-24; Henoch; 2 Chr. 1:3, KJV). After living for years, Enoch was "translated," or taken directly into God's presence without experiencing death (Gen. 5:24).

Nelson's Illustrated Bible Dictionary, Herbert Lockyer, ed., Nashville: Thomas Nelson Publishers, 1986, p. 342

"The expression 'walked with God' denotes a devout life, lived in close communion with God, while the reference to his end has always been understood, as by the writer of Heb. to mean, By faith Enoch was translated that he should not see death; and he was not found, because God translated him.' " (Heb. 11 5).

The International Standard Bible Encyclopedia, James Orr, ed., Mich.: W.M.B Eerdmans, 1960, p. 953

Enoch walked with God; and he was not, for God took him." (Gen. 5:24). This short sentience - a mere nine words in Hebrew - makes Enoch one of the most enigmatic figures of the Bible. Evidently it means that Enoch was spared death because of his righteousness, a reward confirmed by the anonymous author of the New Testament Letter to the Hebrews: "By faith Enoch was taken up so that he should not see death." (Heb. 11:5). Only Enoch and the prophet Elijah (in the chariot of fire) were taken by God without having to die.

ABC's of the Bible, New York: Reader's Digest Association, Inc., 1991, p. 25-6

Enoch was "translated" or taken directly into God's presence without experiencing death (Gen. 5:24, Heb.11:5-6)

Nelson's New Illustrated Bible Dictionary, Ronald F. Youngblood, ed., Nashville: Nelson, 1995, p. 402

The Books of Enoch, Aramaic Fragments of Qumran Cave 4 cites a similar sentiment from Enoch:

"I am Enoch which was translated hither by the word of the Lord...and up to this day we have not tasted death..." (J. T. Milik, ed., Oxford: Oxford University Press, 1976, p. 119)

Enoch pleased God he did not die, but was translated directly to heaven.

The Handbook of Biblical Personalities, George Alexander, Greenwich, CT: The Seabury Press, 1962, p. 83

This verse was traditionally interpreted to mean that he did not die naturally but was transported to heaven on account of his righteousness.

Blackwell Dictionary of Judaica, Dan Cohn-Sherbok, Oxford: Blackwell Publishers, 1992, p. iii

As the same work points out:

Early Christians utilized this interpretation to expound Jesus' immortality. In later Jewish legend he was identified with the angel Metatron. (p. iv)

"'God took him,' the traditional interpretation of the clause being that Enoch did not die like mortals but was transported alive to heaven as was Elijah, with whom he was also connected in the tales of the later Jews."

The Universal Jewish Encyclopedia, Vol. 4, Isaac Landman, ed., N.Y., 1941, p. 131

There can be no question that the clause "and he was not for God took him" (Gen 5:24) refers to the translation; the same expression is used of Elijah's translation (2 Kings 2:11) being identified with the angel Metatron, and a mystical literature grew up around his personality.

The New Standard Jewish Encyclopedia, Seventh Edition, Geoffrey Wigoder, ed., New York: FACTS ON FILE, 1984, p. 307

The Chair of the Religious Studies Department at California State University, Professor R. H. Eisenman and Professor M. Wise strike a similar chord:

The various stories involving the mysterious Enoch who, because he was described as 'walking with God' in Gen. 5:24, was thought not to have died, are another variation of this genre. A lively...tradition developed in Enoch's name...implicit in his having visited Heaven and lived.

The Dead Sea Scrolls Uncovered, New York: Barnes & Noble Books, 1992, p. 96

It is said that "Enoch walked with God" (Gen 5:22), and as a reward for his holy walk he was translated to heaven without tasting death (Heb 11:5).

Wycliffe Bible Encyclopedia, Vol. 1 Charles F. Pfeiffer, Chicago: Moody Press, 1975, p. 529

"Enoch it appears from Genesis 5:24 did not die..."

Judaism, Christianity and Islam, F.E. Peters, Vol. 3, Princeton, New Jersey: Princeton University Press, 1990, p. 191

Finally, Origen, the third-century Church Father, asserts that some of Dositheus's disciples held that he [the Gnostic teacher, Dositheus] had not really died but, like Enoch, Elisha [Elijah] and Jesus had been translated miraculously to heaven.

The Dead Sea Scrolls and the Christina Myth, John Allegro, New York: Prometheus Books, 1992, p. 187

As the first Biblical character to forego death, Enoch had a unique relationship with God. This direct and continuous relationship may be the meaning of the phrase "walked with haelohim"...

The Anchor Bible Dictionary, Vol. 2, David Noel Freedman, ed., New York: Doubleday Co., 1992, p. 508

It is probable that the language of Pss. 49:15, 73:24 reflects the story of Enoch. In that case the example of Enoch's assumption played a part in the origin of Jewish hope for life with God beyond death.

The Illustrated Bible Dictionary, J.D. Douglas, ed., England: Tyndale House, Publishers, 1982, p. 458

It was only after the threat of early Christianity to the integrity of Judaism had come to an end, that Jewish authors began to weave legends about Enoch. A late Midrash asserts that Enoch ascended to heaven in a fiery chariot drawn by a fiery steed. Further, he was one of nine righteous men who did not suffer pangs of death and entered paradise alive. The Zohar, as well as earlier mystic literature, takes up many of the early legends centering on Enoch. Enoch, descendant of Adam's son who walked with God, and was taken into his presence without dying. (Gen. 5:18-24)

The Encyclopedia of Judaism, Geoffrey Wigoder ed., New York: Macmillan Publishing Company, 1984, p. 229

To quote from a section in the *Coptic Encyclopedia* on Enoch written by Professor Gonzalo Aranda Perez of the University of Navarra:

Enoch, father of Methuselah, 'walked with God, and he was not, for God took him' (Gn 5:24). He was taken up into heaven and there received the revelation of the divine mysteries concerning the...end of the world, thus becoming the most important representative of the apocalyptical revelation.

The Coptic Encyclopedia, Vol. 1, Aziz S. Atiya, ed., New York: Macmillan Publishing Co., p. 162

The Dictionary of the Bible characterized Enoch as "an antediluvian patriarch mentioned...in the Sethite genealogy as the Son of Jared and the father of Methuselah (Gen 5:18-24). Enoch differs from the other members of the Sethite list in his age (365 years, notably less than the others) and in the notice that he walked with God and was taken by God; 'he died', explicitly said of the others, is omitted of Enoch."

> John L. McKenzie, S.J., Colliers Books, New York: Macmillan Publishing Co., 1984, p. 238

Citing the Ethiopic Book of Enoch, Stephen L. Harris, author the book *Understanding the Bible*, calls "Enoch the antediluvian patriarch who was reputedy transported alive to heaven (Gen 5:24)..." (London: Mayfield Publishing Co., 1980)

> Enoch Biblical character, son of Jared, father of Methuselah. He was depicted as extraordinary, devout, and therefore as translated directly into heaven without dying. (Gen 5:24 p. 161)

> *Larousse Dictionary of Beliefs and Religion*, Rosemary Goring ed., New York, 1994, p. 161

> The cycle of Enoch not being finished, he was taken up to heaven, but did not die.

> *Anacalypsis*, 2 vols., Godfrey Higgins, University Books, New York, p. 196

> Enoch, meaning...dedicated one...The son of Jared of the godly line of Seth who walked with God and was translated to heaven without dying (Gen 5:18-24); 1 Chron 1:3). As a hero of faith (Heb 11:5) he is known as a man who pleased God. Enoch prophesized against ungodly men (cf. the Book of Enoch).

> *Zondervan Pictorial Encyclopedia of the Bible*, Vol. 2, Merill C. Tenney, ed. Regency Reference Library, Michigan, 1984, p. 309

ENOCH, THE DIVINE

> Enoch is also said to officiate in paradise at the sanctuary before God...In some later parts of this literature, Enoch himself

becomes a divine figure who dwells in heaven and executes justice...

The Encyclopedia of Religion, Vol. 5, Mircea Eliade, ed., New York: Macmillan Publishing Co., 1987, p. 117

Enoch is given that heavenly knowledge; and the tradition in which he stands, as we shall see, believed that such knowledge conferred angelic status and made one, in effect, like God. Compare this with Genesis 2-3. In the story of the Garden of Eden the serpent promises Adam and Eve that they would have knowledge to open their eyes and make them like God. Whoever wrote the Genesis story believed that this knowledge was wrong, and the cause of all subsequent evil. Yet the other, lost tradition says that this knowledge brought one to the presence of God. The wise, like Enoch, walked with God.

The Lost Prophet, (The Book of Enoch and its influence on Christianity), Margaret Barker, Great Britain: SPCK, 1988, p. 24

The International Standard Bible Encyclopedia in referring to a previous work of Enoch describes how "God, overcoming the protests of the heavenly hosts, transfigured him with the rays of heavenly glory and made him as one of themselves, in order that he might serve before His throne as one of the highest angel princes...the Angel of Wisdom at God's command, had instructed him in all wisdom and knowledge (compare ib. xxii, 11, 12 and xxiii.) and had imparted to him all the mysteries of creation, of heaven and earth, of past and future things, and of the world to come (compare ib. xxiv-xxxiii 2).

Grand Rapids, Michigan: William Eerdman Publishing Co., 1982, p. 677

Professor Emeritus of Biblical Criticism, Matthew Black, compares 3 Enoch with 2 Enoch in relationship to Enoch's identification with the supremely elevated angel, Metatron:

Like Enoch in 2 Enoch, Ishmael ascends to the seventh heaven, where he is admitted by the archangel Metatron, who informs Ishmael that he, Metatron, is really Enoch, son of Jared, translated to heaven to become a vice-regent of deity, "the lesser YHWH."

The Oxford Companion to the Bible, Bruce Metzger and Michael Coogan, Eds., Oxford: Oxford University Press, 1993, p. 185

Professor Hugh Nibley informs us of a Christian writer who remarked that "Enoch is next to God, but not God,"...*Enoch the Prophet*, Salt Lake City, Utah: Deseret Book Company, 1986. p. 39

Elsewhere along the same lines, Professor Nibley indicates that:

Enoch's transcendent virtue qualifies him as a vital link in "the order" of the Lord himself. (p. 258)

Writes Professor R.J. Bauckham:

In the Similitudes (*1 Enoch* 37:71) he is identified with the Messianic Son of man (71:14-17) and some later Jewish traditions identified him with the nearly divine figure Metatron (*Targum of Pseudo-Jonathan*, Gn. 5:24; *3 Enoch*). Early Christian apocalyptic writings frequently expect his return to earth with Elijah before the End.

The Illustrated Bible Dictionary, J.D. Douglas, ed., England: Tyndale House, Publishers, 1982, p. 458

According to the writings incorporated into the Hebrew, Enoch-Metatron is an almost divine being, an intermediary between God and creation, and he is identified with the patriarch Enoch who was lifted up to heaven.

The Books of Enoch, Aramaic Fragments of Qumran Cave 4, J. T. Milik, ed., Oxford: Oxford University Press, 1976

Enoch and the Growth of An Apocalyptic Tradition touches on a similar point:

When Enoch is pictured as a divine figure, he appears as the one who in effect saves Noah from the flood by disclosing salvific information to him...In the passages in which he assumes a superhuman role, Enoch serves as a mediator between God and man or God and the world.

James VanderKam, Washington, D.C.: The Catholic Biblical Association of America, 1984, p. 13

Writes Professor Hugh Nibley:

the Odes of Solomon report that Enoch is "raised up to become the Son of God," or when an Ethiopian text teaches that only the prophets by ascending a high mountain to a high place "can hear the fearful name of God," pending which God is known only by epithets, the first of the list being Enoch.

Enoch the Prophet, Salt Lake City, Utah: Deseret Book Company, 1986, p. 39

On this grandiose tableau, which is dominated by the theological aspect of the history of the universe, Enoch is now projected, a hero who is at the same time human and divine (12:1-2, anticipated by the fleeting reference to the Son of Lamech, 10:1-3).

The Books of Enoch, Aramaic Fragments of Qumran Cave 4, J. T. Milik, ed., Oxford: Oxford University Press, 1976, p. 34

ENOCH, THE SUPERHUMAN (SUPERMAN)

The superhuman Enoch inherited traits of both the divine and quasi-human sides of this complex figure.

Enoch and the Growth of An Apocalyptic Tradition, James VanderKam, Washington, D.C.: The Catholic Biblical Association of America, 1984, p. 14-5

Aprocryphal works attributed to Enoch. From Gen. v.24 ("Enoch walked with God" and "God took him") a cycle of Jewish legends...naturally ascribed to such a man, credited with superhuman knowledge, found their literary expression in the Books of Enoch.

The Jewish Encyclopedia, Vol V., KTAV Publishing House, Isidore Singer, Ph.D Managing Editor, 1967, p. 179

In Gen. v. 24 it is said of Enoch that he walked with God. This expression was taken in later times to mean not only that he led a godly life, but also that he was the recipient of superhuman knowledge.

The Book of Enoch, transl. from Professor Dillmann's Ethiopic Text, R. H. Charles, ed., Oxford: Clarendon Press, 1893

Harvard Theological Review makes reference to "...the term "Son of Man." The role of the Son of a Man...a late, Christian work a book devoted largely to the prediction of the coming of a super-human Son of Man, existent in the thought of God before crea-tion...Son of Man is identified as Enoch." (70:1-2, January-April 1977, Missoula Montana Scholars Press, p. 57)

The second Similitude (chs 45-57) brings in the Son of Man as a superhuman if not also superangelic being, who is to come to earth as the Messiah. The third Similitude occupies chs 58-71, and gives an account of the glory of the Messiah and of the subjugation of the kings of the earth under Him.

The International Standard Bible Encyclopedia, James Orr, ed., Mich.: W.M.B Eerdmans, 1960, p. 165

Professor of Religion at North Carolina State University and the world's greatest authority on the Book of Jubilee, James Van-derKam reminds us that:

At this early point in the tradition the man Enoch has already assumed astonishing superhuman traits.

Enoch and the Growth of An Apocalyptic Tradition, James VanderKam, Wash-ington, D.C.: The Catholic Biblical Association of America, 1984, p. 135

Later on he adds: "They enlivened the remarkable person of Enoch with a variety of mythological traits and thus created...a primeval hero who outshone the legendary supermen or even divinities of any other people". (p. 189)

ENOCH, OMNISCIENT SAGE

The Oxford Companion to the Bible mentions the fact that:

There are parallels...in Greek and Near Eastern sources, and the later picture of Enoch as omniscient sage...

Bruce Metzger and Michael Coogan, Eds., Oxford: Oxford University Press, 1993, p. 184

ENOCH, THE ALL WISE

From the section entitled CATALOG in the book *Scrolls From Dead Sea* we read the following about Enoch:

Rabbinic sources and pseudepigraphic literature attach many tales and legends to the figure. He is all wise, knowing the secrets of the universe and being the source of information for natural and supernatural occurrences. The fullest portrait of Enoch emerges in I Enoch, a work preserved in its entirety only in Gecez (Old Ethiopic). Reference: J.T. Milik The Books of Enoch: Aramaic Fragment of Qumram Cave 4, Oxford, 1976. [George Braziller, Inc., Library of Congress, 1993, p. 76]

Similarly, Professor VanderKam, a leading world scholar, says that in the First Book of Enoch "...the Epistle...develops the theme that Enoch's words are truly wise as are those who heed them" (cf. also 82:2-3). He himself is described as "the wisest of men" (Milik. The Books of Enoch; 260).

Enoch and the Growth of An Apocalyptic Tradition, James VanderKam, Washington, D.C.: The Catholic Biblical Association of America, 1984, p. 173

ENOCH, THE UNIVERSAL

He is identified with more other great characters than any other figure of the past. He is the most mysterious individual, and unique of characters, yet he is the most universal type of them all. How can we account for "the extraordinary strength and persuasiveness of the Enoch legend" ?

Enoch the Prophet, Hugh Nibley, Salt Lake City, Utah: Deseret Book Company, 1986, p. 19

Enoch was a generic title, applied to, and borne by, scores of individuals, at all times and ages, and in every race and nation...

Some say Enoch was a great Saint, beloved by God, and taken alive to heaven (i.e., one who reached Mukti or Nirvana, on earth, as Buddha did and others still do)...

This shows only that Enoch, or its equivalent, was a term, even during the days of the later Talmudists, which meant "Seer,"

"Adept in the Secret Wisdom," etc., without any specification as to the character of the title-bearer.

When Josephus, speaking of Elijah and Enoch (Antiquities, ix., 2), remarks that "it is written in the sacred books they (Elijah and Enoch) disappeared..."

The Secret Doctrine, H.P. Blavatsky, Vol. 11, London: Anthropogenesis, The Theosophical Publishing Co., 1888, p. 532

G. A. Gaskell, author of *Dictionary of all Scriptures and Myths*, defines "walking with God" as:

"A symbol of the potential life of the unmanifest...'Enoch walked with God is a symbol of the latent individuality on the higher mental plane, which is able to survive three attached personalities with their terrestrial incarnations and their first (physical) and second (astral deaths).

The 365 'days of Enoch' indicate the length of the solar year, or Zodiac, a symbol of the great cycle of life, during which the individuality (Enoch)...'God took him,' or 'he abode in God,' signifies that individuality was potential or yet in the bosom of the Absolute."

"Some of the writers interested in the subject - especially Masons - have tried to identify Enoch with Thoth of Memphis, the Greek Hermes, and even with the Latin Mercury. As individuals, all these are distinct one from the other; professionally - if one may use this word, now so limited in its sense - they belong one and all to the same category of sacred writers, of Initiators and Recorders of...ancient Wisdom."

The Secret Doctrine, H.P. Blavatsky, Vol. 11, London: Anthropogenesis, The Theosophical Publishing Co., 1888, p. 366

H.P. Blavatsky continues:

Those who in the Koran (see Surat XIX) are generically termed the Edris, or the "Learned" (the Initiated), bore in Egypt the name of "Thoth," the inventor of arts, sciences, writing or letters, of music and astronomy.

Among the Jews the Edris became "Enoch," who, according to Bar-Hebraeus, "was the first inventor of writing," books, arts, and sciences, the first who reduced to a system the progress of the planets.

In Greece he was called Orpheus, and thus changed his name with every nation. The number Seven being attached to, and connected with, each of those primitive Initiators, as well as the number 365, of the days in the year, astronomically, it identifies the mission, character, and the sacred office of all those men...

Enoch is the seventh Patriarch; Orpheus is the possessor of the phorminx, the 7-stringed lyre, which is the seven-fold mystery of initiation. Thoth, with the seven-rayed Solar Discus on his head, travels in the Solar boat, the 365 degrees, jumping out every fourth (leap) year for one day. (Khanoch, or Hanoch, or Enoch means the "Initiator" and "teacher" as well as the "Son of Man," Enos (vide Genesis iv., 26), estoterically.

"Enoch," writes G.A. Gaskell, is "a symbol of the individuality; that part of the soul which survives physical...deaths, and is immortal." (*Dictionary of all Scriptures and Myths*, p. 250)

He is the great observer and recorder of all things in heaven and earth, of which God grants him perfect knowledge. The great learner, he is also the great teacher. Enoch the Initiator into the higher mysteries of the faith and the secrets of the universe.

Enoch the Scribe, keeper of the records, instructor in the ordinances, aware of all times and places, studying and transmitting the record of the race with intimate concern for all generations to come. He offers the faithful their greatest treasure of knowledge. He is the seer who conveys to men the mind and will of the Lord.

Enoch the Prophet, Hugh Nibley, Salt Lake City, Utah: Deseret Book
    Company, 1986, p. 21

ENOCH, THE COLOSSUS

It is strange that the man to whom the Bible gives only a few brief sentences should be the colossus who bestrides the Apocryphas as no other. Everywhere we catch glimpses of him.

Enoch the Prophet, Hugh Nibley, Salt Lake City, Utah: Deseret Book
Company, 1986, p. 19.

Significantly, Enoch's importance in the Old Testament pseude-
pigrapha is equaled by his central role in the book of Moses.
In "A Strange Thing in the Land: The Return of the Book of
Enoch" (which appeared serially in the Ensign in 1976-77), Pro-
fessor Nibley demonstrates at great length the richness of the
Old Testament pseudepigraphic Enoch literature...

The Lost Prophet, (The Book of Enoch and its influence on Christianity),
Margaret Barker, Great Britain: SPCK, 1988, p. vii.

ENOCH THE VICAR, THE LITTLE GODHEAD (YAHWEH)

After having been installed as ruler over the angels, Metatron
was given a new distinctive name: "the Lesser YHUH (Yahweh)"
(or "the little YHUH," "after the name of his Master," chh.
12.5, 48 c7, d1 no. 102, cf. no. 14.

The name, "the Lesser YHUH," is in chh. 12 and 48 c7 used
as indicative of Metatron's character of representative vicarius, of
the Godhead; it expresses a sublimation of his vice-regency into
a second manifestation of the "Divine Name" are, besides his
being enthroned, the conferment upon him of (part of) the Divine Glory, honor, majesty and splendor" (ch. 48 c7), "a garment of glory, robe of honor," but especially a "crown of king-
ship" (10 1-4) on which the mystical 'letters', representing cosmic and celestial agencies, are engraved - after the pattern of
the Crown of the Holy One...and lastly knowledge of all the
secrets of Creation, otherwise in possession of the Most High
alone, chh. 13, 48 c7, d5.

Being named like his Master, Metatron is also said to have seventy names "corresponding to the seventy nations of the world"
, ch. 3....the 70 names of Metatron are "taken from the names
of the Holy One" (ch. 48 c9, d1,5), they are a reflection of the
Divine 70...

3 Enoch or The Hebrew Book of Enoch, Hugo Odeberg, ed., New York:
KTAV Publishing House, Inc., 1973, p. 82.

Professor of Anthropology at Dropsie University, R. Patai recounts a passage from 3 Enoch concerning Metatron:

But when Aher came to gaze at the vision of the Chariot and set eyes upon me, he was affrighted and trembled before me, and his soul was terrified into departing from him because of his fear, dread and terror of me when he saw me seated upon a throne like a king, with ministering angels standing about me as servants, and all the princes of kingdoms crowned with crowns surrounding me. In that hour he opened his mouth and said: 'There are indeed two powers in heaven'!

Gates To The Old City, Raphel Patai, Detroit: Wayne State University Press, 1981, p. 387.

Professor Odeberg indicates why Metatron was so highly honored:

Metatron the enthroned vice-regent of the Holy One...He is enthroned. 'Because of the great love of His Master, Metatron has authority to be seated on a Throne like the Throne of Glory... The Holy One made him the ruler over his celestial and terrestrial household'...'Little less than God'(i.e. probable, Ps 8, 5 refers to him: "Thou hast made him a little lower than Elohim...He represents the Godhead to the 'outside'celestial and terrestrial world...

Hugo Odeberg, ed., New York: KTAV Publishing House, Inc., 1973, p. 111.

According to Gustav Davidson, a university fellow at Wroxton College, England:

Metatron is perhaps the greatest of all the heavenly hierarchs...He has been called king of angels, prince of the divine face or presence, chancellor of Heaven, angel of the covenant, chief of the ministering angels, and the lesser YHWH (the tetragrammaton)

He is charged with the sustenance of mankind. In Talmud and Targum, Metatron is the link between the human and divine. In earthly incarnation he was the patriarch Enoch...

A Dictionary of Angels, New York: The Free Press, 1967, p. 192.

Professor of Biblical Studies at the University of Notre Dame John J. Collins said that "...he (Enoch) was identified with Metatron, 'Little Yahweh,' an angel closest to God Himself."

Harper's Bible Dictionary, Paul J. Achtemeier, ed., San Francisco: Harper & Row Publishing, 1971.

Metatron will naturally be identified with any angel-prince that before had been regarded as the angel nearest to the godhead or as the representative of the Most High - or will take over the functions assigned to that angel.

3 Enoch or The Hebrew Book of Enoch, Hugo Odeberg, ed., New York: KTAV Publishing House, Inc., 1973, p. 139.

ENOCH, THE FIRST "SON OF MAN"

It is generally held that this "Son of Man" is identified with Enoch himself at the end of the Similitudes. In I Enoch 71:14, Enoch is greeted by an angel on his ascent to heaven: "You are the Son of Man who was born to righteousness, and righteousness remains over you and the righteousness of the Head of Days will not leave you...

The Scepter and the Star: The Messiahs of the Dead Sea Scrolls and other Ancient Literature, John J. Collins, New York: Doubleday Co., 1984, p. 178.

The book *Jewish Writings of the Second Temple Period*, points out that in "...an appendix to The Similitudes, the Son of Man is specifically identified as Enoch."

Michael E. Stone, ed., Van Gorcum, Philadelphia: Assen Fortress Press, 1984, p. 399

The Son of Man and Enoch have one distinct characteristic in common. They were both brought into the assembly of God.

Roots of Apocalyptic, Helge S. Kvanvig, Norway: Neukirchener Verlag, 1988, p. 130

ENOCH, THE MESSENGER OF GOD

According to M. Barker except for a few brief sentences in the Bible:

That is all the Old Testament tells us about him, yet books and visions in his name had once been widely known and very influential.

It is clear that there was more to the figure than appeared in Genesis, and a considerable cult of Enoch did undoubtedly exist, even though the Biblical writers gave no place to it.

A belief grew that he did not die; like Elijah he was taken up to heaven. Enoch was to be revealed in the last days as a messenger of judgment.

The Lost Prophet, (The Book of Enoch and its influence on Christianity), Margaret Barker, Great Britain: SPCK, 1988, p. 6

ENOCH, THE LEGENDARY

"He figured in a rich body of legend and literature that accumulated in Palestine".

Collier's Encyclopedia, New York: P. F. Collier, 1995, p. 253

The author of the book *Scrolls From the Dead Sea* shares a similar view:

Rabbinic sources and pseudepigraphic literature attach many tales and legends to the figure. He is all wise, knowing the secrets of the universe..."

George Braziller, Inc. Library of Congress, 1993, p. 76

From Memoirs of the patriarchs A. Lamech in the section entitled "The Birth of Noah" (Cp. Enoch 106.1-2) mentions the "legend that when the hero of the flood was born, the house was filled with a sudden and wondrous light; where upon his father Lamech suspected that the child was of supernatural origin and sought to discover the truth from his grandfather Enoch, who, in reward for his piety, had been translated to heaven...and made privy to celestial lore. (cp, Gen. 5:24)

The Dead Sea Scriptures, 3rd ed., (English translation), New York: Anchor books, Doubleday, 1976, p. 358

A noted Enoch scholar reports that:

Christian writings in many languages - Latin, Greek, Arabic, Coptic, Ethiopic - show how widely this aspect of the Enoch legend was known.

The Lost Prophet, (The Book of Enoch and its influence on Christianity), Margaret Barker, Great Britain: SPCK, 1988, p. 6

Along the same vein, a well-respected American scholar talks about a study of the Enoch tradition that begins with "Gen. 5:21-24, the most ancient passage about him, and then follows the evolution of Enochic lore until approximately the middle of the second pre-Christian century. By that time a substantial corpus of literature had accumulated about his name..."

Enoch and the Growth of An Apocalyptic Tradition, James VanderKam, Washington, D.C.: The Catholic Biblical Association of America, 1984, p. 1

"Shortly before the Christian era, Enoch became the hero of a whole cycle of legends,' which enjoyed immense popularity."

Enoch the Prophet, Hugh Nibley, Salt Lake City, Utah: Deseret Book Company, 1986, p. 96

ENOCH, THE FIRST WISE MAN

In the intertestamental period Enoch became a popular figure: see Ecclus. 44:16; 49:14, 16 (Heb.); *Jubilees* 4:14-26; 10:17...[in] the legend of Enoch...[He] became the initiator of the art of writing and the first wise man, who received heavenly revelations of the secrets of the universe and transmitted them in writing to later generations.

The Illustrated Bible Dictionary, J.D. Douglas, ed., England: Tyndale House, Publishers, 1982, p. 458

ENOCH, THE CHAMPION OF THE HUMAN RACE

Enoch is the great advocate, the champion of the human race.

Enoch the Prophet, Hugh Nibley, Salt Lake City, Utah: Deseret Book Company, 1986, p. 21

ENOCH, THE GREAT

P. Johnson characterizes as "a great historical figure..."*A History of the Jews*, Paul Johnson, Harper Perennial, 1987, p. 19

A pairing of Enoch and Noah, similar to that in Ecclesiasticus, is found in Jub. 10:17: '(Noah) during his life on earth surpassed the children of men by his perfect justice, with the exception of Enoch. For the work of Enoch was created as a testimony for the generations of the world, in which he recounted to all generations their actions up to the day of judgment.'

The Books of Enoch, Aramaic Fragments of Qumran Cave 4, J. T. Milik, ed., Oxford: Oxford University Press, 1976, p. 11

Thus, for Jansen some aspects of the portrait of Enoch as a prophet-sage and the entire picture of him as a heavenly being pointed to non-Jewish sources for their inspiration.

Enoch had learned all this through his travels and heavenly contacts. Such knowledge is an eschatological gift now made available to the last generations through the chosen sage Enoch.

Enoch and the Growth of An Apocalyptic Tradition, James VanderKam, Washington, D.C.: The Catholic Biblical Association of America, 1984, p. 173

Enoch...was a wise man, a scribe and a priest.

The Lost Prophet, (The Book of Enoch and its influence on Christianity), Margaret Barker, Great Britain: SPCK, 1988, p. 18

Ephraem of Syria (fourth century) stresses that Enoch, like Jesus, in conquering sin and death and in regaining paradise in spirit as well as body, is the antipode of Adam. Because Enoch precedes the covenant of law (he is said to be uncircumcised and unobservant of the Sabbath), his faith and reward are of particular importance to Christianity in its polemic against Judaism and in its mission to the gentiles.

The Encyclopedia of Religion, Vol. 5, Mircea Eliade, ed., New York: Macmillan Publishing Co., 1987, p. 117

The book Gates To The Old City, contained the following passage:

And the Holy seed had no power to materialize, except in two or three persons such as Seth, Enoch, Mehtuselah...

Raphel Patai, Detroit: Wayne State University Press, 1981, p. 467

Ben Sira (44:16) associated great knowledge with Enoch...

Enoch and the Growth of An Apocalyptic Tradition, James VanderKam, The Catholic Biblical Association of America, Washington, D.C., 1984, p. 29

George Washington Ivery Distinguished Professor in Christian Origins, W.D. Davies and the A.A. Bradford Distinguished Professor of Texas Christian University, Louis Finkelstein cite a second century B.C.E. author, Eupolemus, who "identifies the Greek Atlas - because of his connection with astrology - with Enoch."

The Cambridge History of Judaism, W.D. Davies and Louis Finkelstein, ed., Cambridge: Cambridge University Press, 1989, p. 400

ENOCH, THE EXTRAORDINARY

The Universal Jewish Encyclopedia says of Enoch that he was the "son of Jared and the father of Methuselah (Gen. 5:18-24; Sirach 44:16;49:14). Even in Gen. 5:18 et seq. Enoch is pictured as a very unusual man, for we are told that he "walked with God"...

Vol. 4, Isaac Landman, ed., N.Y., 1941, p. 131

As one author notes:

In the Book of the Watchers, Enoch ascends to heaven, sees the great throne of God, and then travels through the heavens observing their secrets.

The Lost Prophet, (The Book of Enoch and its influence on Christianity), Margaret Barker, Great Britain: SPCK, 1988, p. 49

This work is an amplification of Genesis 5:21-32; that is, it covers events from the life of Enoch to the onset of the Flood. The first and larger part, chapters 1-68, describes how Enoch was taken up to the Lord through the seven heavens and then returned to report to his family what he had learned.

The Old Testament Pseudepigrapha, Apocalyptic Literature and Testaments, Vol. I, James H. Charlesworth, New York: Doubleday & Company, Inc., 1984, p. 95

To which the eminent scholar J.T. Milik insightfully adds:

The...discourses of Enoch claim universal scope for their appeal: in space ('to those who inhabit the dry land', 37:2) and in time (from the first right up to the last generations, 37:2-3)...

The Books of Enoch, Aramaic Fragments of Qumran Cave 4, ed., Oxford: Oxford University Press, 1976, p. 90

The angels showed to Enoch all that was "on earth and in the heavens"...

The Book of Jubilees or Little Genesis, trans. from The Editor's Ethiopic Text, by R. H. Charles, London: D.D., Adam and Charles Black, 1902, p. lvii

The angel Uriel reveals to Enoch all the laws which govern the movements of the heavenly bodies.

The Lost Prophet, (The Book of Enoch and its influence on Christianity), Margaret Barker, Great Britain: SPCK, 1988, p. 24

Enoch's uniqueness is shown by a statement by Professor VanderKam regarding an appeal made by rebellious angels:

Enoch becomes an official mediator for the angels because their crimes had made them too ashamed to approach their former heavenly home again (13:5). They assume rightly that Enoch will have access to God himself. (*Enoch and the Growth of An Apocalyptic Tradition*, James VanderKam, Washington, D.C.: The Catholic Biblical Association of America, 1984, p. 132)

ENOCH, THE VISIONARY

The ancients recognize that others, from Adam to Daniel, also had the great Universal Vision, but give Enoch a special rating. Enoch alone, says the Ethiopian Book of Mysteries, saw it all from the beginning to end, before it happened.

Enoch the Prophet, Hugh Nibley, Salt Lake City, Utah: Deseret Book Company, 1986, p. 222

Enoch was able to see the past and future of mankind.

Asimov's Guide to the Bible, Vol. 1, Isaac Asimov, Garden City, New York: Doubleday & Co., Inc., p. 37

Enoch, as we shall see, become the central figure in a great man visionary accounts of the upper world.

Judaism, Christianity and Islam, F.E. Peters, Vol. 3, Princeton, New Jersey: Princeton University Press, 1990, p. 192

When Enoch ascends to the heavenly places, he not only receives the message of judgment, he also learns the secrets of the creation. This association of the vision of God and scientific knowledge...is very important...because it is entrusted to those who have a special calling into the presence of God. Knowledge of the workings of creation is part of the vision of God.

The Lost Prophet, (The Book of Enoch and its influence on Christianity), Margaret Barker, Great Britain: SPCK, 1988, p. 53

Some biblical Apocrypha as the Book of Enoch...individuals...through the mechanics of a visionary revelation where by the suspect is carried to the highest heaven where the mysteries of creation are revealed. [on the parallel experience credited to Muhammad by the Islamic tradition see G. Widengren *Muhammad, the Apostle of God, and His Ascension* (Uppala: 1955)]

Children of Abraham, F.E. Peters, Princeton: Princeton University Press, 1982, p. 143

According to the *Encyclopedia Dictionary of Religion:* "Chapters 83-90 are a historical section describing visions of the flood and the history of the human race from Adam to the coming of the Messiah." (Vol. I, Paul Kevin Meagher, ed., et al., Corpus Publications, Washington DC, 1979, p. 1208)

The author of *The Story of Scripture*, Daniel Jeremy Silver asserts that in "Daniel (2:21-22)...Visionaries like Enoch are pictured entering heaven to receive the knowledge of the future..." (Basic Books, Inc., N.Y., 1984, p. 179)

ENOCH, THE INVENTOR OF URBAN CIVILIZATION

Enoch, the first citizen, is thus the inventor of urban civilization, sciences and techniques included.

The Books of Enoch, Aramaic Fragments of Qumran Cave 4, J. T. Milik, ed., Oxford: Oxford University Press, 1976, p. 13

ENOCH, THE CIVILIZER

Enoch's "firsts" include contributions that constitute the basis of civilized life...

Enoch and the Growth of An Apocalyptic Tradition, James VanderKam, Washington, D.C.: The Catholic Biblical Association of America, 1984, p. 181

ENOCH, THE PERFECT LEADER AND RULER

He is the wise and obedient servant, the friend and helper of all, hence the perfect leader and ruler...Abraham is our model (D&C 132:29ff.) and is as notable as Enoch for a peculiar combination of intelligence, independence and humanity..

Enoch the Prophet, Hugh Nibley, Salt Lake City, Utah: Deseret Book Company, 1986, p. 30

ENOCH, THE MASTER

As early as the 2d century B.C. this was interpreted to mean that Enoch had been conducted by angels through earth and the underworld and made privy to the secrets of the universe and the purpose of God. He was therefore regarded as the prime master of several sciences...

Encyclopedia Americana, Int'l Edition, Vol. 10, Danbury, CT: Grolier Inc., p. 472

ENOCH, THE SCIENTIST

The name of the patriarch Enoch served as a pseudepigraph to numerous literary and scientific works in several national literatures of the Middle Ages.

The Books of Enoch, Aramaic Fragments of Qumran Cave 4, J. T. Milik, ed., Oxford: Oxford University Press, 1976, p. 116

The *Encyclopedia Judaica* suggests that in "The Book of the Courses of the Heavenly Luminaries....the nature of the 'true' calendar of 364 days per year, i.e., 52 weeks, is also explained (by means of a description of the procession of the sun through the 'gates' and 'window' of the heavens." (Jerusalem, Israel: Keter Publishing House, L.T. D, David Flusser, ed.,1971, p. 796)

Likewise, Biblical scholar, theologian and Dead Sea Scrolls expert teaching at Sidney University, Barbara Thiering observed that: "A scheme of world history based on the solar calendar, and showing every sign of having been written as the first of several schemes, is found in the Apocalypse of Enoch." (1 Enoch 93:3-10, 91: 12-16)

Jesus and the Riddle of the Dead Sea Scrolls, San Francisco: Harper, 1992, p. 166

ENOCH, THE CONVEYOR OF COSMIC KNOWLEDGE

The author of *Enoch the Prophet*, states that Enoch has been portrayed "as the conveyor of cosmic knowledge."

Hugh Nibley, Salt Lake City, Utah: Deseret Book Company, 1986, p. 219.

ENOCH, THE PRINCE AND CHIEF OF ALL THE HEAVENLY HOSTS

"God arrayed him in a magnificent garment and a luminous crown, opened to him all the gates of wisdom, gave him the name 'Metatron' prince and chief of all heavenly hosts, transformed his body into a flame, and engirded him by storm, whirlwind, and thundering."

Encyclopedia Judaica, David Flusser, ed., Jerusalem, Israel: Keter Publishing House, 1971, p. 797.

ENOCH, THE COMPANION OF GOD

Professor J. VanderKam focuses our attention on the fact that there exists but two Biblical figures who were given the singular honor to have..." 'walked with God' (as the phrase is usually rendered) for 300 years. Only Enoch and Noah, of all the characters in the Bible, enjoyed this kind of relationship with the deity or this quality of life (Gen 5:22; 24; 6:9)..."

Enoch and the Growth of An Apocalyptic Tradition, Washington, D.C.: The Catholic Biblical Association of America, 1984, p. 30

Enoch is described as having "walked with God and he was not, for God took him" (Gen 5:24)...[some] regard Enoch as a predecessor of the prophet Elijah who, because of his intimate relationship with God, was gathered up to heaven while still alive (Heb 11:5). Enoch lived 365 years. He is mentioned in the genealogy of Jesus (Luke 3:37).

Almanac of the Bible, Geoffre Wigoder, Shalom M. Paul and Benedict T. Vivians, New York: Prentice Hall, 1991, p. 300

ENOCH, THE SEER WHO CONVEYS TO MEN THE MIND AND WILL OF THE LORD

He offers the faithful their greatest treasure of knowledge. He is the seer who conveys to men the mind and will of the Lord.

Enoch the Prophet, Hugh Nibley, Salt Lake City, Utah: Deseret Book Company, 1986, p. 21.

ENOCH, THE ANGELIC

The idea of Enoch's elevated status, his identification with the 'Man' (I Enoch 71) or his transformation into an angel (2 Enoch A 22:1-10 = Vaillant, p. 27)...is his identification with Metatron in 3 Enoch. See the valuable observations of Greenfield, 'Prolegomena' xxxi-xxxii. The tradition of Enoch's heavenly journeys and his subsequent return to the earth may be related to the exegesis of 'and Enoch walked with God' in Gen 5:22. This could have been understood to refer to a walking with God, that is a heavenly ascent, after the birth of Methuselah and before his translation which is related in Gen 5:24. "See particularly Sjoberg, *Menschensohn*, 47-189.)

Jewish Writings of the Second Temple Period, Michael E. Stone, ed, Van Gorcum, Philadelphia: Assen Fortress Press, 1984, p. 396

ENOCH, THE CREATOR'S FAVORITE

In 3 Enoch it reads:

I have chosen this one in preference to all of you, to be a prince and a ruler over you in the heavenly heights....because your Creator has favored you.

The Old Testament Pseudepigrapha, Apocalyptic Literature and Testaments, Vol. I, James H. Charlesworth, ed., New York: Doubleday & Company, Inc., p. 259

ENOCH, THE EGYPTIAN MASTER

As to Enoch, Thoth or Hermes, Orpheus and Kadmus, these are all generic names, branches and offshoots of the seven primordial sages (incarnated Dhyan Chohans or Devas, in illusive, not mortal bodies) who taught Humanity all it knew, and whose earliest disciplines assumed their master's names. This custom passed from the Fourth to the Fifth Race.

Hence the sameness of the traditions about Hermes (of whom Egyptologists count five) Enoch, etc., they are all inventors of letters; none of them dies but still lives, and they are the first Initiators into, and Founders of the Mysteries...

The Secret Doctrine, H.P. Blavatsky, Vol. 11, London: Anthropogenesis, The Theosophical Publishing Co., 1888, p. 267

ENOCH, THE CUSTODIAN OF SUPREME WISDOM

Enochian tradition - The significance of the name Enoch, otherwise Henoch...connects in Hebrew with instruction, which offer to masonic minds of the past a path of easy transition to the notion of initiation.

To him therefore is referred the first institution of Mysteries, or alternatively, their specific development and direction. Such a notion is of course implied by the attribution of the secret tradition to which I have referred.

The heads of tradition in the Zohar may be summarized shortly thus...the Book of Genesis of Man, containing the Mysteries of the Name of God, was communicated to the first man, and it taught him the Supreme Wisdom...

Adam had authority from the transmission of the book to his son Seth, its later custodians being Enoch, Noah and Abraham.

A New Encyclopedia of Freemasonry, Arthur Edward Waite, New York: Wings Books, 1984, p. 261

ENOCH, THE HIGH INITIATE

The generation which followed Cain and Abel refer to the principle of both man and Cosmos on the evolutionary scale culminating in Enoch, which is both a generic title for high

Initiates or Adepts (Sages) and a personification of the degree of unfoldment at which the human Ego develops the capacity for abstract thought.

This is a most important phrase because the synthesizing intelligence makes possible awareness of the innermost spiritual SELF the Divine in man - a mystical experience which can be transmitted to the mind - brain.

The Greek word Enoichion means literally the inner eye of the Seer, and is reference to the so-called third or spiritual eye. Entry upon this stage is referred to in the text in the words: "...then began men to call upon the name of the LORD."

The Hidden Wisdom in the Holy Bible, Vol. II, Geoffrey Hodson, Illinois: The Theosophical Publishing House, 1984, p. 149.

ENOCH, THE INVENTOR OF ALL SCIENCES

Enoch was the son of Jared (Gen 5:18), the seventh generation after Adam...The Bible declares that he "walked with God, then he was no more for God took him" (Gen 5:23). This unusual description of Enoch's death sparked the imaginations of the writer of the pseudepigrapha...Enoch's translation to heaven (interpreted as a bodily assumption) betokened his role there as a heavenly scribe. According to these sources, Enoch was the inventor of all sciences and knowledge since he was privy to the secrets of God and could decipher the writing on the heavenly tablets.These and similar legends are to be found throughout the Apocrypha and Pseudepigrapha...Early Christian sources...(CHURCH FATHERS), contain many legends about Enoch.

The New Standard Jewish Encyclopedia, Seventh Edition, Geoffrey Wigoder, ed., New York: FACTS ON FILE, 1984

ENOCH, THE ELEVATED ONE

The traditions regarding the elevation of Enoch play a pivotal role in the longer forms of 3 Enoch...The largest collection of 3 Enoch traditions is to be found in the manuscripts Vatican 228 and Oxford 1656.

Enoch, in the course of his elevation and transformation into a high angel-prince, is not officially pronounced in the heavens as Metatron until immediately on his having been enthroned by the Most High: ch. 10.3.

3 Enoch or The Hebrew Book of Enoch, Hugo Odeberg, ed., New York: KTAV Publishing House, Inc., 1973, p. 139

Professor Perez of the University of Navarra draws a comparsion with Enoch apocryphon and 3 Enoch when the eminent scholar suggests that:

The ascension and exaltation of Enoch is similar to that shown in the Parables of Enoch or 3 Enoch. His task in the judgment is to act as scribe of the sins and good deeds of the just, which are then weighed in the balance, and this connects with the Testament of Abraham and other apocryphal works.

The Coptic Encyclopedia, Vol. 1, Aziz S. Atiya, ed., New York: Macmillan Publishing Co., p. 163

ENOCH, THE ANOINTED

"Go and extract Enoch from [his] earthly clothing. And anoint him with my delightful oil, and put him into the clothes of my glory." And so Michael did, just as the Lord had said to him. He anointed me and he clothed me.

And the appearance of that oil is greater than the greatest light, and its ointment is like sweet dew, and its fragrance myrrh, and it is like the rays of the glittering sun. And I looked at myself, and I had to become like one of his glorious ones...

The Old Testament Pseudepigrapha, Apocalyptic Literature and Testaments, Vol. I, James H. Charlesworth, ed., New York: Doubleday & Company, Inc., p. 138

ENOCH, THE HEAVENLY MAN INCARNATE

The apparent identification of Enoch with the Son of Man at 71:14 remains a problem...If the two figures are indeed identified, then the author...must have regarded Enoch as the heavenly man incarnate, although Enoch was apparently unaware of his own identity throughout his visions, and was separated from his heavenly form during his earthly career.

The Scepter and the Star: The Messiahs of the Dead Sea Scrolls and other Ancient Literature, John J. Collins, New York: Doubleday Co., 1984, p. 180

ENOCH, THE GREAT AUTHORITY

In Levitical literature and traditions Enoch is regarded as a great authority...

Roots of Apocalyptic, Helge S. Kvanvig, Norway: Neukirchener Verlag, 1988, p. 143

ENOCH, THE PRINCE OF THE DIVINE PRESENCE

Metatron as the angel who has access to the Divine Presence, the 'Face' of the Godhead (and in this sense the appellation "Prince of the Presence" is understood here), hence possesses knowledge of the Divine secrets and decrees.

3 Enoch or The Hebrew Book of Enoch, Hugo Odeberg, ed., New York: KTAV Publishing House, Inc., 1973, p. 79

ENOCH, THE FAVORITE OF GOD

Lamech dispatches his father Methuselah to the far-distant Enoch in order to "...learn everything from him with certainty, since he (Enoch) is a favorite and [one cherished...]"

The Adepts In the Esoteric Classical Tradition, Part 2, Mystics and Mysteries of Alexandria, Manly P. Hall, Los Angeles, CA.: The Philosophical Research Society, Inc., 1984, p. 217

ENOCH, THE GREAT ANCESTOR

In a subject entitled "Praise of the Ancestors" from an old manuscript by Ben Sira "...there [is] a section which serves as an introduction to the historical panorama of Israel's heroes who are worthy of praise...Enoch is the first individual named (44:16)..."

The Wisdom of Ben Sira, Patriack W. Skehan, trans., New York: Doubleday, 1987, p. 499

In Luke 3:37 he has a place among the ancestors of our Lord.

A *Dictionary of the Bible*, Vol. 1, James Hastings, ed., Mass: Hendrickson
  Publishers, 1984, p. 705

A sermon of St. Gregory Palamas in the fourteenth century ex-
plores the idea of a remnant of the elect children of God who
can be traced through the Virgin's ancestors from Seth to Enoch
and King David.

Christian Mythology, George Every, London: Hamlyn Publishing Group
  Limited, 1970, p. 85

ENOCH, THE ULTIMATE REVEALER OF WISDOM

...the Jewish community choose Enoch as the ultimate revealer
of wisdom...

Roots of Apocalyptic, Helge S. Kvanvig, Norway: Neukirchener Verlag,
  1988, p. 17

ENOCH, THE GREAT SCHOLAR

Director of the International Center for the Study of Christian
Origin, Professor Charlesworth comments on the secret book(s)
that speak "about the taking away of Enoch the just, a wise man,
a great scholar, whom the Lord took away...to see, to love the
highest realm..."

The Old Testament Pseudepigrapha, Apocalyptic Literature and Testaments, Vol. I, James H. Charlesworth, ed., New York: Doubleday
  & Company, Inc., p. 103

In Islamic literature Enoch is the first man to practice the art
of writing. Major Jewish works of prophesy and religious instruction are attributed to Enoch. The most important of these
is a complex work of 108 chapters, compiled sometime between
the third century B.C. and the first century A. D. known as 1
Enoch. It includes a history of the world from the time of
Adam. Once widely read and highly influential, 1 Enoch is
quoted by Jude: "Behold the Lord came with his holy myriads,
to execute judgment on all."

ABC's of the Bible, New York: Reader's Digest Association, Inc., 1991, p.
  26

The wise men - and remember that Enoch was a wise man, a scribe and a priest - were learned in all the knowledge of their day. They knew about medicine and mathematics, metallurgy and engineering...

The Lost Prophet, (The Book of Enoch and its influence on Christianity), Margaret Barker, Great Britain: SPCK, 1988, p. 25

ENOCH, THE TEACHER OF HEAVEN AND EARTH

But everywhere Enoch is credited with being the scribe and transmitter par excellence, "the Righteous Scribe, the Teacher of heaven and earth, and the Scribe of Righteousness."

Enoch the Prophet, Hugh Nibley, Salt Lake City, Utah: Deseret Book Company, 1986, p. 138

ENOCH, THE DISCOVERER OF COSMIC GEOGRAPHY

"The variety in the Enoch sources becomes clear when one recognizes the distinguished characteristics connected with Enoch...as the discoverer of cosmic geography..." (see The Astronomical Book, the Book of Watchers, Jubilees)

Roots of Apocalyptic, Helge S. Kvanvig, Norway: Neukirchener Verlag, 1988, p. 148

ENOCH, THE RIGHTEOUS

Enoch lived in a secret place as a hidden righteous man...

Enoch was among the nine righteous names who entered paradise without suffering the pangs of death "He ascended to heaven on God's command..." (Targ. Yer. to Gen. 5:4.)

Encyclopedia Judaica, David Flusser, ed., Jerusalem, Israel: Keter Publishing House, 1971, p. 797

As VanderKam notes:

...in Ezek. 28:13 Eden is identified as the garden of God. Jub. 8:19 considers the garden God's residence. Hence the writer inferred that God had brought the righteous patriarch to his home.

Enoch and the Growth of An Apocalyptic Tradition, James VanderKam, Washington, D.C.: The Catholic Biblical Association of America, 1984, p. 185

"In an encomium on Saint Michael the Archangel attributed to Theodosius, archbishop of Alexandria, 'Enoch the righteous man' "is given a noteworthy reference.

The Books of Enoch, Aramaic Fragments of Qumran Cave 4, J. T. Milik, ed., Oxford: Oxford University Press, 1976, p. 105

An excerpt for the Zohar (1:56a-b) reads:

And the Holy One, blessed be He, postponed their punishment while those righteous men, Jered, Methuselah, and Enoch, were alive. But when they departed from the world, the Holy One, Blessed be He, let the punishment descend upon them and they perished.

Gates To The Old City, Raphel Patai, Detroit: Wayne State University Press, 1981, p. 473

ENOCH THE "SCHOLAR" PAR EXCELLENCE

In the *Ethiopic Book of Enoch,* Enoch's involvement with angelic forces and his incredible journeys gave rise to the following:

Enoch had been conducted by angels through earth and underworld and made privy to the secrets of the universe and the purpose of God. He was therefore regarded...as the "scholar" par excellence.

Encyclopedia Americana, Int'l Edition, Vol. 10, Danbury, CT: Grolier Inc., p. 472

ENOCH, THE ULTIMATE REVEALER OF DIVINE SECRETS

In the Jewish material Enoch is primarily portrayed as a primeval sage, the ultimate revealer of divine secrets.

Roots of Apocalyptic, Helge S. Kvanvig, Norway: Neukirchener Verlag, 1988, p. 27

ENOCH, THE HEAVENLY SAINT

According to the Apocalypse of Zephaniah, an angel meets Abraham, Isaac, Jacob, Enoch, Elijah, and David in paradise

(James, p. 540). In the Descent into Hell, added to the Gospel of Nicodemus (Acta Pilati) no earlier than the fifth century, Christ descends to hell and frees Adam and other saints; upon entering paradise they meet Enoch, Elijah, and the good thief: "And there met with them two men, ancients of days, and...they were asked of the saints: "Who are ye that have not yet been dead in hell with us and are set in paradise in the body?"...

The Books of Enoch, Aramaic Fragments of Qumran Cave 4, J. T. Milik, ed., Oxford: Oxford University Press, 1976, p. 119

ENOCH, THE CELESTIAL PATRIARCH

Enoch was the patriarch who moved in celestial realms, learning astronomical facts and observing punishments and rewards meted out to men and angels.

New Encyclopedia Brittanica, Vol. 4, Chicago, 1995,

ENOCH, THE KEEPER OF THE BOOK OF LIFE

Enoch [was a] celestial scribe, keeper of the Book of Life, and judge of all men in Coptic and Byzantine literature...

The Books of Enoch, Aramaic Fragments of Qumran Cave 4, J. T. Milik, ed., Oxford: Oxford University Press, 1976, p. 263

ENOCH, THE KNOWER OF "SECRET KNOWLEDGE"

According to Dr. Albert Churchward: There was "the legend which existed that Enoch had deposited certain invaluable secrets in a consecrated cavern deep in the bowels of the Earth..."

The Origin and Evolution of Religion, London: Unwin Bros. Ltd., 1924, rep. 1986 Heath Research, p. 352,

To quote the Encyclopedia Americana:

Enoch is shown the secrets of nature, the Eternal Fire, the Abyss...the Tree of Life, the center of the earth...the valley of the Damned, and the Tree of Wisdom. (Int'l Edition, Vol. 10, Danbury, CT: Grolier Inc., p. 472)

ENOCH, THE HERO OF FAITH

Of Enoch, son of Jared and father of Methuselah (not to be confused with Enoch, son of Cain, mentioned in Gen. 4.17), it is written that, after walking "with God for 365 years", "he was no more, because God took him" (Gen. 5.22-24; cf. Sir 44.16; 49:14).

From these words has grown the Enoch legend and its literature, the books of Enoch. Traces of the legend are found in Hebrews 11:5, where Enoch has become a hero of faith.

The Oxford Companion to the Bible, Bruce Metzger and Michael Coogan, Eds., Oxford: Oxford University Press, 1993, p. 184

Enoch walked with God; and he was not, for God took him" (v.24) The expression "walked with God" denotes a devout life, lived in close communion with God, while the reference to his end has always been understood, as by the writers of Hebrews, to mean that "by faith Enoch was taken up so that he should not see death, and he was not found, because God had taken him" (Heb 11:5).

The Interpreter's Dictionary of the Bible, An Illustrated Encyclopedia, New York: Abingdon Press, 1962, p. 103

The son of Jared (Gen.5:18) and the father of Methuselah (Gen. 5:21 Lk 3:37). He [was] incited as a hero of faith (Heb. 11:5)

Wycliffe Bible Encyclopedia, Vol. 1 Charles F. Pfeiffer, Chicago: Moody Press, 1975, p. 528

The New Testament mentions Enoch's name twice; at Jude 14, where he is said to have been the "seventh generation of Adam," and at Heb. 11:5-6 where he is listed as the...hero of faith,

Quoting the LXX nearly verbatim, the author of Hebrews focuses on Enoch's faith as a prequisite for a life well-pleasing to God.

The Eerdmans Bible Dictionary, Allen C. Meyers, ed., 1987, p. 336

ENOCH, THE PIONEER

Enochic "firsts" are: learning, writing, knowledge, and wisdom; recording and systematizing astronomical / calendrical data; and writing a testimony. All of these activities can be documented in more ancient Enochic literature, but Jubilees itself scores a "first" by claiming that Enoch was the pioneer in each area.

Enoch and the Growth of An Apocalyptic Tradition, James VanderKam, Washington, D.C.: The Catholic Biblical Association of America, 1984, p. 181

ENOCH, THE SOLAR HERO

According to the Encyclopedia Brittanica:

"he appears as the seventh in descent from Adam in the line of Seth...The fact that his years are given as 365 suggests that he is a solar hero. (William Benton, Chicago, 1973, p. 604)

He lived 365 years (some have suggested that he was a solar hero).

Illustrated Dictionary and Concordance of the Bible, Geoffrey Wigoder, ed., The Jerusalem Publishing House Ltd., 1986, p. 319

ENOCH, THE LEGENDARY HERO

He early became a favorite legendary hero, as appears from the passages cited from Sirach and from Josephus (Antiquities, book I, chap. 3, section 4), and he maintained that character in later Judaism (e.g. Testament of the Twelve Patriarchs, Levi 10:14 and Dan 5, mentions other books of Enoch) as well as in Christianity and Islam, which tells of 366 Books of Enoch.

The Universal Jewish Encyclopedia, Vol. 4, Isaac Landman, ed., N.Y., 1941, p. 131

ENOCH, THE MATHEMATICIAN

According to Jubilees, Enoch acquired knowledge and wisdom; another Jewish tradition makes him a teacher of astronomy and mathematics and the one to whom an angel revealed the true calendar.

ABC's of the Bible, New York: Reader's Digest Association, Inc., 1991, p. 26

He was esteemed as the inventor of writing, arithmetic and astronomy, and the Arabs called him Idris, which is explained by Baidawi as meaning one of great knowledge.

The Universal Jewish Encyclopedia, Vol. 4, Isaac Landman, ed., N.Y., 1941, p. 131

ENOCH, THE COLLECTOR OF THE HEAVENLY TABLETS

He is "the collector of the tablets," ...such is the office of Enoch:

"Bring out the books from my store house," says God to his angels in the Slavonic Enoch, "and a reed of quick-writing [shorthand], and give it to Enoch, and deliver to him the choice books out of my hand." (2 Enoch 22:12.) Enoch sees the heavenly tablets on which human deeds are recorded. This section is dated between 150 and 100 B.C.

Encyclopedia Americana, Int'l Edition, Vol. 10, Danbury, CT: Grolier Inc., p. 473, p. 140

Enoch (seventh in Adam's line); he too learned God's mysteries and had access to the heavenly tablets.

Encyclopedia Judaica, David Flusser, ed., Jerusalem, Israel: Keter Publishing House, 1971, p. 797

ENOCH, THE RECIPIENT OF SECRET KNOWLEDGE FROM GOD

"he was later believed to be the recipient of secret knowledge from God".

Encyclopedia Britannia (Micropoedia III Coleman Exclusi, 1978

ENOCH, THE KNOWER OF DIVINE SECRETS

Enoch's supernatural disappearance led to the belief that he became privy to the divine secrets. These heavenly secrets were purportedly revealed in the...books of Enoch.

Who's Who in the Bible, Reader's Digest, New York: Reader's Digest Association, Inc. Pleasantville, 1994, p. 102

With ch 37 begins the Book of Similitude (chs 37-44) represents the future kingdom of God, the dwelling of the righteous and of the angels; and finally all the secrets of the heavens.

The *International Standard Bible Encyclopedia*, James Orr, ed., Mich.: W.M.B Eerdmans, 1960 p. 165

ENOCH, THE KNOWER OF HEAVENLY KNOWLEDGE

Professors Eisenman and Wise explains that Enoch was "conversant with 1. Heavenly Knowledge - in particular 'Knowledge' of an esoteric kind, and 2. scientific knowledge of the kind alluded to in this text - knowledge of the heavenly spheres and their courses. Since he had been there, he could actually measure them."

The *Dead Sea Scrolls Uncovered*, by Robert H. Eisenman and Michael Wise, New York: Barnes & Noble Books, 1992, p. 96

Enoch had been translated to heaven, where the secrets of the heavenly regions and the course of human events predetermined in heaven were disclosed to him.

The *International Standard Bible Encyclopedia*, Vol. 2, Geoffrey Bromiley, ed., Grand Rapids, Michigan: William B. Eerdmans Publishing Co., 1982, p. 103

ENOCH, THE MEDIUM FOR REVELATION

Enoch is depicted as a medium for the revelation of heavenly secrets to humanity: secrets of cosmology, sacred history, and eschatology. The principal sources for these traditions are 1 and 2 Enoch, Jubilees, Pseudo-Eupolemus, and previously unknown writings among the Dead Sea Scrolls.

The *Encyclopedia of Religion*, Vol. 5, Mircea Eliade, ed., New York: Macmillan Publishing Co., 1987, p. 117

ENOCH, THE LEARNER OF THE MYSTERIES OF LIFE

According to Gen. 5:24, Enoch was caught up from the earth to be with God...he learned...the coming of the kingdom of God, but also secrets about many of the mysteries of life and the world.

The *International Standard Bible Encyclopedia*, Vol. 1, Grand Rapids, Michigan: William B. Eerdmans Publishing Co., 1982, p. 156

ENOCH, THE REVEALER OF THE DEEPEST MYSTERIES

This modest presentation points to significant relations with Hebrew - and also Aramaic - parallelistic features within the Bible.

This can be expected in a corpus of traditions ascribed to the patriarch Enoch who, thanks to his special closeness to God was believed to be able to reveal the deepest mysteries.

The use of word patterns known from the sacred texts enhanced the authority of revelations for Jews and Christians.

Intertestamental Essays In Honour of Jozef Tadeusz Milik, Zdzislaw J. Kapera, ed., Krakow: The Enigma Press, 1992, p. 201

ENOCH, KNOWER OF HIDDEN COSMOLOGICAL AND HISTORICAL KNOWLEDGE

Enoch's "life" and the secrets revealed to him are summarized in Jubilees 4:16-26 and detailed in the Books of Enoch.

Enoch receives these revelations first in nocturnal visions, and then in a heavenly journey lasting three hundred years, during which he dwells with angels and is instructed by them in hidden cosmological and historical knowledge. After a brief return to earth...he is removed to the garden of Eden....

The Encyclopedia of Religion, Vol. 5, Mircea Eliade, ed., New York: Macmillan Publishing Co., 1987, p. 117

ENOCH, "THE SIGN OF KNOWLEDGE FOR ALL GENERATIONS"

In Ecclesiastics 44:16 he is described as a "sign of knowledge to all generations implying that he was the source of esoteric knowledge. The idea that Enoch was transported alive to heaven is prevalent in later Judaism and Christianity (see Heb. 11:5)

Illustrated Dictionary and Concordance of the Bible, Geoffrey Wigoder, ed., The Jerusalem Publishing House Ltd., 1986, p. 319

For the function of Enoch in his role as 'sign of knowledge for all generations' because he was sent down there [to the earth after his removal] as the sign that he might witness against all the children of men and foretell every work of the generations until the day of judgment' (4:24). This legendary framework certainly corresponds to the situation described in En. 81 and in the Book of Watchers, En. 1-36.

The Books of Enoch, Aramaic Fragments of Qumran Cave 4, J. T. Milik, ed., Oxford: Oxford University Press, 1976, p. 11

ENOCH, THE VISIONARY OF SACRED HISTORY

In *The Books of Enoch, Aramaic Fragments of Qumran Cave 4*, Enoch is referred to as a "visionary of sacred history...."

J. T. Milik, ed., Oxford: Oxford University Press, 1976, p. 60

ENOCH, TEACHER OF DIVINE KNOWLEDGE

Professor at the University of Iowa George W. Nickelsburg in his chapter entitled, *"The Bible Rewritten and Expanded"* indicates that:

Enoch appears in the literature of the Second Temple period primarily as a recipient and teacher of divine knowledge; as a scribe, inventor of writing and of the calendar.

Jewish Writings of the Second Temple Period, Michael E. Stone, et, al. eds. Philadelphia: Fortress Press, 1984, p. 104

ENOCH, THE INTERMEDIARY OF SECRET DOCTRINE

Thus Metatron is represented as the intermediary through whom the secret doctrine was brought down to man. And as such he defends the rights of men to obtain these secrets against the angels in general who do not desire that the terrestrials should know the 'mysteries'.

3 Enoch or The Hebrew Book of Enoch, Hugo Odeberg, ed., New York: KTAV Publishing House, Inc., 1973, p. 84

ENOCH, THE HEAVENLY WITNESS

The Anchor Bible Dictionary informs "...that the motif of Enoch as a heavenly witness is very old (see Jub. 10:17)."

Vol. 2, David Noel Freedman, ed., New York: Doubleday Co., 1984, p. 525

In another vein, it is stated that the reason or object of Enoch's translation was the function prescribed for him of be-ing a witness - in the world to come - to the sinfulness of his generation and the justice of the Holy One in eventually destroying the men of that generation through the Deluge: see chh. 4, 48c2. Thus Enoch is defined as Scribe-Witness in agreement with Book of Jubilees 4.21 seqq. and Targ. P. to Gen. 5.24.

3 Enoch or The Hebrew Book of Enoch, Hugo Odeberg, ed., New York: KTAV Publishing House, Inc., 1973, p. 80

ENOCH, THE EXALTED ONE

Enoch, at the end of his life, is exalted to the presence of the Son of Man.

The Scepter and the Star: The Messiahs of the Dead Sea Scrolls and other Ancient Literature, John J. Collins, New York: Doubleday Co., 1984, p. 179

With Enoch who in the "Enoch Literature" tended to occupy the most exalted position in the Presence of the Godhead. (In fact, this derivation seems to give the only reasonable explanation why the figure of Metatron was at all introduced into the Enoch Literature.) See 2 En. 21.3, 22.4,6,10, cf. I En. 70.

3 Enoch or The Hebrew Book of Enoch, Hugo Odeberg, ed., New York: KTAV Publishing House, Inc., 1973, p. 140

The New Standard Jewish Encyclopedia tells us that:

Only after the Christians had become quite distinct from the Jews did Enoch regain his popularity in Jewish lore, being identified with the angel Metatron, and a mystical literature grew up around his personality.

7th edn. Geoffrey Wigoder, ed, New York: Facts On File, 1992, p. 307

ENOCH, THE METATRON, THE BELOVED OF GOD

I said to Metatron, "Why are you called by the name of your Creator with seventy names? You are greater than all the princes, more exalted than all the angels, more beloved than all the ministers, more honored than all the hosts, and elevated over all potentates in sovereignty, greatness, and glory; why, then, do they call you 'Youth' in the heavenly heights?" He answered, "Because I am Enoch, the son of Jared".

The Old Testament Pseudepigrapha, Apocalyptic Literature and Testaments, Vol. I, James H. Charlesworth, ed., New York: Doubleday & Company, Inc., p. 258

ENOCH, THE CHOSEN ONE

From the book *Gates to the Old City* the question is asked of Metatron (Enoch). What is the nature of this one who ascends the heights of heights:

I have chosen this one in preference to you all, to be a prince and a ruler over you in the heavenly heights'. Instantly they all went to me, prostrated themselves before me, and said: "Happy are you, and happy your parents, because your Creator has favored you!' And since I am young in their company, and a mere youth among them in days and months and years, therefore they call me Youth.' "

Detroit: Wayne State University Press, 1981, p. 390

ENOCH, THE AGENT OF GOD

He became the archangel Metatron (3 Enoch 4-16). He was a messianic figure, the agent of God (3 Enoch 10.3-6). Enoch was a figure who aroused considerable passions.

The Lost Prophet, (The Book of Enoch and its influence on Christianity), Margaret Barker, Great Britain: SPCK, 1988, p. 19

ENOCH, THE REPRESENTATIVE AND VICE-REGENT OF THE HOLY ONE

But the characterization of the translated Enoch is not restricted to describing him as a celestial Scribe-Witness. The various honors and offices conferred upon him are in chh. 7 seqq. set forth in successive stages, progressing towards a climax (in chh. 12 and 48 c7,8). Thus he is made:

As a ruler and judge over the angelic hosts and the princes of kingdoms, he is also the representative and vice-regent of the Holy One, the intermediary between the Most High and the angelic world as well as the insignia of his dignity by the Holy

One Himself. The Holy One makes him sit on a Throne similar to His own, gives him a Curtain similar to the Curtain spread over the Throne of Glory, 10.1, 48 c5.

The Throne of the man-angel is placed at the door of the Seventh Hall (the innermost of the Divine Hekalop or Palaces), 10.2, 48 c8. After this the heavenly herald is sent out into the heavens to announce him as "Metatron, the (Servant) of the Holy One," His representative and vice-regent, 10.3.

3 Enoch or The Hebrew Book of Enoch, Hugo Odeberg, ed., New York: KTAV Publishing House, Inc., 1984

From the book *Gates to the Old City* the question is asked of Metatron (Enoch) why is he so favored:

The angel Metatron, Prince of the Face, who dwells in the heights, said to me: "because of the abundant love and great compassion with which the Holy One, blessed be He, loved and cherished me more than all the children of the heights, He wrote with his finger [as] with a pen of flame, upon the crown which was on my head, the letters by which heaven and earth were created".

Raphel Patai, Detroit: Wayne State University Press, 1981, p. 393

ENOCH, THE TESTIFIER

Metatron retains the functions of Scribe, Witness, Testifier associated with him on the ground of his identity with Enoch. Scribe, Witness, Testifier (of men's deeds).

3 Enoch or The Hebrew Book of Enoch, Hugo Odeberg, ed., New York: KTAV Publishing House, Inc., 1973, p. 119

ENOCH IS METATRON

Metatron, the steward of the angelic hosts, who acts as a kind of intermediary between God and man. Metatron is depicted as the transfigured Biblical character Enoch who was taken up to heaven from the midst of a sinful generation and transformed into an angel.

Jew, Their Religious Beliefs and Practices, Alan Unterman, London: Routledge, 1981, p. 93

Metatron's identity with Enoch symbolizes into earthly life, into the existence as a terrestrial man, and the ascent of the terrestrial man into a celestial being.

3 Enoch or The Hebrew Book of Enoch, Hugo Odeberg, ed., New York: KTAV Publishing House, Inc., 1973, p. 319

Raphel Patai of Fairleigh Dickinson University, a noted anthropologist and Biblical scholar, cites the following passage from the Midrash about Metatron:

You are greater than all the [celestial] princes, higher than all the angels, more beloved than all the servants, more honored than all the host, and more exalted than all the powers in sovereignty, greatness, and glory... Why, then, do they call you 'Youth' in the heavenly heights ? He answered and said to me: 'Because I am Enoch the son of Jared. For when the generation of the deluge sinned and turned to evil deeds and said to God, *Depart from us! For we desire not the knowledge of Thy ways* (Job 21:14), the Holy One, blessed be He, took me from their midst to be a witness against them in the heavenly heights to all those who walk on earth so that they should not say, 'the Merciful One is cruel!'

Gates To The Old City, Detroit: Wayne State University Press, 1981, p. 387

In an ancient writing on the "Ascension of Moses...Metatron announces himself to Moses as "Enoch, the son of Jared." He is the guide of Moses during his ascent through the heavens..."

3 Enoch or The Hebrew Book of Enoch, Hugo Odeberg, ed., New York: KTAV Publishing House, Inc., 1973, p. 99

Ishmael asks Metatron to identify himself and in particular to explain the title "Youth" (Na'ar) with which the Merkaba angels addressed him. Metatron reveals that he is Enoch the son of Jared (Gen. 5:18-24); as the youngest of the angel princes he is known as "Youth." He recounts in detail to Ishmael how as Enoch he was taken up to heaven and transformed into Metatron, one of the highest of the archangels who acts as God's vice-regent. Having established Metatron's impeccable credentials as a heavenly guide...

The Anchor Bible Dictionary, Vol. 2, David Noel Freedman, ed., New York: Doubleday Co., 1992, p. 140

Metatron identified with the Prince of the World, God's vice-regent over the world, etc. There Rabbi Ishmael narrates that when he ascended on high to behold the vision of the chariot he was greeted by Metatron, who has several names, including Enoch, son of Jared. Metatron tells him how he was taken up from the generation of the Flood, and how "the Holy One, blessed be he, made for me (i.e. Metatron) a throne like the throne of glory" (10:1).

The Scepter and the Star: The Messiahs of the Dead Sea Scrolls and other Ancient Literature, John J. Collins, New York: Doubleday Co., 1995, p. 141

Professor Odeberg narrates about the pilgrimage of Metatron's spirit or the "Spiritual Essence of the Righteous" and indicates that:"

"Two earthly men were made into angels: Enoch who became Metatron and Elijah who became Sandalfon.

3 Enoch or The Hebrew Book of Enoch, edited by, Ph.D., New York: KTAV Publishing House, Inc., 1973, p. 123

The Hebrew Book of Enoch describes Enoch's transformation in this fashion:

"instantly my flesh turned into flames, my sinews into blazing fire, my bones into embers of broom-fire, my eyelids into lightning flashes, the wheels of my eyes into fiery torches, the hairs of my head into flame and flares, all my limbs into wings of burning fire, and the body of my stature into blazing fire. (Excerpts from 3 Enoch 3-16) The Enoch Metatron ideas are connected with Gen. 5.24, "he was not for God took him," and Enoch's elevation into Metatron-Na'ar is based on Proverbs 22.6...The sequence 'Enoch Metatron' or sometimes, 'Metatron Enoch' is very frequent. Cf. e.g. Zohar iii. 189 a b.

3 Enoch or The Hebrew Book of Enoch, Hugo Odeberg, ed., New York: KTAV Publishing House, Inc., 1973, p. 119

The book *A Dictionary of Angels* declared that:

Metatron was considered...mightier than either Michael or Gabriel [which] is the view expressed in the *Chronicles of Jerahmee*...In *Yalkut Hadash*, also, Metatron is said to be 'appointed over Michael and Gabriel.'

Gustav Davidson, New York: The Free Press,1967, p. 193

Metatron is the ladder in Jacob's vision, on which ladder the angels were descending and ascending.

3 Enoch or The Hebrew Book of Enoch, Hugo Odeberg, ed., New York: KTAV Publishing House, Inc., 1973, p. 123

Gershom Scholem, a professor at the Hebrew University of Jerusalem, indicated that:

Metatron is the angel of whom it is said in Exod. xxiii 20 ff.: "Beware of him for my name is in him."

Major Trends in Jewish Mysticism, New York: Schocken Books, 1974, p. 68

It is said that Exodus 23:20 refers to Metatron: 'behold, I send an angel before thee, to keep thee in the way and to bring thee unto the place which I have prepared' (usually applied to John the Baptist), and Exodus 23:22: 'My name is in him.' In addition, Metatron has been identified as the Liberating Angel..

A Dictionary of Angels, Gustav Davidson, New York: The Free Press, 1967, p. 192

Proverbs 22:6, is interpreted: "Enoch was made into the Na'ar Metatron by the Holy One who took him from on earth and made him a ruler on high for ever."

3 Enoch or The Hebrew Book of Enoch, Hugo Odeberg, ed., New York: KTAV Publishing House, Inc., 1973, p. 123

Throughout this literature Metatron, or whatever name is given to him, remains in the position of the highest of all created beings...

Major Trends in Jewish Mysticism, Gershom Scholem, New York: Schocken Books, 1974, p. 70

Adds Gustav Davidson, a University Fellow at Wroxton College (England), in the book *A Dictionary of Angels*: Metatron is the tallest angel in Heaven, and the greatest...

[and] legend relates that upon Metatron (while still Enoch, a mortal) arriving in Heaven, he was transformed into a spirit of fire... (New York: The Free Press, 1967, p. 192)

...he is a living record of the spirit's journey from its earliest beginnings to its last phases. The spirit's descent and ascent are also brought into connection with the mystical language of Ezek. 1:14. The descent is the 'running', the ascent is the 're-turning'.

3 *Enoch or The Hebrew Book of Enoch*, Hugo Odeberg, ed., New York: KTAV Publishing House, Inc., 1973, p. 123

Metatron has also been credited with the authorship of Psalms 37:25 according to Talmud...and the authorship, in part, of Isaiah 24:16. In the *Zolar* I, Metatron is spoken of as Moses' rod...

A Dictionary of Angels, Gustav Davidson, New York: The Free Press, 1967, p. 193

CHAPTER III

ENOCH, THE MIGHTIEST PROPHET OF GOD

IF YOU THINK ENOCH'S ATTRIBUTES ARE EXAGGERATED THEN consider this. What kind of human being do you think would have the qualifications to "walk with God."? How many of us have them?

To "be taken up" into heaven, body and soul would stagger the human imagination. Yet, Scripture verifies that all this and more was experienced by Enoch.

Those two lines found in Genesis speak volumes for the depth of righteousness and holiness that Enoch the Ethiopian must have possessed. The many characteristics we have outlined only reflect the phenomenon known as Enoch.

The greatest heroes of Israel's past - Abraham, Moses, David, Amos - were shepherds...

ABC's of the Bible, New York: Reader's Digest Association, Inc., 1991, p. 165

But Enoch by his deeds is greater than all of the Biblical personalities in Scripture.

Enoch was an IMMORTAL, not Abraham or Moses. He, also, "walked with God," something that was not said of Abraham or Moses in the Bible.

Enoch the Ethiopian has the highest religious stature in Scripture next to Jesus Christ if one considers the biblical accounts of his life.

He is the first and only example of both "having walked with God and ascending bodily into heaven." (Gen. 5:21-24).

Enoch sets the biblical standard for the word legend. He adds new dimensions to the scale of human achievement on a spiritual level. His triumph over adversity, those frailties and weaknesses that plague all earthly existence, expands the known boundaries of human potential.

He stood at the threshold of perfection and passed over, the first perfect human being. He was the consummate biblical character devoted to righteous living, an antediluvian masterpiece of perfection who was a natural forerunner of Jesus Christ.

Forever a stranger to death because of his translation into heaven, Enoch is a precursor to Christ in having both human and divine characteristics.

Enoch the Ethiopian was the original "high father" in the biblical world before Abraham. This biblical superstar casts a colossal shadow over both his predecessors and contemporaries alike. He scaled the heights of perfection and was not found wanting. He sets a precedent for perfected human development.

Enoch, the translated patriarch, is a pivotal figure in biblical history because he plays a major role in establishing the African origins of the Bible. The early African presence in the Bible is clearly established by this Ethiopian's participation at the beginning of Biblical history. He is only seven generations removed from the first Biblical man.

Enoch defeated death and mortality through a righteous life unsurpassed by any other patriarch or prophet. Death stood powerless before Enoch as he arrived in Heaven without the sting of death.

He is the first and only translated patriarch who became the first man to leave a mortal imprint on the "stairway to heavens."

INTIMATE COMPANION OF GOD

Enoch is also reported to have a "special closeness to God," (*Intertestamental Essays In Honour of Jozef Tadeusz Milik*, Zdzis, 1992)

Thus Enoch is the special companion of God. Enoch's supreme love for the Most High resulted in a special relationship with the Creator. He was anointed with the "holy" oil of Immortality and blessed with such a high spirit of love that he "walked with God."

As The New International Dictionary of the Bible explains:

Walking with God is a relic of the first paradise when men walked and talked with God in holy familiarity, and it anticipates a new paradise (Rev. 21:3; 22:3-4).

Regency Reference Library, Grand Rapids, Michigan: Zondervan Publishing House, 1987, p. 313

The cryptic statement which related to Enoch as a man who "walked with God and he was not, for God took him." (Gen. 5:24) gave rise to various mystical and esoteric interpretations, suggesting a miraculous translation of Enoch alive from earth to heaven, where he enjoyed an intimate fellowship with God...

Illustrated Dictionary and Concordance of the Bible, Geoffrey Wigoder, ed., The Jerusalem Publishing House Ltd., 1986, p. 319

The Interpreter's Dictionary of the Bible testifies that:

Enoch lived in such intimate association with God (Gen. 5:22,24) that he was not, for God took him (cf. Ecclus. 44:16; 49:14, Heb. 11:5) Enoch's translation produced a large growth of later legend (Wisd. Sol. 4:10, Jude 14)...

George Arthur Butttrick, ed., New York: New Abingdon Press, 1962, p. 103

Furthermore, Enoch is the first to be found in paradise still in his earthly body - absent was death's universal influence.

According to The Anchor Bible Dictionary:

Enoch had a unique relationship with God. This direct and continuous relationship may be the meaning of the phrase "walked with haelohim," ... (New York: Doubleday Co., 1992)

By faith Enoch 'was translated that he should not see death ... for before his translation he had this testimony, that he pleased God." Hebrews 11:5. In the midst of a world by its iniquity doomed to destruction, Enoch lived a life of such close communion with God that he was not permitted to fall under the power of death. The godly character of this prophet represents the state of holiness which must be attained by those who shall be "redeemed from the earth..." (Revelation 14:3)

Patriarchs and Prophets, Ellen G. White, California: Pacific Press Publishing Association, 1958, p. 89

The wise, like Enoch, walked with God.

The Lost Prophet, (The Book of Enoch and its influence on Christianity), Margaret Barker, Great Britain: SPCK, 1988, p. 24

He himself is described as "the wisest of men" (Milik. The books of Enoch; 260)

Enoch and the Growth of An Apocalyptic Tradition, James VanderKam, Washington, D.C.: The Catholic Biblical Association of America, 1984, p. 173

In like manner, George Braziller author of the book *Scrolls From the Dead Sea* writes that "[the] literature attach many tales and legends to the figure. He is all wise, knowing the secrets of the universe..." (Library of Congress, 1993, p. 76)

Enoch is the first among men.

And he was the first among men that are born on earth who learnt writing and knowledge and wisdom...

Enoch and the Growth of An Apocalyptic Tradition, Washington, D.C.: The Catholic Biblical Association of America, 1984, p. 9

Only two men were reputed to have attained the equivalent of "King of Kings." Enoch was the first, and Jesus Christ, naturally, was the other.

Enoch is the Supreme Head of Kings.

The Hebrew Life of Enoch has the kings of the earth hailing Enoch as their supreme head.

Enoch the Prophet, Hugh Nibley, Salt Lake City, Utah: Deseret Book Company, 1986, p. 258

Enoch is a heavenly king.

As a reward for instructing mankind, God, resolved to install him as king over the angels in heaven too...He made a powerful impression on all he taught, including kings and princesses and they acclaimed him as their king...

Encyclopedia Judaica, David Flusser, ed., Jerusalem, Israel: Keter Publishing House, 1971, p. 797

This immortal heavenly regent was the first man to enter God's house, the divine garden of paradise (Heaven) without the "touch of death.." This is the Eerdmans Bible Dictionary's description of Enoch:

A descendent of Adam and Eve through Seth, Enoch is described as one who spent his relatively short life in spiritual communion with God (vv 22-23; cf. LXX "was well-pleasing to God" cf. Jub. 4:17-21).

Enoch's ascension to heaven is thought to be indicated at v.24 ("and he was not") [LXX "he was not found"], for God took him [LXX "translated him"]; cf. 2 Kings 2:1;11).

Outside of the Genesis narrative his name occurs only in the royal genealogy at 1 Chr. 1:3 (KJV "Henoch") [Allen C. Myers ed., 1987, p. 336]

ENOCH IS THE RIGHTEOUS IMMORTAL ONE.

In the Bible Enoch becomes the first example and personification of Immortality. He is the first Biblical "phoenix," the symbol of immortality who was translated miraculously into heaven without a visit by "the angel of death." Enoch became an Immortal man, a man who never "tasted" death. Naturally, therefore, he becomes the first man to forego the need of a future "resurrected" body.

He typifies the saints living at Christ's coming who will be removed from mortality to immortality without passing through death (1 Cor 15:51-52).

The New International Dictionary of the Bible, J.D. Douglas & Merrill Tenney, Editors, Regency Reference Library, Grand Rapids, Michigan: Zondervan Publishing House, 1987, p. 313

Death was not a pre-requisite for Enoch to enter heaven. His earthly vehicle remained intact as he crossed "the gates of paradise." As a result, he becomes the first man to enter heaven in his mortal wrappings.

Enoch is clearly the most righteous man in Biblical history. His achievements extend beyond the realms of human imagination.

How can one imagine a perfect human being or an Immortal man who traveled back and forth from heaven only to be changed into a perfect angelic figure.

He is an example of human potential realized on divine levels. Through Enoch the Ethiopian, we can see why in the African tradition we are called the "children of God."

In the Biblical universe he is the brightest sun among *all* the Patriarchs and Prophets. He stands in Biblical history as a shining example of humanity perfected by righteous living.

In an ancient writing from the 1st century, we note how Enoch's premature departure from this earthly plane was ordained by God to prevent him from being contaminated by evil and thus preserve his perfect sainthood.

According to Emeritus Professor W.D. Davies of Duke University and A.A. Bradford Distinguished Professor at Texas Christian University, Louis Finkelstein:

> "he is said to have been 'taken' to be with God, because of his sanctity, whereas the other patriarchs underwent the experience of death."

> *The Cambridge History of Judaism*, ed., Cambridge: Cambridge University Press, 1989, p. 425.

Enoch strides along the corridors of greatness, the first among the legendary heroes of the Bible.

> Enoch was the inventor of all sciences and knowledge since he was privy to the secrets of God and could decipher the writing on the heavenly tablets....Early Christian sources...(CHURCH FATHERS), contain many legends about Enoch.

> *The New Standard Jewish Encyclopedia*, Seventh Edition, Geoffrey Wigoder, ed., New York: FACTS ON FILE, 1984

As "the inventor of all sciences and knowledge" Enoch was the *first* Genius and multi-genius in Biblical history.

"FACE TO FACE" WITH GOD

Like Enoch, Moses is said to have conversed with God "face to face." But Enoch not only talked with God "face to face," he *saw* God's "face." He was God's companion having "walked with God" as the Bible says.

> I saw the view of the face of the Lord, like iron made burning hot in a fire [and] brought out, and it emits sparks and is incandescent. Thus even I saw the face of the Lord. But the face of the Lord is not to be talked about, it is so very marvelous and supremely awesome and supremely frightening.

> *The Old Testament Pseudepigrapha, Apocalyptic Literature and Testaments*, Vol. I, James H. Charlesworth, ed., New York: Doubleday & Company, Inc., p. 136

"The New Testament affirms the notion that people are not allowed to see God. Paul tells his traveling companion, Timothy: 'No man has ever seen or can see God." (1 Tim 6:16)

No one maybe except Enoch, we might add.

To quote from the Curator of Hebrew books and manuscripts at the British Library, George Every:

> In Exodus Moses is accorded a partial revelation of God. He is not permitted to see God's glory. But God places him 'in a crevice of the rock', and as God's glory passes by he is allowed to see only God's 'back' while his face 'shall not be seen'. On the very same mountain, Horeb, Elijah too gains his most intimate knowledge of the divine presence. 'The Lord was passing by', and Elijah was in a cave, perhaps the very same 'cleft' which had sheltered Moses. The revelation here, however, is not a sight but a sound, the 'still, small voice.'

> *Christian Legends*, New York: Peter Bedrick Books, 1987, p. 130

Professor John Metford of the University of Bristol records the same Biblical portrayal of Elijah's experience with God:

While sheltering in a cave from an earthquake and fire, he was made aware of the presence of God in 'a still small voice' (1 Kg. 19:21).

Dictionary of Christian Legend, London: Thames and Hudson, 1983, p. 94

However, it is quite clear that Elijah's "small voice" experience is not comparable to Enoch's "face to face" experience with God.

ENOCH IS GREATER THAN MOSES.

Professor of Biblical Theology T.K. Thordarson says that Moses was "something more than just a prophet, he was a servant of the Lord. Generally speaking, these narrative (Numbers) tell how Moses welded the Hebrew tribes and the rabble (Num. xi, 4) that accompanied them into the ordered community of life and worship.

He is at the same time the precursor of Christ (I Cor. x, 1, ff) and a witness to him (John i, 45). Moses (with Elijah) appears to Jesus in the scene of the transfiguration, thus heralding the coming of the Kingdom of God in Christ (Mark, ix, 4 ff). On the other hand, Jesus (it can be inferred) is seen as the new Moses giving the new law on the Sermon on the Mount (Matt. v-vii). Conversely, the law of Moses contrasted with the grace of Christ (John i, 17)."

Encyclopedia Britannica Vol. 8, Chicago, Ill., William Benton Publ., 1973, p. 882

The same work concluded: "Moses remains one of the outstanding figures of all time. In Judaism Moses is a towering figure from whom the entire religious system is derived and on whose authority it rests. In past Biblical Jewish literature Moses became an eschatological figure and a heavenly being who will appear at the end of time. Traditionally, he was regarded as the author of the first five books of the Bible, which are known as the books of Moses and the Jewish law is called Mosaic because it was traditionally revealed through him."

About 1300 BC. came Moses, the mightiest man in Hebrew history. Guided by God through crisis after crisis, Moses set his people free and led them back toward the Promised land.

The World's Great Religions, Henry R. Luce, ed., New York: Time Inc., 1957, p. 157

And yet with all that Moses had accomplished in Biblical history, Enoch still surpasses him. Enoch is a heroic figure of mythical proportions. Enoch, the Servant of God, Enoch the Ethiopian reached such high levels of spiritual development and oneness with the Supreme Reality that he "walked with God" in "holy familiarity." He was a companion of the Most High, a man who lived a God-Conscious life so well that God, Personally, took him straight up into heaven in his earthly body according to the Bible (Gen. 5:24).

One changed the definition of a people. The other changed the definition of humanity.

ENOCH IS THE FLAWLESS PATRIARCH-PROPHET.

All of the prophets displayed, at one time or another, some character flaw like anger, despair, drunkenness, covetousness and so forth, all except Enoch.

As *The Encyclopedia of Religion* says "God prematurely terminated Enoch's life on earth so that wickedness would not infect his perfect saintliness."

He stands in Biblical history as the first perfect man.

This African man showed us how to be in the world yet above its profane demands. Enoch lived and made his life sacred by first serving God completely, then his family and his fellow man.

Enoch's commitment to family life and guidance is made clear when Enoch returns from paradise to instruct his family, so great was his dedication to family life.

For instance, Professor L. Schiffman calls our attention to the fact that:

Enoch's journey to the seven heavens is described, followed by God's revelation of the history of the world up to Enoch's time and the prediction of the flood. Then Enoch returns to earth, where he instructs his children of belief and behavior, emphasizing the importance of his books.

From *Text to Tradition*, Lawrence H. Schiffman, Ktav Publishing House, New Jersey, 1991, p. 128

Along the same line of thought *The Cambridge History of Judaism* points out that:

In Ethiopic Enoch (91:1-19) Methuselah calls together all the sons of Enoch for Enoch to make known to them what is to happen to them in eternity. Enoch invites them to live in righteousness and reveals to them what has been called 'the Apocalypse of Weeks' (chapter 93).

A man who does his duty to his family, who does right and is committed to truth and justice within his own home first, with his wife and with his children, there lies a man who "walks in the light." A man of divine greatness, a man like Enoch.

The author of *Patriarchs and Prophets* expressed it this way:

Enoch's walk with God was not in a trance or a vision, but in all the duties of his daily life. He did not become a hermit, shutting himself entirely from the world; for he had a work to do for God in the world. In the family and in his intercourse with men, as a husband and father, a friend, a citizen, he was the steadfast, unwavering servant of the Lord.

Ellen G. White, California: Pacific Press Publishing Association, 1958, p. 85

"and was called by an angel to leave his retreat to go to teach man to walk in the ways of God. He taught for 243 years, during which peace and prosperity reigned in the world."

Encyclopedia Judaica, David Flusser, ed., Jerusalem, Israel: Keter Publishing House, 1971, p. 797

Enoch is our African ancestor who was a primeval example of righteous living. In knowing his story, there is a lesson for all of us in how to live life, in sacredness and holiness.

He achieved the ultimate freedom, freedom from death and became history's Ist Immortal Man (Gen. 5:24). Enoch is the first to enter paradise in his mortal coil. His was the first ascent into heaven without the burden of death.

The Bible says Enoch and Elijah are the only two men who never died. Even Jesus Christ experienced death, "Father, into thy hands I commit my spirit." (Luke 23:46); until three days later when he, according to the Bible, rose from the dead, "He is not here; for he has risen..." (Matthew 28:6) and ascended into heaven. The New Testament says [Jesus was] "taken up into heaven" (Mark 16:19).

Who then is this great man we call Enoch and where are his racial origins? The answer can only be that he had to be an African because the Hebrews as a nation was not even in existence during his time. He was Adam's 7th Seed. Abraham was not born until 21 generations later. The same Abraham who is the recorded "Father of the Hebrews." Obviously, Moses came even later. So what else could he have been except a Black Ethiopian. According to Carl Conrad Nickols, Enoch was the "ancestor to the 'shepherd' people that later migrated as nomads into Egypt, who were named by the Egyptians Habiru meaning Hebrews." (See C.C. Nichols lecture tapes "The Bible in Africa.")

White supremacists have an obvious discomfort with black origins in anything except crime and intellectual inferiority. Therefore, many of them would like to put the emphasis on Abraham because they feel they can obscure his racial identity by saying he is from the "mythical" land of the "Middle East."

Enoch, on the other hand, has his racial identity too undeniably close to Africa which in the mind of the white supremacists encourages dismissal and obscurity. Enoch, it would seem, is too closely linked to Mother Africa for their "discriminating" taste.

His Ethiopian origins leave less room for distortion and misleading geographical locations like the so-called "Middle East," a geopolitical term which was non-existent during those times.

If that doesn't work they will start stressing Mesopotamia in the hope that Abraham's blackness would be compromised.

Some take a dubious comfort in locating Abraham in Mesopotamia which has a greater appeal to them because they believe it makes his black/African roots more open to debate and question (deception?).

As the Winston's Original African Heritage Study Bible Encyclopedia Concordance points out:

> this African Edenic prophet of God...has been one of the biblical characters most neglected by European Bible scholars.

> James W. Peebles, Tenn.: James C. Winston Publishing Company, Inc., 1996, p. 212

Now there are several reasons why we maintain that Enoch is an Ethiopian. To briefly state some of them. First of all, his first book is found complete only in Ethiopic. Secondly, his work is canonized almost exclusively by the classic Ethiopian Falasha Temple (Church) and the Coptic Church in Ge'ez which points to a recognition of a native son and ancestor since Ethiopia houses the oldest Hebrew-Israelite and Christian traditions and peoples. And, Enoch comes from a very old tradition, "the seventh from creation."

In addition, Ge'ez is actually the oldest Semitic language in existence and it is known as classic Ethiopic. Moreover, out of Ge'ez came "Amharic, the official language of Ethiopia," according to *Funk & Wagnalls, New Standard Encyclopedia of Universal Knowledge*, pp. 297-8

Thirdly, the First book of Enoch is in fact called Ethiopic Enoch, and parts of it were found among the Dead Sea Scrolls. And lastly, Ethiopia is the only country which comes closest to the Enoch figure in terms of geography and chronology since Ethiopia is thought to be the place where one can find the origins of man himself, and Enoch is known as the seventh seed from the first Biblical man, Adam. In later chapters we will explore his African roots in greater detail. But for now permit us to continue our comparisons and exploration of the Enoch character.

Regarding the nation state known as Israel, "God raised up the greatest leader of their history, Moses, [who was a] deliverer, lawgiver, and prophet...Moses grew in moral stature to become what God called him to be, and in that process he showed himself to be the model of a hero of faith. Moses transformed the Israelites into a nation living by a covenant with God - they had been delivered...by God, and in return they vowed that they would obey God's law."

ABC's of the Bible, New York: Reader's Digest Association, Inc., 1991, p. 94

YET, ENOCH "THE DEDICATED ONE" IS THE FIRST AND GREATEST HEROIC FIGURE OF FAITH.

Enoch is the great living example of the power of faith. He merits immortality and an escort by God Himself into Heaven because of his unwavering faith. According to the Bible, he was the first man to "cheat" death.

In the priestly genealogy of Adam, Enoch is the son of Jared and father of Methuselah...The Epistle to the Hebrews holds him up as a example of faith: "By faith Enoch was taken away without dying."

Winston's Original African Heritage Study Bible Encyclopedia Concordance, James W. Peebles, Tenn.: James C. Winston Publishing Company, Inc., 1996, p. 212

The Bible says that "Enoch was spared death because of his righteousness, a reward confirmed by...the New Testament Letter to the Hebrews: 'By faith Enoch was taken up so that he should not see death.'" (Heb. 11:5).

ABC's of the Bible, New York: Reader's Digest Association, Inc., 1991, p. 25-6

The Oxford Companion to the Bible revealed the following about the legendary Enoch: "Traces of the legend are found in Hebrews 11:5, where Enoch has become a hero of faith."

Wycliffe Bible Encyclopedia maintains a similar point of view: "He [was] incited as a hero of faith (Heb. 11:5)."

Likewise, *Zondervan Pictorial Encyclopedia of the Bible* asserts that: "As a hero of faith (Heb 11:5) he is known as a man who pleased God."

ENOCH IS THE HOLY ONE.

He was so pure and lived such "a godly life" that he would be the first to have "walked with God." He was the first in Scripture to accomplish this spiritual feat. Enoch's "story is so exceptional that it sets...Enoch quite apart from all other mortals as one who did not die."

"Blessed are the pure in heart: for they shall see God." Matthew 5:8. For three hundred years Enoch had been seeking purity of soul, that he might be in harmony with Heaven. For three centuries he had walked with God.

> *Patriarchs and Prophets*, Ellen G. White, California: Pacific Press Publishing Association, 1958, p. 87

As *The Interpreter's Dictionary of the Bible* stated:

> "Enoch walked with God; and he was not, for God took him" (v.24) The expression "walked with God" denotes a devout life, lived in close communion with God. (An Illustrated Encyclopedia, New York: Abingdon Press, 1962, p. 103)

Enoch was a lawgiver before Moses.

> Enoch is also said to officiate in paradise at the sanctuary before God. Elsewhere, certain religious laws are said to have originated with Enoch and his books...
>
> Enoch himself...executes justice...Thus, Enoch combines the functions of...lawgiver, sage and judge.

> *The Encyclopedia of Religion*, Vol. 5, Mircea Eliade, ed., New York: Macmillan Publishing Co., 1987, p. 117

The combination of certain traits - independence, intelligence, compassion, and power - is Enoch's signature, setting him apart from all others by the superlative degree to which he possesses them.

Enoch the Prophet, Hugh Nibley, Salt Lake City, Utah: Deseret Book Company, 1986, p. 21

Nibley continues:

As Van Andel puts it, the great line including Enoch, Abraham, Noah, Moses, and Elijah "all crystallizes around Enoch," fulfilling the promise to him by "a logical process from Adam to the Messianic kingdom" at the end of the world. (p. 32)

His translation out of a wicked world was an appropriate testimony to the truth ascribed to him in Jude 14-15, "See, the Lord is coming...to judge everyone."

The New International Dictionary of the Bible, J.D. Douglas & Merrill Tenney, Editors, Regency Reference Library, Grand Rapids, Michigan: Zondervan Publishing House, 1987, p. 313

The same biblical reference is made by *The New Smith's Bible Dictionary*: He is mentioned by Jude (vs.24) along with a quoted testimony of warning as to the Lord's coming in judgment.

William Smith, rev. Reuel G. Lemmons, New York: Doubleday & Company, Inc., 1966, p. 97

The renowned Dead Sea Scrolls expert, J. T. Milik, states how Enoch mirrors this same divine decree:

"For the work of Enoch was created as a testimony for the generations of the world, in which he recounted to all generations their actions up to the day of judgment."

The Books of Enoch, Aramaic Fragments of Qumran Cave 4, J. T. Milik, ed., Oxford: Oxford University Press, 1976, p. 11

Likewise, "Enoch himself becomes a divine figure who dwells in heaven and executes justice..."

The Encyclopedia of Religion, Vol. 5, Mircea Eliade, ed., New York: Macmillan Publishing Co., 1987, p. 117

To which the Zondervan Pictorial Encyclopedia of the Bible adds:

Enoch prophesied against ungodly men (cf. the Book of Enoch).

Vol. 2, Merill C. Tenney ed. Regency Reference Library, Michigan, 1984, p. 309

According to the book *ABC's of the Bible*:

Holiness is the attribute that defines God; without it, he is not God. When Moses and the people praise the Lord, they ask: 'who is like thee, majestic in holiness [Ex. 15:11] ?'... In the old Testament, God's holiness is often represented by fire, which expresses purity and danger. (Reader's Digest Association, Inc., New York, 1991, p. 75)

Enoch so reflected this God-like quality of "holiness" that he was recorded as "walking with God [which] is a relic of the first paradise when men walked and talked with God in holy familiarity..." (Rev. 21:3; 22:3-4) says *The New International Dictionary of the Bible*.

As the book Patriarchs and Prophets suggests:

The godly character of this prophet represents the state of holiness which must be attained by those who shall be "redeemed from the earth..." (Revelation 14:3)

Ellen G. White, California: Pacific Press Publishing Association, 1958, p. 89

According to the *Wycliffe Bible Encyclopedia*: [Enoch] "as a reward for his holy walk...was translated to heaven...(Heb 11:5)."

Moreover, it is written in the book The Scepter and the Star: The Messiahs of the Dead Sea Scrolls and other Ancient Literature that:

In I Enoch 71:14, Enoch is greeted by an angel on his ascent to heaven: "You are the Son of Man who was born to righteousness, and righteousness remains over you and the righteousness of the Head of Days will not leave you..." (John J. Collins, New York: Doubleday Co., 1984, p. 178)

He is righteousness personified. "Enoch" it was written "was created as a testimony for the generations of the world."
he did not die naturally but was transported to heaven on account of his righteousness.

Blackwell Dictionary of Judaica, Dan Cohn-Sherbok, Oxford: Blackwell Pub-
    lishers, 1992, p. iii

By translation of Enoch, the Lord designed to teach an important lesson. There was danger that men would yield to discour-
agement, because of the fearful results of Adam's sin. Many
were ready to exclaim, 'what profit is it that we have feared the
Lord and have kept His ordinances, since a heavy curse is rest-
ing upon the race, and death is the portion of us all?' But the
instructions which God gave to Adam, and which were repeated
by Seth, and exemplified by Enoch, swept away the gloom and
darkness...

Patriarchs and Prophets, Ellen G. White, California: Pacific Press Publish-
    ing Association, 1958, p. 88

The Church Fathers "hailed Enoch as a historic witness 'to the
possibility of a resurrection of the body and a true human existence in glory. Rev. 11:3' " (*Smith Bible Dictionary*, p. 174)

Enoch was the Bible's first paragon, a model of excellence or perfection. He was a paragon of integrity and principled living that
while everyone in his world was turning towards corruption and
wickedness, he stayed on his path of serving God first and always. Enoch stood for righteousness while others proclaimed evil.
Enoch was baptized in the "River of Righteousness" and emerged
"spotless" and pure.

Enoch is the greatest saint in the Biblical world, and "...in reward for his piety, had been translated to heaven...For it is the
testimony of the Scripture that before he was taken he had
pleased God..." (Hebrews 11:1, 5-6)

Judaism, Christianity and Islam, F.E. Peters Vol. 3, Princeton, New Jersey:
    Princeton University Press, 1990, p. 192

According to the words of Enoch himself, "The righteous...will walk in eternal light."

Enoch is the embodiment of a virtuous life as the following will help show.

Enoch is the blessed and righteous man of the Lord

The blessing of Enoch: with which he blessed the elect and the righteous who would be present on the day of tribulation at (the time of) the removal of all the ungodly ones...[Enoch is] the blessed and righteous man of the Lord...

The Old Testament Pseudepigrapha, Apocalyptic Literature and Testaments, Vol. I, James H. Charlesworth, ed., New York: Doubleday & Company, Inc., 1984, p. 13

"Create in me a clean heart, O God, and put a new and right spirit within me." (Psalm 51:10)

He had stood at the threshold of the eternal world, only a step between him and the land of the blest; and now the portals opened, the walk with God...continued and he passed through the gates of the Holy City - the first from among men to enter there.

Patriarchs and Prophets, Ellen G. White, California: Pacific Press Publishing Association, 1958, p. 87

Enoch was so holy that he was changed into the angel, Metatron.

In...3 Enoch, Metatron, "the little Yahweh" declares that he is Enoch,

son of Jared, who was taken up in the generation of the Flood (4:3-5), enlarged until he matched the world in length and breadth (9:2) and installed on a throne of glory (10:1).

In this case, however, it would seem that the human Enoch is transformed into a new angel...

The Scepter and the Star: The Messiahs of the Dead Sea Scrolls and other Ancient Literature, John J. Collins, New York: Doubleday Co., 1984, p. 180

The author of the book *Jews, Their Religious Beliefs and Practices*, Alan Unterman agrees:

[the] Biblical character Enoch...was taken up to heaven from the midst of a sinful generation and transformed into an angel. (London: Routledge, 1981, p. 93)

Here is a description of the transformation of Metatron [Enoch]:

He made me a garment of glory in which there were all kinds of luminaries, and He clothed me in it.

He fashioned for me a glorious cloak in which there were brightness brilliance, splendor and luster of every kind,

and He wrapped me in it, and He made me a royal crown in which were set forty-nine stones of countenance like the wheel of the sun, and its brilliance went out to the four winds of the...firmament, and to the seven firmaments, and the four winds of the world.

And He placed it upon my head and He called me "The Lesser Lord' in the presence of His whole family in the heights,

as it is said, *My name is in him* (Exod. 23:21).

Gates To The Old City, Raphel Patai, Detroit: Wayne State University Press, 1981, p. 393

Enoch is the teacher of righteousness.

"Enoch's cosmological teachings have become extraordinarily bold: his teachings are special disclosures for the end of the ages...

Enoch is a sage who teaches to the last generations the way of righteousness in critical times and exhorts his community to patient hope in the final hours of the world.

The Ethiopic version of 92:1 reads:

"Written by Enoch the scribe - this complete wisdom teaching, praised by all men and a judge of the whole earth..."

Enoch and the Growth of An Apocalyptic Tradition, James VanderKam, The Catholic Biblical Association of America, Washington, D.C., 1984, p. 173

"...let justice roll down like waters, and righteousness like an ever-flowing stream. (AMOS 5:21)

The ancient writings showed that Enoch the Ethiopian, Patriarch-Prophet was a true pioneer of faith. He was the first Biblical *superman* in history.

No star shines brighter in the constellation of Biblical heroes. He exists first among the pantheon of legendary personalities in Scripture.

According to the *Dictionary of the Bible*, Enoch is "a wonder of knowledge for all generations,"

John McKenzie S.J., New York: Touchstone Books, 1995, p. 239

In the same works it adds that: "no one was ever created on earth like him..." (Sirach 49:14)

Enoch is the only perfect servant of God.

He had no marks against his character because he "walked with God" for over three centuries and then "God took him." The Bible finds no fault in Enoch for the revelations of him show that he was without any spiritual weaknesses.

Enoch is the first archetype (perfect example) of the divine man. He entered the "pearly gates" unadorned by the veil of death. Enoch the Ethiopian is the prototype, an original model, of the resurrected man in glory.

Dr. Harold L. Willmington , one of America's leading Bible teachers, calls Enoch "the first recorded preacher in human history". In fact, he maintains that his name means "Teacher."

Willimington's *Complete Guide to Bible Knowledge*, Vol.1, Illinois: Tyndale House Publishers, Inc., p. 108

ENOCH IS THE MOST SANCTIFIED OF THE SAINTS.

He is the first "sanctified saint and the greatest because he is the most perfect one".

As Professor R.J. Bauckham of the University of Manchester indicated:

Enoch was a man of outstanding sanctity who enjoyed close fellowship with God (Gn 5:22,24: for the expression 'walked with

God', cf. Gn. 6:9; Mi 6:8; Mal. 2:6)...he was received into the presence of God without dying (Gn.5:24).

The Illustrated Bible Dictionary, J.D. Douglas, ed., England: Tyndale House, 1982, p. 458

CHAPTER IV

ENOCH'S LINEAGE FROM THE BIBLE:

The Book of Genesis, the King James Version, Chapter 5 verses 1 to 32

The Generations of Adam

This is the book of the generations of Adam. In the day that God created man, in the likeness of God made he him;

2. Male and female created he them; and blessed them, and called their name Adam, in the day when they were created.

3. And Adam lived an hundred and thirty years, and begat a son in his own likeness, after his image; and called his name Seth:

4. And the days of Adam after he had begotten Seth were eight hundred years; and he begat sons and daughters:

5. And all the days that Adam lived were nine hundred and thirty years: and he died.

6. And Seth lived a hundred and five years, and begat Enos:

7. And Seth lived after he begat Enos eight hundred and seven years, and begat sons and daughters:

8. And all the days of Seth were nine hundred and twelve years: and he died.

9. And Enos lived ninety years, and begat Cainan:

10. And Enos lived after he begat Cainan eight hundred and fifteen years, and begat sons and daughters:

11. And all he days of Enos were nine hundred and five years: and he died.

12. And Cainan lived seventy years, and begat Mahalaleel:

13. And Cainan lived after he begat Mahalaleel eight hundred and forty years, and begat sons and daughters:

14. And all the days of Cainan were nine hundred and ten years: and he died.

15. And Mahalaleel lived sixty and five years, and begat Jared:

16. And Mahalaleel lived after he begat Jared eight hundred and thirty years, and begat sons and daughters:

17. And all the days of Mahalaleel were eight hundred and ninety and five years: and he died.

18. And Jared lived a hundred sixty and two years, and he begat Enoch:

19. And Jared lived after he begat Enoch eight hundred years, and begat sons and daughters:

20. And all the days of Jared were nine hundred sixty and two years: and he died.

21. And Enoch lived sixty and five years, and begat Methuselah:

22. And Enoch walked with God after he begat Methuselah three hundred years, and begat sons and daughters:

23. And all the days of Enoch were three hundred sixty and five years:

24. And Enoch walked with God: and he was not; for God took him

25. And Methuselah lived a hundred eighty and seven years, and begat Lamech:

26. And Methuselah lived after he begat Lamech seven hundred eighty and two years, and begat sons and daughters:

27. And all the days of Methuselah were nine hundred sixty and nine years: and he died.

28. And Lamech lived an hundred eighty and two years, and begat a son:

29. And he called his name Noah, saying, This same shall comfort us concerning our work and toil of our hands, because of the ground which the Lord hath cursed.

30. And Lamech lived after he begat Noah five hundred ninety and five years, and begat sons and daughters:

31. And all the days of Lamech were seven hundred seventy and seven years: and he died.

32. And Noah was five hundred years old: and Noah begat Shem, Ham, and Japheth.

Having laid out the genealogy of Adam, we will begin exposing the reason why so many individuals have been misled. Because up to this point certain people were trying to promote White Supremacy through religious doctrine.

They knew Enoch was Black but they tried to make him "the-forgotten-man-of-the-Bible." However, it is the aim of this book to help resurrect him from the grave of neglect and obscurity. To reveal him in all his glory and magnificence.

Once you establish a Black seed in the middle of a lineage (a family line that goes back through the ages) then everything before and after contains that dominant Black Seed.

If Enoch is an Ethiopian and therefore Black, then all those who came before or after him would logically be Black too. They would have that dominant genetic trait, that BLACK SEED.

Thus, 1st Seed Adam is a Black Man, then Seth is Black, and so forth and so on.

If Enoch is an Ethiopian and a Black Man, then he must have come naturally from Black (African) lineage.

Tracing back his lineage (Adam's 7th Seed) it makes Adam and Eve Black, and tracing it forward it shows that all of his descendants are Black also. Which is why Moses is Black and Abraham, too.

Quite appropriately, on the cover of *Newsweek* magazine also revealed the racial identity of Adam and Eve as Black and African.

THE IMAGE IS THE MESSAGE

Hollywood and Euro-centric theologians do not have an objective concern for historical fact.

As might be expected, they have a particular interest in projecting certain kinds of images into the subconscious mind, in order to promote their perception of "reality" and "historical truth."

Whether some of them do it deliberately or not, is really not the point because the effects of these projected Euro-centric images on people of African descent are so devastating and destructive to their mental health.

Like a poisonous gas that cannot be seen, felt or tasted, but it kills nonetheless. It destroys self-esteem, self-worth, self-reliance and motivation thereby promoting deep levels of inferiority and self-hatred.

For people of European descent, it gives them a false sense of pride, arrogance and power over those for the expressed purpose of mental control and dominance which leads to unspeakable acts of human exploitation and abuse. "As a man thinketh so he is."

These are the associations and connections your subconscious mind makes with or without your awareness or permission.

Certain images are created to send messages in your spirit which you think or act on in very subtle ways.

The most effective techniques are those that people are not conscious of and still believe themselves to be basically unaffected.

Throughout the religious depiction of major Biblical personalities, a definite Euro-centric viewpoint has been constantly promoted. This can be seen in the following illustrations and in many other instances in the book:

1. AN EURO-CENTRIC VERSION OF MOSES ON MOUNT SINAI

According to Carl Conrad Nichols, we have "an Euro-centric version of Moses on Mount Sinai in Africa with the 10 Commandments written in Hebrew! while Moses only spoke Ge'ez and Egyptian. Hebrew did not become the language of the Habiru people until after they crossed the Jordan river into Canaan 192 years after Moses was dead.

Moses died on Mount Pisgah this side of the Jordan River and he never went into Canaan where the Phoenician language was adopted by the Habiru people and renamed Hebrew ca. 1000 B.C.

Seven hundred years before the Greeks came, what is a Caucasian white man doing in Black Africa? The Sinai is really in Egypt, the so-called Sinai Peninsula is part of Africa in general and Egypt in particular. The construction of the Suez Canal and European mythology created what is now known as the "Middle East."

2. THE EURO-CENTRIC VERSION OF JESUS CHRIST

"Jesus Christ was born in Northeast Africa (Bethlehem). His parents were naturally two Africans named Mary and Joseph. Jesus was born in Africa, raised in Africa, lived in Africa all his life. He never left Africa a day in his life! So how could he be white," asks Mr. Carl Conrad Nichols.

3. THE EURO-CENTRIC VERSION OF SOLOMON AND SHEBA

"This picture was suppose to be a biblical reproduction of Africa - (King Solomon's Court) in 975 B.C. Where does all these white Europeans come from? King Solomon was a Black Hebrew and the Queen of Sheba (Makeda) was a Black Ethiopian, so where did all of these Caucasian white people come from? Hollywood has a great imagination which is very deceptive and misleading.

The first white Europeans to come to Africa were the Greeks. They came to be civilized' they came as students, to study at the universities of Egypt. The picture was about a meeting that took place roughly about 400 years *before* the European came to Africa (Egypt)."

[Source: Carl C. Nichols lecture tapes "The Bible in Africa."]

History as portrayed by Michelangelo, who was one of the main myth makers of white supremacy in religion, shows that his conception of a white God still dominates the Euro-centric minds of the western world. [See *Nelson's Illustrated Bible* and *The Disappearance of God*]

MOSES WAS BLACK.

Sir T. W. Arnold indicated that:

"According to Mohammedan tradition, Moses was a black man as may be seen from the following passage in the Koran, 'Now draw thy hand close to thy side; it shall come forth white but unhurt'- another sign (XX, 23). 'Then he drew forth his hand and lo! it was white to the beholders. The nobles of Pharaoh said, 'Verily this is an expert enchanter.' "

THE PREACHING, OF ISLAM, London, 1913, p. 358

When Jehovah wished to give Moses a sign, so runs the famous legend, he told him to put his hand into his bosom.

The hand came out white, proving that it could not have been white before.

The miracle lay in turning a black skin white, and turning it black again. Hence the perfect logic of the Mohammedan belief that Moses was a Black."

J. A. Rogers, Sex and Race, Vol. I

Moses, "origins is certainly Egyptian, for the name is Egyptian provenance."

Encyclopedia Britannica Vol. 8, Chicago, Ill., William Benton Publ., 1973

As the Bible says,

Moses "was learned in all the wisdom of the Egyptians." ACTS 7:22

JESUS CHRIST WAS BLACK

"Josephus, the Jewish historian, wrote that Christ 'was a man of simple appearance, mature age, dark skin with little hair.' "

J. A. Rogers, NATURE KNOWS NO COLOR LINE

Life magazine discloses that:

> "The African knows a dark-skinned Jesus, the Swede, a blond one. Americans picture the bearded Jesus of a billion prayer book covers. Look at the pieces of art on the facing page. We see Jesus in our own image. It helps us to know him. (December 1994, p. 67)

Yet, Godfrey Higgins, asks this revealing question about the color of Jesus:

> Was he of a *black* tribe? Indeed I believe that the Christ, whose black icon I saw in Italy, was; and I believe that he came to Italy when his black mother arrived at Loretto (Near the Fossiones Taratrum, or Italian Tartary) from Syra-strene, for Satrun-ja or Regna Saturnia or Pallitana, even before the foundation of the Rome of Romulus.

> *Anacalypsis*, 2 vols., New York: University Books, rep. A & B Books, Brooklyn, 1965, p. 751

The African origins of Jesus is gaining such popular acceptance that even in the movie *"Waiting to Exhale"* a huge stain-glassed portrait of a Black Jesus Christ is given special emphasis as the camera focuses on him with his black hands prominently extended in one of the church scenes.

Should the color of Jesus be of any interest to Black people living in America?

One scholar offers this view:

> "It is an understandable concern of African-Americans, given our history in this country and given the way the Bible and Scriptures have been used against us," says the Rev. Renita J. Weems, assistant professor of the Hebrew Bible at Vanderbilt University School of Divinity in Nashville, referring to whether it should matter to Black people if Jesus is or is not a person of color.

> "Is Jesus Black"?, *Emerge*, Vol 6, No.6, Brenda L. Webber, April 1995, p. 28

As "one white perceptive theologian, Kyle Haselden had observed:

The white man cleaves Christian piety into two parts: the strong virile virtues he applies exclusively to himself; the apparently weak, passive virtues he endorses especially for the Negro [Black]..."

Troubling Biblical Waters, Cain Hope Felder, New York: Orbis Book, 1994, p. 207

For too long in the history of Western civilization, persons of African descent have been stereotyped in negative ways which caused them to question not only their own identity but also their part in God's plan of salvation.

The Original Africa Heritage Study Bible, Hope Cain Felder, ed., Nashville: Dr. James Peebles, Winston-Derek Publishers, 1993, p. v

"Vincent Harding reminds us that the Black encountered the American white Christ first on the slave ships that brought them to these shores."

Troubling Biblical Waters, Cain Hope Felder, New York: Orbis Book, 1994, p. 207

It was at this point in history that Western culture determined all evil as black and Satanic, and all good as white and of God.

The Original Africa Heritage Study Bible, Hope Cain Felder, ed., Nashville: Dr. James Peebles, Winston-Derek Publishers, 1993, p. 3

"Artists like Michelangelo painted Jesus and other Biblical characters like themselves in order that Europeans could relate to them more easily ~ people all over the world do the same today," says its literature.

"Is Jesus Black?," *Emerge*, Vol 6, No.6, Brenda L. Webber, April 1995, p. 30

William Mosley, author of *What Color Was Jesus*, maintained that:

"Not long after the first slaves were taken from Africa by Europeans, Pope Julius II in 1505 commissioned the painting of certain Biblical works for artist Michelangelo and in doing...so initiated the concept of God as being White. Included in the painting is the portrait of Mary, mother of Jesus whose prominent Black features were distorted to resemble a Florentine Italian woman. (Chicago, Illinois: African American Images, 1987, p. 7)

In the newspaper, THE WASHINGTON POST (May 4, 1979), a similar view is expressed.

"Many of the Madonnas painted in the earliest centuries of Christendom were BLACK, according to historians, and it wasn't until the Renaissance that it became popular to give the Mother of Christ the features of a Florentine Maiden [a white woman]."

"Mary, the mother of Jesus was Afro-Asiatic and probably looked like a typical Yemenite, Trinidadian or African-American of today," says Felder who is founder and chairman of the Biblical Institute for Social Change, housed at Howard University, and general editor of the *Original African Heritage Study Bible*.

"Is Jesus Black?" *Emerge*, Vol 6, No.6, Brenda L. Webber, April 1995, p. 28

But, as W. Mosley points out:

"...in the Michelangelo paintings, the images of the Christ child, the three wise men, the Lord's Supper and the resurrection, were changed until no trace of their original Blackness remained. Not only were there images changed but entire nations, peoples, empires were changed, like the ancient Egyptians, the Israelites, Babylonians, Persians..."

What Color Was Jesus, William Mosley, Chicago, Illinois: African American Images, 1987, p. 7

Which gives new meaning to what "Goethe wrote of Michelangelo's work in the Vatican: 'he who has not seen the Sistine Chapel can form no comprehensive idea of what man is capable.'
"

The World's Great Religions, Henry R. Luce, ed., New York: Time Inc., 1957, p. 210

In fact, in the movie *"Waiting to Exhale"* the character named Robin was wearing a dark brown shirt with the white Eurocentric

version of Adam painted originally by Michelangelo as the principal design on the shirt.

By the same token, the eminent Biblical scholar Professor Cain
Hope Felder asserts that:

"Matthew 2 relates the story of Mary and Joseph's harrowing
escape from King Herod, who sought to kill the young child
who had been declared to be King of the Jews. Herod wanted
no competition as supreme ruler. An angel of the Lord called
him out of Egypt. Black scholars believe the family of Jesus was
dark enough to blend in with the people of Egypt and not
draw attention to themselves.

'Imagine the divine family as Europeans hiding in Africa. This
is quite doubtful,' Felder submits, taking the position that Egypt
has always been a part of Africa, despite European scholarship
that places Egypt at the southern extension of Europe. "

"Is Jesus Black ?" *Emerge*, Vol 6, No.6, April 1995, p. 31

The writer Ben Ammi made this observation:

"The features came to resemble those of Caucasian ancestry.
Thus, we have Michelangelo, Leonardo de Vinci and others to
thank for artistically changing the face of the worlds from Black
to White." (*God, the Black Man and Truth*, Communicators Press,
Chicago, 1982)

What Color Was Jesus, William Mosley, Chicago, Illinois: African American Images, 1987, p. 7

The Bible offers contrary evidence that points to an African presence as opposed to the manufactured images of whiteness or
European ancestry.

For example, in the book of Revelations it reads:

"A throne stood in heaven, with one seated on that throne!
And he who sat there appeared like jasper and carnelian. Both
of these are rare stones that are dark."

In like manner, a passage from Revelations Chapter 1 verse 5
reads:

His feet were like brass....

"In the Bible (Rev. 1:14) 'The Ancient of Days' God is described as having *Hair Like Pure Wool.*'"

One description that has influenced countless illustrations of the deity comes from the Book of Daniel, where God is described as "ancient of Days....his raiment was white as snow, and the hair of his head like pure wool."

ABC's of the Bible, New York: Reader's Digest Association, Inc., 1991, p. 40

States Brenda L. Webber of *Emerge* magazine:

"It is not unusual for people to create images out of their own history and culture.

What is unusual is that Black people, for so long, have used images out of European and White culture for their idea of God.

'It is not unusual to go to China and see God looking like the Chinese,' Cone says, 'Or go to Japan and see God...coming out of Japanese culture."

"Is Jesus Black ?," April 1995, p. 31.

"The same damage to our racial community," says Walter Williams, "is being repeated Sunday morning from the pulpits of Christian churches all over America and the world.

Consider how these Christian ministers hold before their congregations the icon/image of Jesus Christ and reiterate over and over that this is our Lord, God, and Savior.

They are encouraging us to worship this European image which causes us to become the principal agent in our own spiritual destruction and confusion.

We end up hating ourselves as a race of people and each other individually, but loving and emulating the European race."

The Historical Origin of Christianity, Chicago, Illinois: Maathian Press, Inc.,
    p. iv

If you worship another image of God that is alien to you, are
you not already vulnerable to enslavement and ridicule.

How then are you an equal when even your image of God becomes a foreign reality.

From the worship of a white God grows the destructive fruits of
internalized "feelings of inferiority" which leads to self-hatred and
ultimately to self-destructive behavior. The final result is drug
abuse, imprisonment and most, if not all, of the ills that affect
Black men and women today.

It all starts with the image and the message it sends to the un-
suspecting subconscious mind. How can one compete fairly with
"God's children."

This explains, in large measure, why we support others before we
support ourselves.

Who wouldn't buy from those who "look" like God. "As a man
thinketh so is he."

ABRAHAM WAS BLACK

Abraham known as the "Father of Nations" is from Ur in
Chaldea.

Francois Lenormant, the French archaeologist and member of the
Academy of Inscriptions and Belles-Lettres, in his Volume One
publication of the *Ancient History of the East*, argued:

"Of these two great nations who constituted the mass of the
population of the Chaldea, one was of the race of Ham and of
the Cushite branch.

The presence of Cushites in Chaldea and Babylonia is attested
by the Bible, by Berosus, and by the universal testimony of antiquity."

Rev. Walter Arthur McCray maintains, along with several reputa-
ble scholars, that "Cushite has traditionally been synonymous with
Black or dark-skinned people."

"The myths, legends, and traditions of the Sumerians definitely point to AFRICA as the ORIGINAL HOME OF THE SUMERIANS.

The first Sumerian remains were unearthed in the middle of the nineteenth century by Hincks, Oppert, and Rawlinson.

Sir Henry Rawlinson called these people Kushites...Rawlinson anticipated Perry by tracing the Sumerians back to Ethiopia."

John G. Jackson, Man, God and Civilization

In the section entitled "Kushitic Civilization," Professors of History Edward Burns and Philip Lee Ralph focus our attention on these facts:

The origin of the Negroid southerners, long shrouded in mystery, is beginning to come to light through recent archaeological discoveries.

We are now fairly certain that from at least 2200 B.C...groups from the...southern Sahara were dispersing to more fertile parts of Africa.

Others wandered southward to the upper Nile in a region later known to the Egyptians as 'Kush'.

By 1500 B.C. these **black-complexioned Kushites,** *showing remarkable cultural affinities to late pre-dynastic Egypt,* had established their own kingdom."

World Civilizations, 5th Edition, W.W. Norton & Co., N.Y. p. 48

"Professor W. Max Muller of *Bible Exegesis* identifies Cush in the *Jewish Encyclopedia* as 'the ancestor of the Nubians' who inhabit modern Ethiopia and Sudan."

God The Black Man and Truth, Ben Ammi, Communicators Press, Wash. D.C., 1990, p. 13

Elsewhere Ben Ammi writes:

The *Encyclopedia Americana* further substantiates the idea that Nimrod was a "cushite. "Abraham's father Terah was a relative of Nimrod and a minister in his government in Mesopotamia, modern day Iraq. (p. 15)

SOLOMON WAS BLACK

Look not upon me because I am Black....(Solomon Songs 1:6)

The Queen of Sheba is discussed in the "Great Queens of Ethiopia" by authors Larry Williams and Charles S. Finch who make a very revealing point concerning her:

"One thing we can safely surmise, the empire that Makeda ruled was at least as important as Solomon's and if any of the traditions about the extent and scope of the empire are even partially correct, she ruled an even more substantial and more important kingdom than did Solomon. The Biblical version of the story is given in 1 Kings 10 and 2 Chronicles 9. It is said that Makeda 'came to test him with hard questions'."

See: GREAT BLACK WOMEN IN ANTIQUITY, Edited by Ivan Van Sertima

Ethiopia certainly had ancient links with Judaism. The royal house of Ethiopia claims descent from King Solomon. The Queen of Sheba, who visited Solomon, had had a son by him who became the Ethiopian king Menelik.

The Lost Prophet, (The Book of Enoch and its influence on Christianity, Margaret Barker, Great Britain: SPCK, 1988, p. 9

The Director of the African and Afro-American Studies Program at Washington University in St. Louis observed that:

"in the recent television dramatization of the love affair between Solomon and Sheba, Sheba was played by a black actress and Solomon by a swarthy Hispanic. In the 1959 Hollywood film version of Solomon and Sheba, directed by King Vidor - who, incidentally, made the first all-black Hollywood film - Solomon was played by Yul Brynner and Sheba by Gina Lollobridgida."

"Understanding Africentrism," *Civilization*, Vol. 2 No. 4, Gerald Early, July-August 1995, p. 32

A contemporary illustration of the racial identity of the Hebrews is given in the *New York Times*, Friday, March 4, 1955:

Falasha Jews From Ethiopia Studying in Israel

Their Tribe Practices Hebrewish-Judaism According to the Laws of Moses by Harry Gilroy

"-Twelve young Falasha Jews who might be taken as living proof of the legend that today's Ethiopians descend from Solomon and the Queen of Sheba are studying at this children's village."

As one can see, the connection between Ethiopia and the Hebrews is very ancient and fundamental despite attempts by some to cloud the issue.

The evidence suggests that what is popularly known and classified as a Jew would best be described as white or Caucasian, and what is classified as Hebrew would have greater historical accuracy if described as Black or African.

Comparing Enoch the Ethiopian to Moses and Abraham, we find the following:

Enoch was about 800 years before Moses.

And, he was about 400 years before Abraham.

The Seeds of Biblical creation are as follows:

Adam (1st Seed) - Enoch (7th Seed)-Abraham (28th Seed) - Moses (50h Seed). Note: We are using the conventional measure for generations (seeds) of 20 year intervals meaning each new generation comes every 20 years.

By tracing Enoch's lineage, it helps to establish the African Origins of the Bible because here we have a Black Man found at the very beginning of Biblical history. This would point to an obvious Bible connection to ancient African Roots.

Because if a Black man is present at the beginning of the Bible's history, then one could conclude that the Bible is a chronicle of Black People put to Scripture. It then becomes more and more an African Story Book. Thus, the *Original African Heritage Bible* has a very logical name and natural purpose.

However, Professor James Cone, the Briggs Distinguished Professor at Union Theological Seminary in New York had this to say on the subject:

"I think what has happened in the past is that people in the dominant culture - the White, European culture - have imposed their understanding of God upon other people throughout the world, and therefore, as long as Whites imposed that position upon the African-American community and made them accept the White God, everything was fine, and that was regarded as objective and true."

"Is Jesus Black"?, *Emerge*, Vol. 6, No.6, Brenda L. Webber, April 1995, p. 31

Consequently, it is in the interest of the historical "myth of white supremacy" to suppress truth as thoroughly as they can. The myth of their introducing to the world the first and only the "true" God (in white face) as something only a superior people can do implies that an inferior people (read black) can not find God on their own.

As the famed German philosopher Hegel once wrote in 1824:

"...Africa is the land where men are children...a land laying beyond the daylight of self conscious history...let us forget Africa...for Africa is no historic part of the world."

But Henrik Clarke said a long time ago that, to control a people you must first control what they think about themselves and how they regard their history and culture. And when your conqueror makes you ashamed of your culture and your history, he needs no prison walls, and no chains to hold you. The chains on your mind are more than enough.

African Link, "The Bell Curve and Africa," Henry M. Codjoe, Vol. 6, No. 6, 1995, p. 10

Says the Reverend Jesse Jackson: "Nothing is more fundamentally important than your own feelings about yourself."

White supremacy is that true "golden idol" of the Bible for it enslaved and dehumanized other for money or gold making the white skin is "better than" and superior to all others.

Or, as Dr. Peebles wrote in the [The Original Africa Heritage Study Bible]

"White supremacy has become modern day Baal and all nations bow to this idol."

Hope Cain Felder, ed., Nashville: Dr. James Peebles, Winston-Derek Publishers, 1993, p.

Brenda L. Webber, who specializes in religious writing, makes this statement:

European truths are no longer readily accepted and African-Americans and other people of color have begun to critically evaluate what they have been taught...("Is Jesus Black"?, *Emerge*, Vol 6, No.6, April 1995, p. 31)

"The difference today," says Professor Cone, "is that "Black scholars for the first time - certainly since the 1960s - have begun to realize that they can challenge the dominant White theological establishment." ("Is Jesus Black"?, *Emerge*)

The need today for such critical thinking could never be more apparent.

CHAPTER V

THE AFRICAN ORIGINS OF MAN

THAT MAN ORIGINATED IN AFRICA ADDS SCIENTIFIC WEIGHT TO the historical reality that Adam must have been a Black Man.

Scientifically speaking, it would seem rather obvious that Adam would be an African since as *Newsweek* magazine reminds us:

"...scientific evidence...has been clear on the African origins of humanity since the 1970's..."

"African Dreams," *Newsweek*, September 23, 1991

According to John Wilford of the *New York Times* (Tuesday, October 30, 1984) the famous scientific family, the Leakeys, achieved the following:

"They proved beyond doubt the AFRICAN ORIGINS OF MAN."

As the Bible says,

"God hath made of one blood all nations."

THE ACTS OF THE APOSTLE

Proclaims Allan C. Wison, of the University of California at Berkeley: "Basically we are all ! Kung." (Botswana)

Egypt, Child of Africa, Ivan Van Sertima, ed., Transaction Publishers, New Brunswick, 1995, p. 323

Even Henry Fairfield Osborn, the late head of the American Museum of Natural History, said that:

"Black stock is even more ancient than Caucasian or Mongolian."

MAN RISES TO PARNASSUS, PRINCETON, N.J., 1928

An identical point was made by Dr. M.G. Seelig:

"the earliest race of beings were Negroid, it is but natural to believe that at one time these were universal, and that their birthplace must have had one common center, which must have been Africa.

Medicine, An Historical Outline, Baltimore: Williams I. Wilkins Company, 1925, p. 15

The *New York Times* declared in a Friday, June 11, 1982 article that

"Ethiopian Bones Called Oldest Ancestor of Man

Fossil bones discovered in Ethiopia were reported yesterday to be from the oldest ancestor of man yet known...

The bones were 400,000 years older than the famous 'Lucy' skeleton found in 1974. The new fossil discovery was announced by Dr. J. Desmond Clark and Dr. Time D. White, anthropologists at the University of California at Berkeley."

Then again twelve years later in the *New York Times* (September 22, 1994) it was reported that "NEW FOSSILS TAKE SCIENCE CLOSE TO DAWN OF HUMANS" by John Noble Wilson:

Fossils of the oldest human ancestors have been discovered in Ethiopia...lived 4.4 million years ago on a forested plain.

In the words of The Original Africa Heritage Study Bible:

the bible provides extensive evidence that the earliest people were located in Africa. The Garden of Eden account, found in Gen. 2:8-14, indicates that the first two rivers of Eden were in ancient Cush, the term that the Greeks would later transpose as "Aithiops," or Ethiopia, meaning literally "burnt face people...Clearly, wherever else "Eden" extended, its beginning was within the continent of Africa."

Hope Cain Felder, ed., Nashville: Dr. James Peebles, Winston-Derek Publishers, 1993, p. x

ELDERS OF THE HUMAN RACE

In *Science* magazine (February 17, 1986) there is an article entitled *"Chromosome maps prove the origins of race"* which begins with this paragraph:

How did mankind develop into the dozens of races we know today? Fossil evidence indicates that Homo sapiens started off in Africa, and then spread into Europe, Asia and the Americas...

Naturally, therefore, the *Science* magazine article would revealingly state that:

All Family Trees Lead to "Eve", An African. Scientists Conclude-Genetic Analysis Indicates Common Ancestry 200,000 Years Ago.

Moreover, in the *Eerdmans Handbook to the Bible* it is interesting to note that:

From Adam to Noah, [the] Family tree (genealogies)...are often given in the Bible attesting a line of descent...The life span of these men is remarkable.

It ranges from 777 years for Lamech to Methuselah's 969 years (apart from Enoch, who God 'took' at 365).

Each of the ten records follows the same formula. When A had lived X years he became the father of B.

He live after the birth of B Y years and had other sons and daughters. Thus all his days were Z years, and he dies.

The somber note of the final phrase 'and he died' is varied only in the case of Enoch, the man who "walked with God." For him God had other plans.

David & Pat Alexander ed., Mich.: William B. Eerdmans Publishing Company, p. 131

Continuing with the article in *Science*:

About 200,00 years ago there lived one woman who was a maternal ancestor of every human being living today, a team of biologists has concluded after analyzing special genes in the cells of people from all the world's major racial and ethnic groups.

The claim is likely to be controversial. But the scientists behind it, from the University of California at Berkeley, have considerable stature...

Their report, in the prestigious British journal *Nature*, is accompanied by an independent commentary that takes the claim seriously and calls it "the strongest molecular evidence so far in favor of the African population being ancestral" to all living humans.

The claim also generally agrees with the view widely shared among anthropologists that anatomically modern forms of Homo Sapiens, the species to which all living people belong, arose more that 100,00 years ago and probably in Africa.

The genetic evidence cited by the Berkeley group also implies that all of today's racial differences evolved after descendant of Eve...and migrated out of Africa into Eurasia.

Sir Godfrey Higgins in his monumental *Anacalypsis* (2 vols.), said as much over a century ago in 1836 with these words:

"Now I suppose, that **man was originally a Negro**, and he traveled Westwards, gradually changing from the jet black of India, through all the intermediate shades of Syria, Italy, France to the fair white and red of the maid of Holland and Britain."

As we can see, if Adam and Eve are the Bible's first human beings then they must have been Black.

Similarly, if man especially the first man was supposedly made into the image and likeness of God, then let us see how Enoch describes this "likeness":

Enoch says "I beheld the ancient of days, whose head was like white wool."

CHAPTER VI

BIBLICAL PERSONALITIES

ENOCH & NOAH

Enoch and Noah lived lives that were pleasing to God.

Enoch and the Growth of An Apocalyptic Tradition, James VanderKam, Washington, D.C.: The Catholic Biblical Association of America, 1984, p. 30

Son of Jared, born when Jared was 162 years old (Gen 5:18), and at 65 years, father of Methusaleh (Gen 5:21). Enoch lived 365 years, "walked with God" (cf. also Noah in Gen 6:9), and was taken by God (Gen 5:22-24).

The Anchor Bible Dictionary, Vol. 2, David Noel Freedman, ed., New York: Doubleday Co., 1992

The infancy tale in 1 Enoch takes the form of a first-person report by Enoch, Noah's great-grandfather, who resides with the angels at the ends of the earth. Despite his great distance from Noah's birthplace, Enoch is a central character in the drama because he alone has access to inside information about the central issues in the tale: who was the child's father and what did the birth of this remarkable child portend. He obtained the answers from the angels and the heavenly tablets. (106:19)

Intertestamental Essays In Honour of Jozef Tadeusz Milik, Edited by Zdzislaw J. Kapera, The Enigma Press, Krakow, 1992, p. 216

Professor J.H. Charlesworth of Duke University relates the following:

And (Noah) took off from there and went unto the extreme ends of the earth. And he cried out to his great grandfather Enoch, and said to him, three times... "Hear me! Hear me! Hear me!"

The Old Testament Pseudepigrapha, Apocalyptic Literature and Testaments, Vol. I, James H. Charlesworth, ed., New York: Doubleday & Company, Inc., 1984, p. 45

Professors Eisenman and Wise cite a scriptural work and state that:

It emphasizes two previous primordial 'Righteous Ones' of the utmost importance to this tradition of Enoch and Noah.

The Dead Sea Scrolls Uncovered, by Robert H. Eisenman and Michael Wise, New York: Barnes & Noble Books, 1992, p. 137

ENOCH & ELIJAH

Enoch, father of Metuselah. It was said of him that he walked with God - a phrase used also by Noah - and also that like Elijah, he was translated to heaven.

The Columbia Encyclopedia, Fifth ed., New York: Columbia University Press, 1993, p. 877

It is said of Enoch, "God took him" (Gen. 5:24), and it is said of Elijah (who did not die).

The Book of Legends, Hayim Nahman Bialik & Hehoshua Hana Ravnitzky, New York: Schocken Books, 1992, p. 530

The Wisdom of Ben Sira records the same:

Like Elijah, who was "taken aloft in a whirlwind" (48:9). Enoch "too was taken up" alive to heaven by God (49:14b; cf. NOTE and 44:16a), a reference to Gen. 5:24; cf. 2 Enoch 18:2. Thus Elijah and Enoch shared a special privilege...

Patriack W. Skehan, trans., New York: Doubleday, 1987, p. 545

Professor Stephen L. Harris of California State University, Sacramento gives this depiction of "Enoch's fate - 'he vanished because God took him' (Gen. 5:24) - have kindled considerable speculation. Like the prophet Elijah, swept heavenward centuries later in a fiery chariot (and then symbol of the sun), Enoch became a figure of myth who, after touring heaven, returned to earth to reveal its mysteries." (*Understanding the Bible*, London: Mayfield Publishing Co., 1980, p. 64)

The prophet Elijah did not die. He was carried bodily to heaven in a whirlwind (2 Kin. 2:1-11). This was an honor previously bestowed only upon Enoch (Gen. 5:24). Elisha the only witness to this event, picked up Elijah's mantle which fell from him as he ascended.

Nelson's New Illustrated Bible Dictionary, Ronald F. Youngblood, ed., Nashville: Nelson, 1995, p. 394

The Dictionary of Christian Legend describes Elijah in the following manner:

a 9th-century BC Hebrew prophet who, like Enoch 'never tasted death' because he was taken up to Heaven in a whirlwind in a chariot of fire (2 Kg 2:11).

John Metford, London: Thames and Hudson, 1983, p. 94

There can be no question that the clause "and he was not for God took him" (Gen 5:24) refers to the translation; the same expression is used of Elijah's translation (2 Kings 2:11)

Zondervan Pictorial Encyclopedia of the Bible Vol 2, C. Teaney Editor, Regency Reference Library Michigan, Merrill. 1976, p. 309

According to the Book Gateway to Judaism:

the Jewish people today do not believe in the doctrine of bodily ascension to heaven. However, there are several references in Scripture to such translation. Enoch (Genesis 5:5) was taken to heaven, bodily, by God. Elijah (II Kings 2) ascended in a fiery chariot. These incidents are the basis for many apocalyptic stories about individuals who penetrated the mysteries of heaven. (Albert M. Shulman, Thoms Yoseloff, New Jersey, 1971, p. 284)

Elijah is soon to disappear from the scene. But he does not die. He, like Enoch, is simply 'taken'. In one of the most skilful literary passages in the whole Bible we are told how Elijah ascends to heaven.

Christian Legends, George Every Peter, New York: Bedrick Books, 1987, p. 130

The Encyclopedia of Religion states that "...the story is so exceptional that it sets Elijah, along with...Enoch, quite apart from all other mortals as one who did not die."(Vol. 5, Mircea Eliade, ed., New York: Macmillan Publishing Co., 1987, p. 93)

In the Epistle to the Hebrews the spring and issue of Enoch's life are clearly marked.

Both Latin and Greek fathers commonly coupled Enoch and Elijah as historic witnesses of the possibility of a resurrection of the body and of a true human existence in glory. Rev 11:3

Smith Bible Dictionary, William Smith, ed., Hendrickson Publishers, Mass., p. 174

The voice of early ecclesiastical tradition is almost unanimous in regarding Enoch and Elijah as the "two witnesses" (Rev. 11:3).

The Unger's Bible Dictionary, R.K. Harrison ed. Chicago: Moody Press, 1988, p. 364

A Latin work, now lost, on Enoch and Elijah's stay in the terrestrial paradise, is summarized in verse by Godfrey of Viterbo...

The Books of Enoch, Aramaic Fragments of Qumran Cave 4, J. T. Milik, ed., Oxford: Oxford University Press, 1976, p. 119

A very common Patristic opinion found as early as Tert.De Anima, 50, Hippo, Antch.43 (cf Bonwetch Txte V. Untersach, xvi, 2, p. 48) identified "the two witnesses" of Rev. 11:3 with Enoch and Elijah.

A *Dictionary of the Bible*, James Hastings, ed., Vol. 1, Hendrickson Publishers, Mass, 1988, p. 705

It would be easy to collect evidence on the eschatological role of Enoch and Elijah. This is the belief of the universal Church, affirms the author of the *Chronicon Paschale*...

The Books of Enoch, Aramaic Fragments of Qumran Cave 4, J. T. Milik, ed., Oxford: Oxford University Press, 1976, p. 120

Verily I say to you that speaking from the heart, I tremble because by the world I (Barnabas) shall be called a god, and for this I shall have to render an account. As God lives, in whose presence my soul stands, I am mortal man as are other men, for although God has placed me as a prophet over the house of Israel...

I am the servant of God, and of this you are witness, how I speak against those wicked men who after my departure from the world shall annul the truth of my gospel by the operation of Satan...

But I shall return toward the end, and with me shall come Enoch and Elijah, and we will testify against the wicked... (The Gospel of Barnabas 52)

The Dead Sea Scrolls, The Gospel of Barnabas and the New Testament, M.A. Yusseff, Indiana: American Trust Publications, 1990, p. 38

A rich iconography on the apocalyptic role of Enoch and Elijah is to be found in manuscripts of the Commentary on the Revelation of St. John compiled by Beatus of Liebana at the end of the eighth century.

The Books of Enoch, Aramaic Fragments of Qumran Cave 4, J. T. Milik, ed., Oxford: Oxford University Press, 1976, p. 120

The theme of the return of Enoch and Elijah at the end of time, of their struggle with the Antichrist, of their death and their resurrection after three (and a half) days was extremely popular in all the Christian churches from the second century (Irenaeus, Hippolytus, Tertullian) until the beginning of the modern era. This belief explains, for instance, the commemoration of Enoch on the Tuesday after Easter by the Jacobite Syrians.

The Books of Enoch, Aramaic Fragments of Qumran Cave 4, J. T. Milik, ed., Oxford: Oxford University Press, 1976, p. 120

A pre-Christian apocalyptic tradition of two messianic precursors men...outside the New Testament the two forerunners are identified as Elijah & Enoch.

The Anchor Bible Dictionary, David Noel Freedman, ed., New York: Doubleday Co., 1992, p. 465

CHAPTER VII

ENOCH IS GREATER THAN ALL THE PROPHETS AND PATRIARCHS

As the record clearly shows, Enoch's uniqueness in Scripture is more singular in its depth and scope than the spiritual accomplishments of all the other Biblical personalities excepting, of course, Jesus Christ. Let us now take a brief survey of the greatest prophets in Biblical history to see how they compare to Enoch.

NOAH'S BIBLICAL PROFILE

"The only righteous, God-fearing man during his time was Noah (Genesis 6:9). According to Scripture he was chosen by God during the Deluge, or as it is known the 'great flood', to keep some of the people and the animals alive when it rained 40 days and 40 nights in the Bible (Gen. 7:12, 24).

Then the Flood sweeps over - only Noah's family is saved-- because 'Noah was a righteous man' he was blameless in his time, with God Noah walked.' " (Gen. 6:9)

The Anchor Bible Dictionary, David Noel Freedman, ed., New York: Doubleday Co., 1992, p. 1123

In the Bible, a righteous person is one who fulfills his or her responsibilities to God and to society. The first time the Bible uses the term is in reference to Noah, who is described as "righteous man, blameless in his generation; Noah walked with God (Gen. 6:9)"...In the Old Testament...God himself was righteous showing mercy and justice in fulfilling his part of the covenant with the people.

ABC's of the Bible, New York: Reader's Digest Association, Inc., 1991, p. 40

One reference source traces the lineage of the righteous patriarch as "the 10th descent from Adam. The Hero of the story
of Deluge (Gen.6-8) he is represented as patriarch who, because
of his blameless piety was chosen by God to perpetuate the
human race...Noah 3 sons, Shem, Ham, Japheth are the reputed
ancestors of the races of mankind."

Encyclopedia Britannica Vol. 8, Chicago, Ill., William Benton Publ., 1973

William Lansdell Wordle, a former Reader in Biblical Criticism
and Exegesis of the Old Testament at the University of Manchester, says that:

Noah is called 'the just [or righteous] man,'...who was found
'without reproach,' or blameless...(44:17a). These two words were
taken from the description of Noah in Gen 6:9 and 7:1. Job is
also described as...(Job 1:1,8, 2:3), 'blameless'. Because of his
righteousness in the midst of a depraved and lawless human
race (Gen 6:5, 11)...

Even though Noah's righteousness is beyond most, he can not be
compared to Enoch, his great grandfather, who is the greatest
Biblical personality in history.

Writes Professor Raphel Patai of Wayne State University:

The phrases "Enoch walked with God," and "God took him,"
have given rise to many legends about this man of Genesis.
(5:24)..."and he was not for God took him," his mystical departure from this earth infers that he did not die a natural death.
He was a very righteous man and lived 365 years. The book
gives an account of Enoch's journey to the upper world, passing
through seven heavens and returning again to earth.

Gates To The Old City, Detroit: Wayne State University Press, 1981, p.
110

Noah, according to the Bible had no such distinction of both
"walking with God" and ascending bodily into heaven without
dying.

ELIJAH'S BIBLICAL PROFILE

Elijah "lived in the 9th century BC during the reign of Ahab and Ahaziah in the northern kingdom of Israel. Elijah shaped the history of the day and dominated Israelite thinking for centuries afterward.

Nelson's New Illustrated Bible Dictionary, Ronald F. Youngblood, ed., Nashville: Nelson, 1995, p. 402

A pre-Christian apocalyptic tradition of two messianic precursors men also explain Elijah's presence at the Transfiguration (Mark 9:2-8; Matt. 17:1-8; Luke 9:28-36) outside the New Testament the two forerunners are identified as Elijah & Enoch, presumably because both had been miraculously translated into heaven.

The Anchor Bible Dictionary, David Noel Freedman, ed., New York: Doubleday Co., 1992, p. 465

Elijah (My God's Yahweh) [is] the most prominent prophet of his time 875-850 B.C. Scripture 1 Kgs 17-19, 21, 2 Kgs 1, 2.

The Revell Bible Dictionary, Grand Rapids, Michigan: Fleming H. Revell, 1990, p. 337

Jesus indicated that John the Baptist was, in a sense, Elijah preparing the way for God's salvation, as Malachi predicted (Mt. 17:10-13).

Malachi "I will send you the prophet Elijah before that great and dreadful day." (4:5)

Elijah saved the religion of Yahweh from being corrupted by the nature-worship of Baal. His decisive intervention ranked him with Moses, the founder of Israel as a nation and religious group, and their two names appear together in old Testament prophesy, which promised Elijah's return as precursor of "the day of Yahweh" (Mal. iv, 4-6). Later Jewish tradition saw him as the great helper in need and the herald or partner of the Messiah. Thus in the New Testament John the Baptist and even Jesus were held by some to be Elijah in person.

Encyclopedia Britannica Vol. 8, Chicago, Ill., William Benton Publ., 1973, p. 281

The assertion that Elijah did not die but rather ascended to heaven strongly influenced late Jewish and Christian traditions, which taught that Elijah would return to the earth as the forerunner of the Messiah.

ABC's of the Bible, New York: Reader's Digest Association, Inc., 1991, p. 110

As Professor of Biblical Studies and Archaelology at Duke University, Carol L. Meyers, pointed out:

"later references to Elijah in the Bible mention or suggest that he will return to announce the coming of the Messiah." (*The New World Book Encyclopedia*, p. 184)

Moreover, a passage on Elijah reads:

"Specific magical powers were ascribed to Elijah's mantle (II Kgs. 2:11) similar to those of Moses's rod...In the Dead Sea Scrolls he appears as one of the forerunners of the messiah...meriting the role in Jewish tradition as the herald of the messiah who would miraculously settle all controversies and make for more peace in the world.

Illustrated Dictionary and Concordance of the Bible, Geoffrey Wigoder, ed., The Jerusalem Publishing House Ltd., 1986, p. 310

According to one Biblical reference book:

Elijah [is] mentioned 29 times in the New Testament. He gained fame as a miracle worker. For example, he miraculously increased the scarce supply of food for a poor widow (1 Kings 17:8-16) and brought the widow's dead son back to life (1 King 17:17-24)...

"1 Kings 17:7-24...Elijah invoked Yahweh's name to raise the dead child of the good widow who acknowledged him..."

The Anchor Bible Dictionary, David Noel Freedman, ed., New York: Doubleday Co., 1992, p. 465

Both Elijah and Jesus miraculously fed many people with scant food.

ABC's of the Bible, New York: Reader's Digest Association, Inc., 1991, p. 110

Elijah hiding from the king's anger, [King Ahab] is fed by ravens and then sheltered by a Phoenician widow whose food is miraculously multiplied and whose son is brought back from the dead by the prophet.

Encyclopedia Britannica Vol. 8, Chicago, Ill., William Benton Publ., 1973, p. 281

Another Biblical reference work indicated that "...in front of 59 sons of the prophets (a guild like society of professional prophesiers), Elijah miraculously split the Jordan by striking the water with his rolled-up mantle, "and the water was parted to the one side and to the other, till the two of them could go over on dry ground." (2 Kings 2:8)

ABC's of the Bible, New York: Reader's Digest Association, Inc., 1991, p. 110

A pilgrimage to Mt. Horeb (Sinai) shows Elijah first disheartened by the long loneliness of his fight, then miraculously sustained and encouraged.

Encyclopedia Britannica Vol. 8, Chicago, Ill., William Benton Publ., 1973, p. 281

Sewell L. Avery Distinguished Service Professor at the University of Chicago, Mircea Eliade explained that: "like the 'specialist in the sacred' of archaic and traditional societies, the prophets are endowed with faculties of divination (Elijah foresees the imminent death of King Ahaziah (2 Kings 3:16-17) and knows that the king has ordered him killed (2 Kings 6:32); he knows the words spoken by the king of Damascus in his bedchamber)."

A History of Religious Ideas, Mircea Eliade, Chicago: University of Chicago Press, 1978, p. 343

Joan Comay, author of *Who's Who, The Old Testament*, portrays Elijah's ascension to heaven in the presence of his successor, Elisha:

They walked on to beyond Jerico they came to the banks of the river Jordan...they walked on talking when 'behold, a chariot of fire and horses of fire separated the two of them and Elijah went up by whirlwind into heaven' (2 Kgs 2:11). As a chariot disappeared from sight, Elisha...then picked up the fallen mantle of Elijah.

New York: Oxford University Press, 1993, p. 92

ABC's of the Bible echoes the same:

"And as they still went on and talked, behold, a chariot of fire and horses of fire separated the two of them. And Elijah went up by a whirlwind into heaven. And Elisha saw it and he cried, 'My father, my father! the chariots of Israel and its horsemen!' And he saw him no more."

Reader's Digest Association, Inc., New York, 1991, p. 110

As The Anchor Bible Dictionary notes:

"Elijah's mysterious assumption to heaven in a whirlwind occurs once the Jordan has been crossed...

David Noel Freedman, ed., New York: Doubleday Co., 1992, p. 465

Finally, he is taken up to heaven in a whirlwind. God is invisible and spiritual, best known in the intellectual word of revelation, (I King xix, 12). The transcendence of God received here one of its earliest expressions.

Encyclopedia Britannica Vol. 8, Chicago, Ill., William Benton Publ., 1973, p. 282

Likewise, Associate Professor of Religious Studies at University of California, Santa Barbara, Richard D. Hecht and Professor of Religious Studies, Ninian Smart remarked that:

Jesus is transfigured...in the company of Moses, (chief founder of ancient Israel), and Elijah (prototype of prophets and herald of the Messiah)....[Mark 8-9]

Sacred Texts of the World, New York: Crossroad, 1982, p. 116

From the *ABC's of the Bible* it reads: "About a week later he [Jesus], Peter, James and John [went] to a mountain top. There the awestruck disciples saw their leader suddenly transformed into a figure of almost blinding radiance. Moses and Elijah - representing the law and the prophets - appeared speaking with Jesus, and from a luminous cloud moving above came a voice saying, 'This is my beloved Son, with whom I am well pleased; listen to him.' "

Reader's Digest Association, Inc., New York, 1991, p. 250

The New Testament also mentions the appearance of Elijah in person. Along with Moses, he appeared with Jesus on the Mount of Transfiguration.

Nelson's New Illustrated Bible Dictionary, Ronald F. Youngblood, ed., Nashville: Nelson, 1995, p. 394

"Moses and Elijah appeared in glory and spake of his decease which he was about to accomplish at Jerusalem." (Luke ix. 31)

Jesus Transfiguration along with Moses and Elijah's appearances in glory is reminiscent of Enoch's transformation into the angel Metatron.

Professor James H. Charlesworth of Duke University records the following passage:

"Go and extract Enoch from [his] earthly clothing. And anoint him with my delightful oil, and put him into the clothes of my glory." And so Michael did, just as the Lord had said to him. He anointed me and he clothed me. And the appearance of that oil is greater than the greatest light, and its ointment is like sweet dew, and its fragrance myrrh; and it is like the rays of the glittering sun. And I looked at myself, and I had to become like one of his glorious ones..."

The Old Testament Pseudepigrapha, Apocalyptic Literature Vol. 1, and Testaments, ed., 1984, p. 138

The Swedish scholar Professor Hugo Odeberg gives this description:

"Enoch, son of Jared, who was taken up in the generation of the Flood (4:3-5), enlarged until he matched the world in length and breadth (9:2) and installed on a throne of glory (10:1)...'Prince of the Presence'. He is addressed by R. Isma'el as 'the Glory of Splendours' (cf. the epithet given to Metatron in chh. 13, 15, 16 et al., 'the Glory of all heavens') ."

3 Enoch or The Hebrew Book of Enoch, New York: KTAV Publishing House, Inc., 1984

Islam also recognized him as a prophet.

Encyclopedia Britannica Vol. 8, Chicago, Ill., William Benton Publ., 1973, p. 281

The Qur'an lists Elijah among the "righteous ones" (Sura 8:85).

The Anchor Bible Dictionary, David Noel Freedman, ed., New York: Doubleday Co., 1992, p. 465

Since some Jews believe that Elijah will announce the coming of the Messiah on a Passover, they put out an additional glass of wine for the prophet and leave the door open for him to enter freely.

The World's Great Religions, Henry R. Luce, ed., New York: Time Inc., 1957, p. 141

Professor John Van Seter of the University of North Carolina at Chapel Hill explains:

At the Passover Seder a cup of wine is placed on the table as the cup of Elijah and is not drunk. This was interpreted eschatologically as an anticipation of the final deliverance from bondage.

The Encyclopedia of Religion, Vol. 5, Mircea Eliade, ed., New York: Macmillan Publishing Co., 1987, p. 93

He further adds:

Elijah was also regarded as healer and guardian of the newborn because of his care for the widow's son. In this respect amulets containing the name of the prophet were good luck charms.

"He is protector of the newborn and the 'Chair of Elijah' is a fixture at circumcision. "

The Anchor Bible Dictionary, David Noel Freedman, ed., New York: Doubleday Co., 1992, p. 465

Professor Emeritus of Theology at the University of Exeter, England, J.R. Porter says that:

When Gabriel announces the forthcoming birth of John the Baptist (Luke 1:13-17), he says that John will be possessed by 'the spirit and power of Elijah' and 'turn the hearts of parents to their children' (Luke 1:17).

The Illustrated Guide to the Bible, Oxford University Press, N.Y., 1995, p. 152

His sudden, mysterious appearances remained a symbol of the unfettered initiative of God in history. The remote austerity of his life was an impressive testimony to other worldly values, just as his being taken to heaven showed Israel the possibility of a life beyond this.

Encyclopedia Britannica Vol. 8, Chicago, Ill., William Benton Publ., 1973, p. 282

Elijah's influence continued even after he ascended into heaven. King Jehoran of Israel received a letter from the prophet seven years after his ascension, indicating that the king would be punished severely for his sins (2 Chr. 21:12-15).

Nelson's New Illustrated Bible Dictionary, Ronald F. Youngblood, ed., Nashville: Nelson, 1995, p. 402

Despite Elijah's obvious Biblical greatness, Enoch's incomparable achievements are more outstanding as the first in "walking with God" and Immortality combined. In addition, he is also the first Patriarch-Prophet in Scripture as well as his legendary "god-like" status as Metatron.

ELISHA'S BIBLICAL PROFILE

Before taking his leave, Elijah fulfilled the final request of Elisha by providing him with a double portion of his prophetic spirit (2 Kings. 2:9-10), making him his spiritual first born. Upon receiving Elijah's mantle, Elisha, the spiritual first son of Elijah, demonstrated this gift by parting the waters of the Jordan River, allowing him to cross on dry land (2 Kgs. 2:14)...

Nelson's New Illustrated Bible Dictionary, Ronald F. Youngblood, ed., Nashville: Nelson, 1995, p. 395

Similarly in the *ABC's of the Bible* it reads:

Elisha picked up Elijah's mantle - the traditional hair shirt symbolizing a prophet's calling...and parted the waters at the Jordan.

New York: Reader's Digest Association, Inc., 1991, p. 110

The transfer of authority from Elijah to Elisha is modeled on the transfer of power from Moses to Joshua (Num. 27:18-23; Deut. 34:9).

The Anchor Bible Dictionary, Vol. 2, David Noel Freedman, Editor-in-Chief, Doubleday Co., p. 472

The chapters on Elisha report 14 miracles, twice as many as are attributed to Elijah.

The Revell Bible Dictionary, Grand Rapids, Michigan: Fleming H. Revell, 1990, p. 338

For example:

Elisha, endowed with miraculous science and power, appears: ...as a kindly, understanding helper in need, as in the house of the Shunammite woman whose dead son he brought back to life (IV, 8-37).

Encyclopedia Britannica Vol. 8, Chicago, Ill., William Benton Publ., 1973, p. 287

Nelson's New Illustrated Bible Dictionary provides confirmation:

While staying at a widow's home, he performed a miracle by bringing her son back to life (1 Kings 17:1-25). Elisha raised him from the dead (2 Kgs. 4:18-37).

Even the bones of the dead had miraculous powers. When a corpse was hidden in Elisha's tomb, it came back to life as it touched the prophet's bones (2 Kgs. 13:21).

Nelson's New Illustrated Bible Dictionary, Ronald F. Youngblood, ed. Nashville: Nelson, 1995, p. 396

An identical point is made by The Anchor Bible Dictionary:

a dead man was revived when he came into contact with Elisha's bones (2 Kgs 13:20-21).

David Noel Freedman,ed., Doubleday Co., p. 472

The words "the chariots of Israel and its horsemen," in which Elisha summed up the greatness of Elijah, were applied by King Joash to the dying Elisha to testify that he had been equal to his inherited task (II Kings ii, 12, xiii, 14).

Encyclopedia Britannica Vol. 8, Chicago, Ill., William Benton Publ., 1973, p. 287

Elisha, the great miracle worker, his achievements in the spiritual realm do not compare to Enoch's greater spiritual accomplishments of perfection.

ABRAHAM BIBLICAL PROFILE

Covenant is a very important word in the Bible; the very names by which the two parts are known, Old Testament and New Testament, actually mean Old Covenant and New Covenant.

The Lost Prophet, (The Book of Enoch and its influence on Christianity), Margaret Barker, Great Britain: SPCK, 1988, p. 79

The first covenant God made was with Noah and his descendants: never again to destroy the earth by flood. Since this was a covenant with all mankind, it differs for the three major Biblical covenants involving Abraham, Moses and David. God's covenant with the patriarch Abraham was a grant of posterity, homeland, and divine protection...Much later, God make a similar covenant with David - this time using the prophet Nathan as an intermediary. God granted David a permanent dynasty.

ABC's of the Bible, New York: Reader's Digest Association, Inc., 1991, p. 47

"As the recipient of God's promise to make a great nation and to give the land of Canaan to that nation, Abraham was revered in the Old Testament as the forefather of the Israelites, who were called the offspring of Abraham [Is. 41:8],"

ABC's of the Bible, New York: Reader's Digest Association, Inc., 1991, p.97

The descendants of Noah who are patriarchs and who lived after the floods are called postdiluvian. Thus Abraham is a postdiluvian patriarch.

Abraham who is referred to as 'the father of a multitude of nations' (Gen. 17:4) is also described in the Bible as 'the friend of God.' (Jas. 2:23).

"In addition, he is referred to as the 'father of all nations,' and the 'model of faith' (See Rom. 4:9, Heb. 11:8). Abraham is second only to Moses among New Testament mentions of Biblical heroes...Ultimately, as the 'father of all believers' (Gal. 3:7), Abraham is to be looked to as a source of unity and harmony..."

The Oxford Companion to the Bible, Bruce Metzger and Michael Coogan, Eds., Oxford: Oxford University Press, 1993, p. 5

The World's Great Religions records Abraham 's death:

And Abraham expired, and died in a good old age, an old man, and full years; and was gathered to his people. And Isaac and Ishmael his sons buried him (Genesis 11:25).

Henry R. Luce, ed., New York: Time Inc., 1957, p. 157

In spite of the fact that Abraham stands as the "father of the multitudes," Enoch the Ethiopian is more outstanding possessing greater spiritual accomplishments as the first Patriarch-Prophet, the first Perfect human being, the first Immortal, the first to have "walked with God" and ascend bodily into heaven.

MOSES' BIBLICAL PROFILE

Moses was the son of Amram and Jochaebed (Num. xxvi), founder and leader of the religious community of Israel. Moses, primary significance is as the prophetic founder of Israel's religious system (Jewish religion) around 1250 B.C.E.

Moses, according to Scripture, had a divine experience where God appeared to him as a fiery blackberry bush, commonly referred to as "the burning bush" that was miraculously not consumed by the fire.

As Scripture would have it, Moses was called on to be a savior of Israel and serve as an intermediary between God and Israel which was the traditional prophet's role.

Moses was the principle leader and teacher of the Israelites and one of the most important characters in the Bible. He declared the Ten Commandments as the law for his people. Under his leadership, the Israelites were established as a nation.

The first five books of the Bible - Genesis, Exodus, Leviticus, Numbers and Deuteron my are called the "Five Books of Moses" or the Pentateuch. In addition, Moses was the one to organize the nation's official forms of worship.

The World's Great Religions points out: "all five books of the Torah are traditionally attributed to Moses."

Henry R. Luce, ed., New York: Time Inc., 1957, p. 166

As the central human figure in the Israelites' history "Moses played several roles. Above all, Moses was the lawgiver of Israel; he received the laws of the covenant on the holy mountain and transmitted them to the people. As intercessor on their behalf, he crossed the "holiness boundary" that separated them from the mountain where God revealed the law. As their moral advocate, he pleaded their case before God..."

ABC's of the Bible, New York: Reader's Digest Association, Inc., 1991, p. 48

In the covenant ceremony at Mount Sinai, where the Ten Commandments were given, he founded the religious community known as Israel.

Nelson's New Illustrated Bible Dictionary, Ronald F. Youngblood, ed., Nashville: Nelson, 1995, p. 859

He established their moral and legal codes, which have been the major force in Judaism and all Western civilization to this day, though, later Jews have adapted and developed the message of Moses, just as Moses did to that of Abraham.

The World's Great Religions, Henry R. Luce, ed., New York: Time Inc., 1957, p. 157

"And Moses was learned in all the wisdom of the Egyptian land was mighty in words and deeds." (ACTS 7:22)

As a spokesman for God, he implemented sacrifice rituals, and after receiving God's blueprint for the tabernacle, he inaugurated daily worship and consecrated the clergy. As the first and greatest of Israel's prophets - "And there has not arisen a prophet since in Israel like Moses" - he was a model for all those who followed.

ABC's of the Bible, New York: Reader's Digest Association, Inc., 1991, p. 48

In the same book we find out that:

Moses made three sacrifices - first, a bull as a sin offering to purify the altar; then a ram as a burnt offering and finally a second ram for the ordination, a peace offering that reached its climax in a sacred meal held at the door of the tabernacle. Some of the sacrifices were repeated for seven days. (p. 65)

Moses then anointed the tabernacle and altar and all their furnishings and 'poured some of the anointing oil on Aaron's head, and anointed him, to consecrate him. (p. 64)

The Pentateuch is both the biography of Moses, greatest Jew of all time, and the history of the Jewish nation's start.

The World's Great Religions, Henry R. Luce, ed., New York: Time Inc., 1957, p. 155

ABC's of the Bible states that:...as in the case of Moses, God's relationship to a person was so special that he spoke to him "face to face, as a man speaks to his friend."

Reader's Digest Association, Inc., New York, 1991, p. 41-2

In the same work later on it reads:

Moses, then, could communicate directly with God - "face to face" - and mediate for his people, a characteristic that the prophets would emulate...(p. 109)

"At one point Moses' patience reached a breaking point and he sinned against the Lord, in anger against the people...Moses lifted his hand and struck the rock twice with his rod."

Nelson's New Illustrated Bible Dictionary, Ronald F. Youngblood, ed., Nashville: Nelson, 1995, p. 862

The death of Moses in *Exodus* is referred to by Professor of Biblical Theology, University of Iceland, Thorir K. Thordarson who remarked that:

Moses vicariously bears Yahweh's wrath against his people. His death alone in Moab takes on a vicarious quality as well. Yahweh buries him and "no one knows the place of his burial to this day" (34:6). There can be no sacred mountain where pilgrims can share in a memorial ceremony for Moses. He must live in the hearts of the people as...one with whom Yahweh spoke 'face to face' (34:10).

The Anchor Bible Dictionary, Vol. 2, David Noel Freedman, ed., New York: Doubleday Co., p. 915.

Striking a similar note, *ABC's of the Bible* adds that: " Moses the servant of the Lord died there" and was buried by God himself. (Dt. 34:5)

Reader's Digest Association, Inc., New York, 1991, p. 180

Despite Moses' lofty position, he still does not compare to Enoch the Ethiopian. A man he had to idolize as a heroic ancestor due to Enoch's spiritual perfection and legendary reputation.

AARON'S BIBLICAL PROFILE

Enoch is greater than Aaron the high priest and brother of Moses.

Nelson's New Illustrated Bible Dictionary asserts that "...with the appointment of Aaron by God as the first High Priest, the priesthood was formally established. Aaron's descendants were established as the priestly line in Israel."

Ronald F. Youngblood, ed., Nashville: Nelson, 1995, p. 1028

Yet, Enoch was a High Priest before Aaron and he was greater in that office.

"Metatron-Enoch belong in the series of Moses and Elijah as heavenly high priests. And so, by an easy transition, to Elijah, more often paired with Enoch than any other figure..."

Enoch the Prophet, Hugh Nibley, Salt Lake City, Utah: Deseret Book Company, 1986. p. 33

Writes Professor VanderKam:

Jubilees...posits that all ancient worthies in the Sethite line were priests who transmitted sacerdotal legislation from father to son.

Enoch and the Growth of An Apocalyptic Tradition, James VanderKam, Washington, D.C.: The Catholic Biblical Association of America, 1984, p. 186

The widely-recognized authority on the Dead Sea Scrolls, J.T. Milik, says that "Enoch and Methusaleh" [are] "antediluvian high priests"...

The Books of Enoch, Aramaic Fragments of Qumran Cave 4, ed., Oxford: Oxford University Press, 1976, p. 114

As Professor Hugh Nibley pointed out: For his work Enoch is endowed with power - the power of the priesthood.

Enoch the Prophet, Salt Lake City, Utah: Deseret Book Company, 1986, p. 21.

SAMUEL'S PROFILE

Enoch is greater than the popular prophet Samuel.

Samuel is given the following description by a well-known Biblical reference book:

Samuel (name of God) [is] the earliest of the great Hebrew prophets (after Moses) and the last judge of Israel. Samuel led his people against the Philistine oppressors. When he was an old man, Samuel anointed Saul as the first king of Israel and later anointed David as Saul's successor. Samuel is recognized as one of the greatest leaders in Israel. (Jer. 15:1, Heb. 11:32)

Nelson's New Illustrated Bible Dictionary, Ronald F. Youngblood, ed., Nashville: Nelson, 1995, p. 1122.

George Bradford Caird, Senior Tutor at Mansfield College, Oxford, defines him thusly:

Samuel, the most outstanding character in Israel's history between Moses and David, is represented in I Samuel in every role of leadership open to a man of his day - seer, Nazerite (dedicated to the defense of Yahweh religion), priest, judge and military leader. The traditions concerning him have been much edited and embellished.

Encyclopedia Britannica Vol. 8, Chicago, Ill., William Benton Publ., 1973, p. 924.

Continuing in the same book:

Samuel's greatest claim to fame was the establishment of monarchy in Israel...Samuel prompted by God, took the initiative in anointing Saul as King...

A noted editor and professor at the University of Chicago made this observation regarding all the great prophets:

All the great prophets are sincerely and passionately convinced of the genuineness of their vocation and the urgency of their message. They do not doubt that they are proclaiming the very word of God....Their divine possession is sometimes manifested by ecstasy, though exaltation or an ecstatic trance do not seem to be indispensable.

A History of Religious Ideas, Mircea Eliade, Chicago: University of Chicago Press, 1978, p. 343

Samuel is "the only person in the Bible who though dead spoke with the living (1 Sam. 28:13). Samuel appeared like "a God coming up out of the earth.....He spoke with king Saul when the king consulted a medium reputed to be able to call up the dead. "

Nelson's New Illustrated Bible Dictionary, Ronald F. Youngblood, ed. Nashville: Nelson, 1995, p. 140

Yet, Enoch surpasses this famous prophet by great lengths in spiritual flawlessness and heavenly achievements.

ISAIAH'S BIBLICAL PROFILE

Isaiah is the first of the Major Prophets in both Jewish and Christian tradition.

The Oxford Companion to the Bible, Bruce Metzger and Michael Coogan, eds., Oxford: Oxford University Press, 1993, p. 325

Isaiah known as one of the heroes of the faith "of whom the world was not worthy." (Heb 11:38). One of the more famous of the Old Testament prophets who is reputed to have predicted the coming of the Messiah.

Nelson's New Illustrated Bible Dictionary, Ronald F. Youngblood, ed., Nashville: Nelson, 1995, p. 609

Isaiah is more often quoted in the New Testament than is any other book of the Hebrew Bible apart from Psalms...

The Oxford Companion to the Bible, Bruce Metzger and Michael Coogan, Eds., Oxford: Oxford University Press, 1993, p. 329

Additionally, in the same work, it states that "the Book of Isaiah also reveals...the coming Messiah...No other book of the bible contains as many references to the coming Messiah as this magnificent book. "

Isaiah's famous dynastic oracles in ix 2-7 (Heb. ix, 1-6) and xi, 1-9...were applied to the Messiah...

The oracles of the late period culminating on those proclaiming that Yahweh would defend Jerusalem against Sennacherib (5-16; xxxvii, 22-29), concentrating on the sovereign purpose of God in determining the course of history and the fate of nations.

Encyclopedia Britannica Vol. 8, Chicago, Ill., William Benton Publ., 1973, p. 656

By comparison, in a chapter entitled *"The Bible Rewritten and Expanded,"* Professor George W. Nickelsburg of the University of Iowa wrote that: "Enoch's oracle consists of two major parts...he announces the flood which will destroy the human race. The second part of the oracle deals with events after the flood...Iniquity will again increase for many generations until generations of righteousness will arise and 'evil and wickedness come to an end...' "

At all events the supramundane character of the Son of Man in I Enoch has no counterpart in the Old Testament expectation of an ideal king or the prophet description of the Servant. Its influence on the concept of the Son of Man in the gospels is widely acknowledged.

Funk & Wagnalls, New Standard Encyclopedia of Universal Knowledge, Vol. X, Funk & Wagnalls Co., 1931.

The book of Isaiah has played a central role in Christian liturgy and theology. It is sometimes called the "Fifth Gospel" because in the words of Jerome, Isaiah recounts the life of the Messiah in such a way as to make one think he is 'telling the story of what has already happened rather than what is still to come.'

The Oxford Companion to the Bible, Bruce Metzger and Michael Coogan, Eds., Oxford: Oxford University Press, 1993, p. 328-9

However, Enoch in the book of Jubilees foretold the coming of a Messiah way ahead of Isaiah's pronouncements. Enoch still is a more significant and powerful figure than Isaiah despite Isaiah's popularity. Enoch had no "uncleanliness."

Isaiah, on the other hand, says "'Woe is me for I am undone because I am a man of unclean lies. (Is. 6:5). Because of this confession his lips were cleaned by live coal."

COMPARISON OF FAMOUS PROPHETS

At the time of the Israelites' flight from Egypt, God gave them their first great miracle worker, Moses...Two of the greatest miracle workers were Elijah and Elisha...

ABC's of the Bible, New York: Reader's Digest Association, Inc., 1991, p. 208

Elijah is supported by several details which suggest a parallel between Elijah and Moses. Elijah's return to Horeb is obvious enough, but there is also the fact that Elijah is accompanied and succeeded by Elisha as Moses was by Joshua.

The Illustrated Bible Dictionary, J.D. Douglas, ed., England: Tyndale House, 1982, p. 441

Like Moses' staff, the prophet's mantle of Elijah became an instrument for enacting God's miracles. By striking the water with the mantle both Elijah and Elisha made the Jordan River part. Elisha also used a branch to make an ax-head float, salt to purify water, and flour to remove poison from stew.

ABC's of the Bible, New York: Reader's Digest Association, Inc., 1991, p. 208

As one Biblical reference work puts it:

"Like Moses and the Israelites Elijah is fed by Yahweh (17:6); cf. Exod. 16:8,12); Yahweh's miraculous food takes the form of cakes baked with oil (17:12-16; cf. Num. 11:7-9); Elijah and Moses complain about Yahweh's mistreatment of a faithful servant (17:19-21; cf. Num. 11:11-12)."

The only miracle of Jesus ministry recorded in all four gospels is the story of feeding a throng of 500 men, women and children...these miracles of Jesus recalled the time the Old Testament prophet Elisha fed a hundred people with 20 small barley loaves with food to spare.

ABC's of the Bible, New York: Reader's Digest Association, Inc., 1991, p. 212

Like Moses, Elijah was sustained for 40 days and nights in the wilderness while fleeing the wrath of Queen Jezebel.

Nelson's New Illustrated Bible Dictionary, Ronald F. Youngblood, ed., Nashville: Nelson, 1995, p. 393

Scripture reports only a few periods marked by multiple miracles; the age of Exodus, the time of Elijah and Elisha, the years of Christ's ministry, and the early days of the Church.

The Revell Bible Dictionary, Grand Rapids, Michigan: Fleming H. Revell, 1990, p. 337

JESUS CHRIST'S BIBLICAL PROFILE & COMPARISONS

The Gospel of Matthew (1:1-17) recorded Christ's descent from the patriarch Abraham.

Nelson's New Illustrated Bible Dictionary, Ronald F. Youngblood, ed., Nashville: Nelson, 1995, p. 481

Many expected Jesus to repeat the earlier miracles of Moses, Elijah, and Elisha...Elijah and his disciple Elisha each brought a child back to life. Elijah revived a grieving woman's son who had "no breath left in him" (1 Kings 17:17) the prophet "stretched himself upon the child three times...and the soul of the child came into him again." ((1 Kings 17:21). In the case of Elisha, he enabled a childless woman to bear a son; then when the boy died some years later, the prophet "lay upon the child, putting his mouth upon his mouth' his eyes upon his eyes, and his hands upon his hands; and...the flesh of the child became warm...and the child opened his eyes" (2 Kings 4:34). In a very similar act of compassion for a widow whose only son had died, Jesus touched the bier of the youth and told him to rise. "And the dead man sat up, and began to speak" (Luke 7:15) - one of three times Jesus revived the dead. Both Elisha and Jesus miraculously fed many people with scant food.

ABC's of the Bible, New York: Reader's Digest Association, Inc., 1991, p. 110

The book further adds:

And when Jesus healed a leper by touching him, it recalled acts of both Elisha and Moses. Elisha cured the leprous Syrian general Naaman by having him bathe in the Jordan River; Moses begged God to heal his sister Miriam's leprosy, and God did so. (p. 112) Jesus acts through words or touch. For example, when he raised Jairus' daughter from the dead, he took her by the hand and said, "Little girl, I say to you arise [Mk. 5:41]. (p. 210)

CHAPTER VIII

ETHIOPIC CHURCH CANONIZATION OF ENOCH

The canonization of Enoch by the Abyssinian Church in Ethiopia is but another proof that Enoch was an Ethiopian.

By canonizing his works as a legitimate and inspired Ethiopian book, the Ethiopic Church was recognizing one of its own native sons called Enoch.

Once you understand the history of Africa in general, and Ethiopia in particular, you will see that Enoch could only have been an Ethiopian, due to his antiquity and reputation.

In Cairo Geniza the passage contains three lines: "Enoch is found blameless, and he walked with God and was taken away, a sign of knowledge for generation after generation. "

Roots of Apocalyptic, Helge S. Kvanvig, Norway: Neukirchener Verlag, 1988, p. 121

Likewise, W.E.B. Dubois notes: "In the dawn of Greek literature, in the Iliad, we hear of the gods feasting "among the blameless Ethiopians."

The World and Africa, International Publishers, New York, 1965, p. 119.

More than a thousand years earlier Homer's proud Achaeans knew of the "most distant of men, the blameless Ethiopian". And almost two thousand years before the clash beneath the walls of Troy, the Fifth Dynasty Sahure sent an expedition to Ethiopia, which he knew was the land of Punt.

"Burnt by the Sun," *American Visions*, Vol.10, No.6, Washington D.C. American Visions Communications, December/January, 1996, p. 14

Lady Flora Louise Lugard says of the Ethiopians:

The Annals of all the great early nations of Asia Minor are full of them. The Mosaic (Biblical) records allude to them frequently, but while they are described as the most powerful, the most just, and the most beautiful of the human race, they are constantly spoken of as black, and there seems to be no other conclusion to be drawn, than that at that remote period of history the leading race of the Western World was a black race.

A *Tropical Dependency*, Lady Flora Louise Lugard, New York: Barnes & Noble, 1964, p. 49

Let us not forget that it is Moses in the Mosaic book known as "Genesis" who introduces Enoch the Ethiopian to the Biblical world.

Professor Herr Eugen Georg, a German scholar of history, indicates that at the "genesis" of the human race:

"A splendid era of black seems to have preceded all the later races! There must once have been a tremendous Negro expansion, since the original masters of all the lands...were...probably...black men. (*THE ADVENTURE OF MANKIND*. E.P. Dutton & Co., 1931, p. 44)

Homer, in an often quoted passage, tells how the Greek gods used to go on their feast days to Ethiopia to commune with their ancestors.

Dionysius wrote:

"Upon the great Atlantic, near the isle of Erithrea, for its pastures famed, the *sacred race* of Ethiopians dwell."

Quoted by J. Bryant, ANALV. OF ANT. MYTHOLOGY, Vol. 3, 1776, p. 185,

The fame of the Ethiopians was widespread in ancient history. Herodotus describes them as:

"The tallest, most beautiful and long-lived of the human races."

And, before Herodotus, Homer, in even more flattering language, described them as:

"The most just of men; the favorites of the gods."

Again, Homer, one of the most ancient and honored writers in the western world, wrote:

"Jupiter today, followed by all the gods, Receives the sacrifices of the Ethiopians."

According to Count Volney in his book, *The Ruins of Empire*:

"What Diodorus says of the Thebans, every author, and himself elsewhere, repeat of the Ethiopians, which tends more firmly to establish the identity of this place of which I have spoken. The Ethiopians conceive themselves, says he, lib. iii, to be of greater antiquity than any other nation and it is probable that, born under the sun's path, its warmth may have ripened them earlier than other men. They suppose themselves also to be the inventors of divine worship, of festivals, of solemn assemblies, of sacrifices, and every other religious practices." (p. 16) [ILIAD, I, 422]

And G. Massey says, and rightly so, that "Africa is man's primordial home." Enoch appears during this primeval period in history. Thus, making him an African man. His books have the mark of antiquity on them as he is only the 7th descent from Adam's lineage. He is a primeval figure in Biblical history.

Enoch the Ethiopian is only, in Biblical terms, seven generations removed from the first man which attests to Enoch's personal antiquity.

As one European scholar pointed out:

"he is not portrayed as one of the great personalities of the Old Testament nor does he belong to the history of Israel. Rather Enoch appears on the stage of primeval history. Strictly speaking he is not even a Jew. "

Roots of Apocalyptic, Helge S. Kvanvig, Norway: Neukirchener Verlag, 1988, p. 18

Hyam Maccoby, a Fellow of Leo Baeck College, London, and a specialist in the study of Judeo-Christian relations, wrote:

We have seen that the Gnostics used non-Jewish biblical characters such as...Enoch..."

The Myth-Maker, San Francisco: Harper, 1986, p. 190

Moreover, Enoch "preceded the covenant of law, uncircumcised and [was] unobservant of the "Sabbath." (*The Encyclopedia of Religion,* 1987, p. 117)

However, The Dead Sea Scrolls made it possible for us to establish that Enoch had a definite place in the foundation and origins of Christianity.

No other Biblical book breaks into double digits, but both First Enoch and Jubilees do.

This means that there were more copies of those books at Qumran than of almost any other book that we now have in our Bible.

We would not have the texts of First Enoch or Jubilees or a number of other works if this very ancient Christian tradition had not preserved them for us and had not preserved an earlier state of canonical development when the question apparently had not been decided uniformly in the early church.

The Dead Sea Scrolls After Forty Years, Hershel Shanks, James C. Vanderkam, P. Kyle McCarter, Jr., James A. Sanders, Washington, DC: Biblical Archaeology Society, 1990

Dr. V.E. Ewing, a theologian and scholar whom Dr. Albert Schweitzer referred to as "the renaissance of Leonardo De Vinci," revealed that:

Among the basic scriptures used by the Brotherhood were the Book of Enoch...Ten manuscripts of the former were found in the Qumran caves, a fact which is not widely publicized.

They were in Aramaic, the mother tongue of Jesus and the Sect of the Scrolls. According to scholars, the book had its origin and growth during the first and late second centuries B.C...

In fact, there are those among the scholars who insist that the Book of Enoch is an original sectarian Scripture.

The Prophet of the Dead Sea Scrolls, California: Tree of Life Publications, 1993, p. 53

"Jubilees, then, has all the traits that mark a book as authoritative at Qumran...[the] book became canonical for some Christian groups, including the Abyssinian Church in Ethiopia. The high esteem it enjoyed in Ethiopia insured its preservation...

The Dead Sea Scrolls Today, James C. Vanderkam, Grand Rapids, Michigan: William B. Eerdmans Publishing Co., 1994, p. 154

Comparing Jude (14-15) to the Book of Enoch, Charles F. Pfeiffer suggests that "excerpts from the Book of Enoch (1:9; 63:8; 93:3)...give a clear-cut sampling of the judgment which was preached by Enoch in this period.

While some may argue as to what source Jude actually used (written or oral tradition), it can be pointed out that inclusion of this quotation in a New Testament book canonizes his [Enoch] message and makes it Holy Writ.

Wycliffe Bible Encyclopedia, Vol.,1, Chicago: Moody Press, 1975, p. 529

The International Standard Bible Encyclopedia revealed that:

After having been quoted in Jude and noticed by several of the Fathers, this work disappeared from the knowledge of the Christian church.

In the last quarter of the 18th century Bruce, the Abyssinian traveler, brought to Europe three copies of the Book of Enoch in Ethiopic, which had been regarded as canonical by the Abyssinian church, and had consequently been preserved by them.

James Orr, Eds., Mich.: W.M.B Eerdmans, 1960,

The existence of a book of Enoch kept by the Abyssinian Church among the sacred books of their Bible had been known in Europe, in a vague way, since the end of the fifteenth century.

The Books of Enoch, Aramaic Fragments of Qumran Cave 4, J. T. Milik, ed., Oxford: Oxford University Press, 1976, Preface

One of the pre-eminent scholars on Enoch, R. H. Charles asserted that 'With the earlier Fathers and Apologists it had all the weight of a canonical book...' "

The Book of Enoch, trans. from Professor Dillmann's Ethiopic Text, edited by R. H. Charles, Oxford: Clarendon Press,1893, p. 1

1 Enoch, as we have seen, made an impact on early Christian thought and left its indelible mark upon the New Testament...On the other hand, it is hardly possible to understand any aspect of the religious tradition and thought of Ethiopia, the country in which it survived, without an understanding of it.

The Old Testament Pseudepigrapha, Apocalyptic Literature and Testaments, Vol. I, James H. Charlesworth, ed., 1984

Adds the author of *Anacalypsis*, Godfrey Higgins:

It is impossible to read the book of, Enoch and not to be struck with the similarity of style to that of the Jewish prophets, particularly Isaiah and Jeremiah: the same expressions are perpetually recurring. (New York: University Books, rep. A & B Books, Brooklyn, 1965, p. 551)

The New Encyclopedia Brittanica remarked that:

What is really a...collection of such books has been found in Ethiopic Gecez. The final section (chapters 39-68) includes Enoch's advice to his sons and an account of his life, including his final ascension. (Vol. 4 Chicago, 1995, p. 506)

Enoch, 1st Book of, also called Ethiopic Book of Enoch, pseudepigraphical work (one resembling in style and content authentic Biblical literature)...is completely preserved in Gecez.

Encyclopedia Britannia Micropoedia III Coleman Exclusi, 1978, p. 604

Enochic literature was to have a full-blown renaissance in the early Christian communities, but this would come about through the medium of Greek translations.

The Books of Enoch, Aramaic Fragments of Qumran Cave 4, J. T. Milik, ed., Oxford: Oxford University Press, 1976, p. 7

The Books of Enoch, Aramaic Fragments of Qumran Cave 4, says that "an important Enochic work, the book of Giants...was admitted to the Manichean canon of sacred books and translated into numerous languages of Asia, Africa, and Europe..."

J. T. Milik, ed., Oxford: Oxford University Press, 1976, p. vi

In Egypt, Ethiopic Enoch was still considered an inspired, canonical work as the following suggests:

Modern knowledge of the work has been derived from the Ethiopic version...probably at a time when all Christendom except Egypt had dropped Enoch from the list of sacred writings.

The Last Chapters of Enoch in Greek, edited by Campbell Bonner & Herbert C. Youtie, London: Christophers, 1937, p. 3

As the German Orientalist in his Life of Peiresc, writes among other things of a certain Capuchin, Aegidius Lochiensis, who had spent seven years in Egypt: He says he mentioned among other things a Mazhapha Einok, or Prophecy of Enoch, declaring what would happen up to the end of the world, a book hitherto not seen in Europe, but written in the character and language of the Ethiopians or Abyssinians among whom it was preserved. By this Peiresc was so excited and so on fire to buy it at any price that he spared no means to make it his own.

Enoch the Prophet, Hugh Nibley, Salt Lake City, Utah: Deseret Book Company, 1986, pp. 100-1

Professor G.A. Perez explains that:

In Christian circles in Egypt the figure of Enoch was important and they gathered many Jewish traditions (see the Pierpont Morgan Fragments of a Coptic Enoch Apocryphon, Coptic Theological Texts 3, fols. 1-9, found in Hou, ed. W.E. Crum, 1913; A Pierson in Nickelsburg, ed., 1976; Latin trans. Garitte in Milik, 1976, pp. 100-103)...

The Coptic Encyclopedia, Vol. 1, Aziz S. Atiya, ed., New York: Macmillan Publishing Company, p. 163

Adding further:

In Pearson's arrangement, the text relates in the first place how the Lord received Enoch into heaven where he saw 'the mysteries that are hidden in the aeons of the Light.' We next find Enoch in a mountain, where an angel of God (possibly Michael) appears to him and instructs him in the...task that he Enoch will have in the judgment.

The only completely extant version...is the Ethiopic one, accepted as canonical in the Abyssinian Church.

Encyclopedia Dictionary of Religion, Vol I, Paul Kevin Meagher, et al., eds., Washington DC: Corpus Publications, 1979, p. 1208

Dead Sea Scrolls After Forty Years provides the reason for Ethiopia's preservation of 1 Enoch since the "text has been preserved in its entirety because the Ethiopic Christian Church considered it part of the Old Testament."

Hershel Shanks, James C. Vanderkam, P. Kyle McCarter, Jr., James A. Sanders, Washington, DC: Biblical Archaeology Society, 1990, p. 2

The Old Testament Pseudepigrapha, Apocalyptic Literature and Testaments confirms this when it says that:

The Falashas, Ethiopian Jews probably dependent on Ethiopian Christianity, however, have an expanded canon, including various apocrypha and pseudepigrapha, especially the...Jubilees, 1 Enoch...

James H. Charlesworth, ed., New York: Doubleday & Company, Inc., 1984, p. xxiv

Jubilees was composed in...Ethiopic, in which language alone it is extant in its entirety. Some halakhoth of the Ethiopian Falashas are derived from Jubilees, and the book continues to be printed in the Ethiopic Bible. (See Schiffman, Halakhah, 19, and the many parallels scattered throughout Albeck, Jubilden.)

Until the discovery of the Qumran Scrolls, the only preserved texts of the Enochic writings [were] derived from Christian circles...The living context of this transmission was a religious community that arose from and for some time continued to draw on the resources of an apocalyptic Judaism transmitted in the Enochic writings. At least some of the Son of Man sayings in Mark and "Q" know the tradition as it was reshaped in the Book of Parables and "christologize" it (see SON OF MAN).

The Anchor Bible Dictionary, Vol. 2, David Noel Freedman, ed., New York: Doubleday Co., p. 77

Dr. Gonzalo Baez-Camargo, a research associate and special con-
sultant in the United Bible Society, wrote that:

Fragments of this book turned up in Qumran Cave 1 and
eight fragmentary copies of it in Aramaic were found in Cave
4. It was evidently one of the favorite apocryphal books of the
Qumran community.

Archaelological Commentary on the Bible, New York: Doubleday & Co., Inc.,
    1984, p. 261

Professor James H. Charlesworth makes an extremely important
point:

This brief overview of the historical development of the canons
reveals that to call the Pseudepigrapha "non-canonical," or the
Biblical books "canonical," can be historically inaccurate prior to
A.D. 100 and the period in which most of these documents
were written. These terms should be used as an expression of
some later "orthodoxy" with regard to a collection that is well
defined regarding what belongs within and what is to be ex-
cluded from it. It is potentially misleading to use the terms
"non-canonical," "canonical," "heresy," and "orthodoxy" when
describing either Early Judaism or Early Christianity.

The Old Testament Pseudepigrapha, Apocalyptic Literature and Testa-
    ments, Vol. I, ed., New York: Doubleday & Company, Inc., 1984,
    p. xxiv

The author of *The Lost Prophet*, strikes a similar chord:

We must not have one set of rules for the Biblical texts and
another for the non-Biblical. The Enoch writings could be as
old as anything in the Old Testament. We must keep an open
mind.

(The Book of Enoch and its influence on Christianity), Margaret
    Barker, Great Britain: SPCK, 1988, p. 22

Similarly, the distinguished and prominent Biblical scholar Professor CainHope Felder drew the following conclusions:

Many inspired books, "holy writings," gospels, and epistles were
ignored and omitted, often for reasons that were quite arbitrary,

dogmatic certainly not scientific....With respect to the New Testament, the process of canon formation begins about A.D. 140. We certainly know of the existence of the Muratorian canon (ca. A.D.190). The work of Eusebius(A.D. 324) and the influence of Bishop Athanasius's list (A.D. 367) help the West fix its canon of 27 books over a span of 350 years.

However, despite Athanasius's list, part of the Eastern church did not agree on all 27 New Testament books until about A.D. 1000 for our immediate discussion, the crucial factor in these long processes is *who* decided which books were to be omitted. Most specifically, what kind of world view, political authority, and cultural/racial self-interest informed their decisions?

Troubling Biblical Waters, Cain Hope Felder, New York: Orbis Book, 1994, p. 14-5

As Professor Morton Smith of Columbia University from an article in *The New York Times*, Tuesday, May 19, 1973, reminds us:

"Everybody knows there were a lot of apocryphal gospels besides the four canonical Gospels - Matthew, Mark, Luke and John."

An example of the relativity of the designation of canonical can be seen in the fact that "Most Jews throughout the world acknowledge only the Old Testament as canonical... "

The Old Testament Pseudepigrapha, Apocalyptic Literature and Testaments, Vol. I, James H. Charlesworth, ed., New York: Doubleday & Company, Inc., 1984, p. xxiv

According to the Winston's Original African Heritage Study Bible Encyclopedia Concordance:

The Book of Enoch was long lost and much desired. Ancient historians have compared its authenticity to that of the Book of Isaiah.

James W. Peebles, Tenn.: James C. Winston Publishing Company, Inc., 1996, p. 769

Elsewhere Professor Charlesworth continues:

The New Testament canon was not closed in the Latin Church until much later, certainly not before the late fourth century and long after Constantine the Great established Christianity as the official religion of the Roman Empire. All the twenty-seven books of the New Testament, for example, are listed for the first time as the only canonical New Testament scriptures by Athanasius...

When R. H. Charles published his edition of the Pseudepigrapha there was widespread agreement that the Hebrew canon, the Old Testament, was fixed finally at Jamnia around A.D. 90. (p. xxiii)

According to *A Dictionary of the Bible* the First Book of Enoch was highly regarded in other works such as "...in the Testaments of the XII Patriarchs its citations are treated as Scripture, and in the later apocalyse of Baruch, and 4 Ezra there are many tokens of its influence. Then, during the first century of the Christian Era it possessed, alike with Jew and Christians, the authority of Deuterocanonical book....with the earlier Fathers and apologists of Christianity it preserved its high position till about the close of the third century."

James Hastings, ed. Vol. 1, Hendrickson Publishers, Mass, 1988, p. 705

The Ethiopic Book of Enoch was written in the second and first centuries. C.E. It was well known to the writers of the New Testament, and to some extent influenced alike their thought and diction. Thus it is quoted as a genuine work of Enoch by Jude. Phrases and at time or entire clauses, belonging to it are reproduced in the New Testament, but without acknowledgement of their service. Barnabas (Ep. iv, 3 xvi 5) quotes it as Scripture.

The Anchor Bible Dictionary, Vol. 2, David Noel Freedman, ed., New York: Doubleday Co., 1992, p. 705

Professor Charleworth emphasizes the fact that "few other apocryphal books so indelibly marked the religious history and thought of the time of Jesus. "

The Old Testament Pseudepigrapha, Apocalyptic Literature and Testaments, Vol. I, James H. Charlesworth, ed., New York: Doubleday & Company, Inc., 1984, p. 8

"The broad Enoch literature...is only preserved in total in Ethiopic...

Biblical Israel, Forge Pixley, Minn.: Fortress Press, 1992, p. 142

The Book of Enoch with which we are concerned here is I Enoch, also known as Ethiopic Enoch, because the whole text has survived only in the language.

The Lost Prophet, (The Book of Enoch and its influence on Christianity), Margaret Barker, Great Britain: SPCK, 1988, p. 6

1 Enoch would have come into its present form only in the Ethiopic version. Of that version, a large number of manuscripts are known, many of them parts of more extensive Biblical manuscripts.

The Anchor Bible Dictionary, Vol. 2, David Noel Freedman, ed., New York: Doubleday Co., 1992, p. 513

Still more significant is the influence of Enochic ideas on Ethiopian Christian theology. What distinguishes Ethiopian Christian theology from that of either Western or Eastern Christendom may well be the Ethiopian emphasis on Enochic thought. Sin does not originate from Adam's transgression alone; Satan, the demons, and evil spirits (the fallen angels) are equally responsible for its origin; they continue to lead man astray, causing moral ruin on the earth. On the other hand, there are the protective angels, with their various orders and ranks, who play an important part in both the religious and social life of the Ethiopian people...

The Old Testament Pseudepigrapha, Apocalyptic Literature and Testaments, Vol. I, James H. Charlesworth, ed., New York: Doubleday & Company, Inc., 1984, p. 10

The book of Enoch gives the fullest account of the doctrine of angels. As the genuineness of the book is not doubted, that is to say, as it is not doubted to be the real book referred to by

St. Jude, and as he was inspired, I do not clearly see how his authority can be denied by Christians.

Anacalypsis, 2 vols., Godfrey Higgins, New York: University Books, rep. A & B Books, Brooklyn, 1965, p. 551

Today, the great interest in angels in America could very likely be traced to Enoch's influence and original emphasis on that subject.

JUDE

Enoch 1:9 is quoted as though it is scripture in Jude 1:14.

Christianity, A Social and Cultural History, H. Kee, E. Hanawalt, C. Lindberg, J. Seban, M. Noll, New York: Macmillan Publishing Co., 1991, p. 116

In the New Testament, Enoch is portrayed as an individual who possessed faith and pleased God, so that he did not die (Heb 11:5-6); his prophecy in Jude 14-15 is a quotation from 1 En. 1:9.

The Anchor Bible Dictionary, Vol. 2, David Noel Freedman, ed., New York: Doubleday Co., 1992, p. 508

Enoch became a canonical book for a number of early Christians, including the writer of the New Testament Epistle of Jude, who quoted 1 Enoch 1:9 as the authentic words of the seventh man (see Jude 14-15).

The Dead Sea Scrolls Today, James C. Vanderkam, Grand Rapids, Michigan: William B. Eerdmans Publishing Co., 1994, p. 156

The Epistle of Jude...quotes it in an authoritative manner as prophetic.

The Old Testament Pseudepigrapha, Apocalyptic Literature and Testaments, Vol. I, James H. Charlesworth, ed., New York: Doubleday & Company, Inc., 1984, foreword

Professor J.R. Porter of the University of Exeter discloses that: He [Jude] is familiar with apocalyptic...literature from Palestine, and quotes from one such work, the first book of Enoch (vv 14-15).

The Illustrated Guide to the Bible, New York: Oxford University Press, 1995, p. 253

My Mother, my hope, pray for us.

Florentine [white] woman

The Image is the Message

Historical Truth: Madonna and Child

THE MADONNA
"the Lord is with thee:blessed art thou
among women." Luke 1:28

PARAMOUNT PRESENTS

CECIL B DEMILLE'S
PRODUCTION

THE TEN COMMANDMENTS

CHARLTON · YUL · ANNE · EDWARD G. · YVONNE · DEBRA · JOHN
HESTON · BRYNNER · BAXTER · ROBINSON · DE CARLO · PAGET · DEREK
SIR CEDRIC HARDWICKE · NINA FOCH · MARTHA SCOTT · JUDITH ANDERSON · VINCENT PRICE

DIRECTED BY CECIL B DEMILLE

TECHNICOLOR

WRITTEN FOR THE SCREEN BY · AENEAS MACKENZIE · JESSE L LASKY JR · JACK GARISS · FREDRIC M FRANK
Based upon THE HOLY SCRIPTURES and other ancient and modern writings · PRODUCED BY MOTION PICTURE ASSOCIATES INC

VISTAVISION

Hollywood's Euro-Centric Version of Moses
From the "The Ten Commandments"

Historical Truth: Moses

From the movie "Kings of Kings"
starring Jeffrey Hunter.

BLACK AMERICA'S NEWSMAGAZINE

WHITE LIES ABOUT WELFARE REFORM

IN HIS IMAGE: A PICTORIAL ESSAY

emerge

IS JESUS BLACK?

Scholars Provide the Gospel Truth

Adopting Black K...

Archbishop George Stallings and His Breakaway Flock

TAXES: THE IRS UNDER FIRE • A TAXING CROSSWORD PUZZLE

U.S.News

& WORLD REPORT

$2.95

APRIL 8, 1996

IN SEARCH OF Jesus

Who was he? New appraisals of his life and its meaning

Newsweek

Rethinking the Resurrection

A New Debate About the Risen Christ

01134

Newsweek

Why Bashing Japan Doesn't Work

The Search for Adam & Eve

Scientists Explore a Controversial Theory About Man's Origins

18201

The Holy Father
The Image is the Maessage

Adam, The first man (Euro-centric image)   GOD, the father
Sistine Chapel

SAMSON and DELILAH
"There hath not come a razor upon mine head..." Judges 16:17

Euro-centric Myth: Solomon and Sheba

Historical Truth: Solomon and Sheba

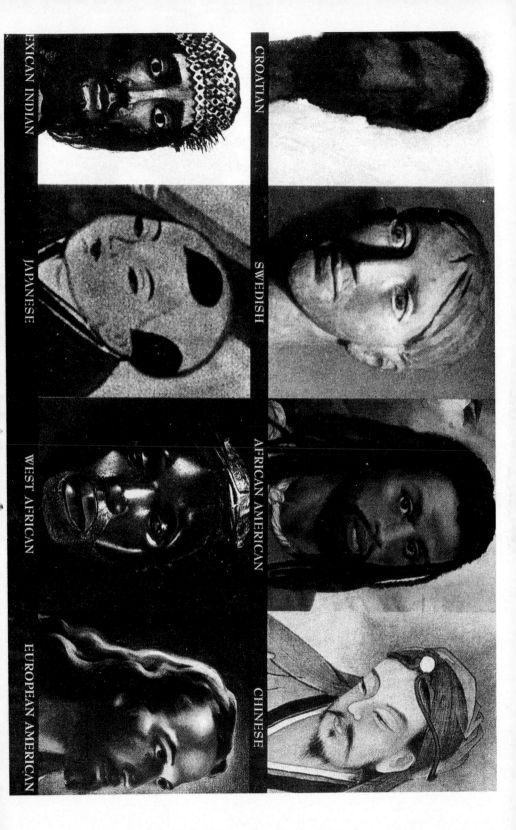

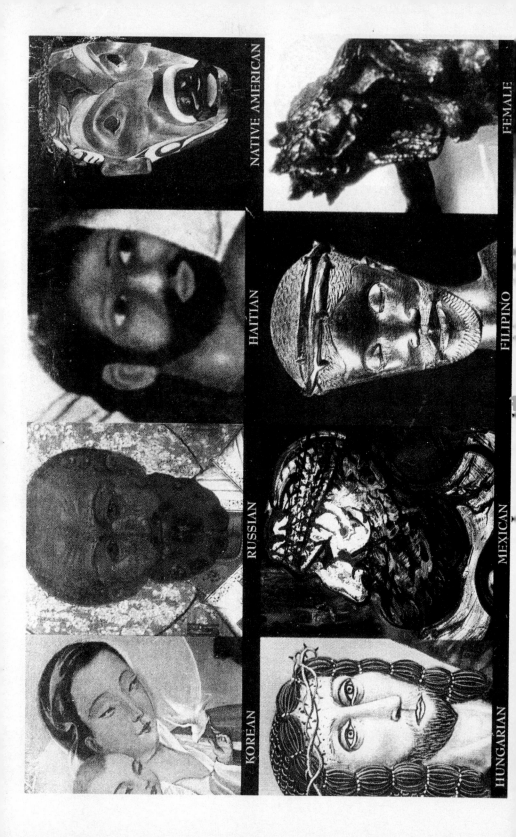

NATIVE AMERICAN

FEMALE

HAÏTIAN

FILIPÍNO

RUSSIAN

MEXICAN

KOREAN

HUNGARIAN

Enoch, book of this book, from which curiously enough, St. Jude quotes as if it were history, shows how richly mythical the history of the mysterious antediluvian Enoch had become...

He was current in the primitive church, and was quoted by the Fathers, but was lost sight of by Christian writers about the close of the 8th century, so that until last century; it was only known by extracts.

Chambers's Encyclopedia, Vol.2, W & R. Chambers, Belford, Clarke & Co., Chicago, 1884, p. 917

For our present purposes it is wise to add to the above insights the recognition that many authors of pseudepigrapha believed they were recording God's infallible words. Early communities, both Jewish and Christian, apparently took some pseudepigrapha very seriously. The author of Jude, in verses 14 and 15, quoted as prophecy a portion of 1 Enoch.

The Old Testament Pseudepigrapha, Apocalyptic Literature and Testaments, Vol. I, James H. Charlesworth, ed., New York: Doubleday & Company, Inc., 1984, p. xxiv

LUKE

Luke is an apostle whose works are considered canonical, that is, authoritative, sacred, holy writ.

Luke himself [was] one of the transmitters of the old Enoch text! "

Enoch the Prophet, Hugh Nibley, Salt Lake City, Utah: Deseret Book Company, 1986, p. 54

It is logical to assume influence from the Enoch text on the phraseology of Luke in cases where the content is the same or related.

New Testament Studies, Vol. 13, October 1966, No. 1; Professor Dr. S. Aalen (Oslo, Norway), St. Luke's Gospel and the Last Chapters of I Enoch, p. 12

Henoch is mentioned in the genealogy of Christ (Luke 3, 37).

A *New Catholic Commentary on Holy Scripture*, Rev. Reginald Fuller, Gen.
ed., Catholic Biblical Association, Thomas Nelson and Sons Ltd.,
London, 1969, p. 457

TERTULLIAN

Tertullian is one of the Founding Church Fathers.

Quintus Septimius Florens Tertullianus (d. post A.D. 220) was
one of the most assiduous readers of the Enochic works in
early Christian times.

The Books of Enoch, Aramaic Fragments of Qumran Cave 4, J. T. Milik, ed.,
Oxford: Oxford University Press, 1976, p. 77

In the second and third centuries, Christian writers (among
them, Tertullian and Irenaeus) place particular emphasis on
Enoch's bodily assumption in support of belief in physical resurrection. Some (Tertullian, Hippolytus, and Jerome) identify
him as one of the two witnesses of Revelations 11:3-13 who
battle and are killed by the Antichrist, are resurrected a few
days later, and are taken to heaven.

The Encyclopedia of Religion, Vol. 5, Mircea Eliade, ed., New York: Macmillan Publishing Co., 1987, p. 117

Some early Church Fathers (like Tertullian) considered the book
to be a part of the canon.

Encyclopedia Judaica, David Flusser, ed., Jerusalem, Israel: Keter Publishing House, 1971, p. 796

The first undeniable piece of evidence on the subject is that of
Tertullian in Apologeticum xxii.

The Books of Enoch, Aramaic Fragments of Qumran Cave 4, J. T. Milik, ed.,
Oxford: Oxford University Press, 1976, p. 97

"Tertullian (Cath. Ency., XIV, p. 525) cites the Book of Enoch
as inspired..."

Who Is This King of Glory, Alvin Boyd Kuhn, rep. ECA Associates Va.,
1944, p. 156

CLEMENT

Clement is a Founding Father and church authority.

Higgins confesses that his exertions to discover the truth are "in opposition to the frauds of the priests of all religions in their efforts to suppress evidence and to keep mankind in ignorance." He charges that Enoch was quoted by Clement and Iraeus like any other canonical Scripture.

Who Is This King of Glory, Alvin Boyd Kuhn, rep. ECA Associates Va., 1944, p. 138

According to Margaret Barker:

Clement of Alexandria...was head of the Christian school there. He knew 1 Enoch's account of the fall of the angels, their heavenly knowledge and their earthly wives. Origen, said by the church historian Eusebius to have been a pupil of Clement, also knew Enoch.

The Lost Prophet, (The Book of Enoch and its influence on Christianity), Great Britain: SPCK, 1988, p. 7

BARNABAS

Barnabas has works that are considered canonical.

Director and Principal Librarian of the British Museum Sir Frederic Kenyon says that the Enoch book "had a considerable popularity in its time. It is twice quoted as Scripture in the Epistle of Barnabas; and the Chester Beatty collection shows that it was included in the library of a Christian community in the fourth century.

The Bible and Archaeology, George G. Harrap & Co. Ltd., London, 1940, p. 248

...it was written before the earliest Christians...and later lost. For a long time all that was known of 1 Enoch was from quotations by early Christian writers. The Epistle of Barnabas, written about AD 140, quotes from Enoch twice...

The Lost Prophet, (The Book of Enoch and its influence on Christianity), Margaret Barker, Great Britain: SPCK, 1988, p. 7

R. H. Charles, a foremost authority on the Enoch works, comments on the "Epistle to the Hebrews. This Epistle was probably written by Barnabas. As we have seen...this writer cites Enoch as Scripture in the Epistle which goes by his name. "

The Book of Enoch, trans. from Professor Dillmann's Ethiopic Text, edited by R. H. Charles, Oxford: Clarendon Press,1893

DANIEL

The same can be said for Daniel whose works are also considered canonical, that is, divine revelation.

Comparing the works of Enoch to that of Daniel the *Encyclopedia Britannica* insists that:

Affinities with the Book of Daniel are evident...in the figure of the Son of Man.

Vol. 8, Chicago, Ill., William Benton Publ., 1973, p. 604

...of which we have examples in our Bible in the latter part of Daniel...

The Bible and Archaeology, Sir Frederic Kenyon, George G. Harrap & Co. Ltd., London, 1940, p. 246

Examples of Enoch's angelic references are provided by the *Encyclopedia Americana* namely: "...those of the rebel angels (see Genesis 6:1-4) and the celestial "watchers" (Daniel 4:13, 17, 23)...originally regarded as a genuine revelation..."

Int'l Edition, Vol. 10, Danbury, CT: Grolier Inc., p. 473

Dr. A.B. Kuhn places Daniel and Enoch as major Biblical authorities when he rhetorically asks:

Does it contain material of equal antiquity and authority as the Biblical Daniel or Enoch.

Who Is This King of Glory, Alvin Boyd Kuhn, rep. ECA Associates, Va., 1944, p. 71

CHURCH AUTHORITIES SUPPORT FOR ENOCH

1 Enoch played a significant role in the early Church; it was used by the authors of the Epistle of Barnabas, the Apocalypse of Peter, and a number of apologetic works. Many Church Fathers, including Justin Martyr, Irenaeus, Origen, and Clement of Alexandria, either knew 1 Enoch or were inspired by it. Among

those who were familiar with 1 Enoch, Tertullian had an exceptionally high regard for it.

The Old Testament Pseudepigrapha, Apocalyptic Literature and Testaments, Vol. I, James H. Charlesworth, ed., New York: Doubleday & Company, Inc., 1984, p. 8

The citations of Enoch by the Testaments of the Twelve Patriarchs and by the Book of Jubilees show that at the close of the second century B.C.E. and during the first century B.C.E, this book was regarded in certain circles as inspired. When we come down to the first century A.D., we find that it is recognized as Scripture by Jude...In the next century this recognition is given amply in the Ep. Barnabas xvi. 5 by Athenagoras, Legatio pro Christianis 24 (referring to Enoch); in the third century by Clem. Alex. Elcog. Prophet. ii...by Irenaeus iv. 6. 12 'Enoch...placens Deo...legatione ad angelos fungebatur'; by Tertullian, De Cultu Fem. i.3, De Idol. xv...by Zosimus of Panopolis, quoted in Syncellus (Dind. i. 24)

The Book of Enoch or 1 Enoch, R. H. Charles, Oxford, Clarendon Press, 1912, p. xiv

Greek excerpts from the book of Enoch have always been available in Jude 14-15 (quote 1 Enoch 4:14); the Epistle of Barnabas 4:3, 16:5-6; Clement of Alexandria, Eclog. Prophet, 53:4; Origen, C. Cels. 5:52; Comm. in John VI, 42 (25); and the long ninth fragment in George Syncellus' Chronicle. (Dindorff, p. 24:2-11.) R. H. Charles lists no fewer than 128 citations from Enoch in the New Testament!

Enoch the Prophet, Hugh Nibley, Salt Lake City, Utah: Deseret Book Company, 1986, p. 116

Professor W.D. Davies and Chancellor L. Finkelstein argue that: It is known that several Latin authors such as Tertullian, Hilary and Priscillian quote passages of Enoch...

The Cambridge History of Judaism, Cambridge: Cambridge University Press, 1989, p. 424

Traditions associated with the Apostle Peter (in Matthew 16, 1 and 2 Peter, and the Apocalypse of Peter) draw on elements in the corpus (Rubinkiewcz). Matthew and probably Luke reflect parts of it. The Apocalypse of John of Patmos uses Enochic traditions about 'Asa'el and is the closest formal counterpart to the Book of Parables. Jude (vv 14-15) and Tertullian (de Idolo- taria 4; de Cultu Feminarum 3:1) ascribe prophetic status to the patriarch Enoch and quote the opening oracle and the Epistle respectively. Barnabas 16 quotes the Animal Vision and the Apocalypse of Weeks as "scripture."

Justin Martyr (2 Apologia 5) and evidently Irenaeus (Adversus Haereses 4.36.4) appear to know the Enochic traditions about the angelic rebellion, and Pseudo-Clement (Homilies 8:12ff.) knows more than is preserved in 1 Enoch. Other allusions and quotations appear in Clement of Alexandria and in Origen. Thus, at a time when the writings ascribed to Enoch were fal- ling into disuse among Jews, these same texts continued to be cited as inspired scripture in sectors of Christianity.

Except in the Ethiopian church and among the Manicheans, however, this authority of Enochic scripture disappeared as the canon of ancient writings was limited to the books contained in the Hebrew Bible or the LXX. Nonetheless, the Enochic influ- ence has continued in the form of traditions that were forma- tive in the writing of the New Testament texts.

The Anchor Bible Dictionary, Vol. 2, David Noel Freedman, ed., Double- day Co., New York,1992, p. 516

The work was not only popular at Qumran, exhibiting definite similiarities with the Essene calendar and angelology, but was used in early Christianity (Jude 14-15 quotes 1 Enoch 1:9) and Tertullian considered the work inspired Scripture (see On the Apparel of Women 1.3; cf. On Idolatry 4)...

Backgrounds of Early Christianity, Everett Ferguson, Grand Rapids, Michi- gan: William B. Eerdmans Publishing Co., 1987, p. 361

It survives entire only in Ethiopic...1 Enoch was occasionally treated as inspired scripture in the early church (Barn 16:4; Tertullian, Cult. fem. 1.3.1).

Encyclopedia of Early Christianity, Editor Everett Ferguson 1990, Associate Editors - Michael P. McHugh, Frederick W. Norris, p. 513

The Book of Enoch edited by R.H. Charles lists the following authoriative works as having been quoted from Enoch:

Irenaeus, iv. 16.2 (quoted in note on xiv. 7). Athenagoras (about 170 A.D.)...Tertullian, writing between 197 and 223, regards Enoch as Scripture, Apol. xxii (quoted in note on xv. 8, 9); De Culture Feminarum, I. 2 (quoted on viii. I).

II. 10 (quoted on viii. I). De Idol. (quoted on xix. I). Cf. also De Idol. ix; De Virg. Veland. vii: ... De Idol. xv: ... Clemens Alex. Eclogae Prophet. ed. Dindorf, iii. 456 (quoted on xix. 3); iii. 474 (quoted on viii. 2. 3); Strom. iii. 9 (quoted on xvi. 3).

The Book of Enoch, trans. from Professor Dillmann's Ethiopic Text, edited by R. H. Charles, Oxford: Clarendon Press,1893, p. 38

"Church Fathers, especially Clement of Rome, Clement of Alexandria, Hippolytus, Tertullian, Origen, and the compiler of the Apostolic Constitutions, as well as by the Byzantine chroniclers (especially George Syncellus [c. 800] and George Cedrenus [c. 1057]" had a noticeably high respect for Enoch works and took special note of him.

The Old Testament Pseudepigrapha, Apocalyptic Literature and Testaments, Vol. I, James H. Charlesworth, ed., New York: Doubleday & Company, Inc., 1984, p. xxiv

Others who hold Enoch in high regard are:

"Anatolius appointed Bishop of Laodicea in 269. Quoted in Euseb. Hist. Eccl. vii. 32. 19:...Hilary, who died 368 A.D., writes in his Comment, in Ps. cxxxii. 3: ... Jerome (346-420) regards Enoch as apocryphal. De Viris Illustr. iv:...Comment. on Ps. cxxxii...Comment. on Epist. ad Titum...Syncellus in his Chronography,...

The Book of Jubilees or Little Genesis, trans. from The Editor's Ethiopic Text, by R. H. Charles, London: D.D., Adam and Charles Black, 1902, p. lxxvii

Irenneus and Origen both show traces of its influence as does the Epistle of Barnabas. Many passages of the New Testament can be cited for the similarity of their thought and expression...

Zondervan Pictorial Encyclopedia of the Bible Vol. 2, C. Teaney Editor, Regency Reference Library, Michigan, Merrill. 1976, p. 312

CHAPTER IX

ENOCH BOOKS - EARLY CHURCH ACCEPTANCE

ENOCH WAS AT FIRST ACCEPTED IN THE CHRISTIAN CHURCH...

New Encyclopedia Brittanica, Vol. 4, Chicago, 1995, p. 506

Enoch "Book II...the Christian origin of the whole book was once advocated by many students..."

Funk & Wagnalls, New Standard Encyclopedia of Universal Knowledge, Vol. X, Funk & Wagnalls Co., 193, p. 491-493

Why scholars have been so slow to see the intimate relation between Revelation and its obvious prototype, the Enoch, is another of the riddles of ecclesiastical history which cry aloud of resolution.

Who Is This King of Glory, Alvin Boyd Kuhn, rep. ECA Associates, Va., 1944, p. 108

Van Andel suggests, as typical of that "edifying literature in Christian circles from the 3rd to the 6th (?) centuries," showing in what high esteem Enoch was held by the early Christians, having been taken into the church with full honors from earlier times.

The Lost Prophet, (The Book of Enoch and its influence on Christianity), Margaret Barker, Great Britain: SPCK, 1988, p. 117

This notion of Daniel was reinforced by the so-called Ethiopic Book of Enoch, written early in the first century AD, which speaks of the 'last day' and the 'day of judgment; when the 'elect' would be favored and come into their kingdom.

A History of the Jews, Paul Johnson, Harper Perennial, 1987, p. 212

William Barclay says that at Qumran:

Parts of about 10 manuscripts...[were] found to contain four out of the five sections of Ethiopic Enoch of the Book of Enoch, and this would indicate that the Book of Enoch too was held in high respect by the Covenanters of Qumran, as they are called.

The Bible and History, Lutterworth Press, London, 1968. p. 196

According to the Professor of Comparative Religion at the Hebrew University of Jerusalem David Flusser:

the figure of Enoch was especially significant from which the Dead Sea Sect originated.

Thus his story and his wrings are treated in the Book of Jubilees, his prophecies are hinted at in the Testament of the Twelve Patriarchs,

and he plays an active role in the Genesis Apocryphon, one of the Dead Sea Scrolls.

Encyclopedia Judaica, Keter Publishing House, Jerusalem, Israel, 1971.

ENOCH, BOOK OF...was highly regarded by the early Christian Church...from the fourth century on..."

Collier's Encyclopedia, 1995, P. F. Collier, L.P. NYC., p. 253,

To quote Funk & Wagnalls:

"The early Christians esteemed the Book of Enoch highly...three complete manuscripts in Ethiopic were discovered in northeastern Africa in the late 18th century." (p. 491-493)

Enoch laid the foundation for some of the major ideas found in the New Testament.

ENOCH'S EARLY CHRISTIAN INFLUENCE

The testimony of the New Covenant documents to such books as Enoch, Jubilees and XII Patriarchs establishes that they were written considerably earlier, so that by the time of the specifically New Covenant writings they already had the force of sacred scriptures.

Secrets of the Dead Sea Scrolls, Hugh J. Schonfield, Thomas Yoseloff, Inc., New York, 1957, p. 136

Enoch has been preserved only as a Christian book, even though it was written long before the time of Jesus. The Christian Churches saw some special importance in this work, and it influenced much of their thinking about the Messiah.

The Lost Prophet, (The Book of Enoch and its influence on Christianity), Margaret Barker, Great Britain: SPCK, 1988, p. 19

Duke University's Professor J. H. Charlesworth reminds us that "the Pseudepigrapha preserve ideas essential for an understanding of Early Judaism and Early Christianity. "

The Old Testament Pseudepigrapha, Apocalyptic Literature and Testaments, Vol. I, James H. Charlesworth, ed., New York: Doubleday & Company, Inc., 1984, p. xxvii

From these books of his forefathers embracing the writings of Enoch and Noah, Abraham instructed Isaac (xxi. 10).

The Book of Jubilees or Little Genesis, trans. from The Editor's Ethiopic Text, by R. H. Charles, London: D.D., Adam and Charles Black, 1902, p. li

The eminent Biblical scholar R. H. Charles delineates the importance of the Book of Jubilee:

It appeals to the Old Testament scholar, as exhibiting further developments of ideas and tendencies which are only in their incipient stages in the Old Testament. It appeals to the New Testament scholar, as furnishing the first literary embodiment of beliefs which subsequently obtained an entrance into the New Testament, and as having in all probability formed part of the library of some of the apostolic writers.

The Book of Jubilees or Little Genesis, trans. from The Editor's Ethiopic Text, by R. H. Charles, London: D.D., Adam and Charles Black, 1902, preface

Professor I. H. Eybers says of Jubilees: It therefore seems that we have a canonical or nearly canonical work of Qumran.

The Canon of Masarah of the Hebrew Bible, Sid Z. Lerman, ed., New York: KTAV Publishing House, Inc., 1974, p. 32

Concerning the "...Epistles of S. Paul. This Apostle, as we know, borrowed both phraseology and ideas from many quarters...We shall find that he was well acquainted with and used the Book of Enoch..."

Rom. viii 38. 'Neither angels, nor principalities, nor powers.'

En lxi. 10. 'Angels of power and angels of principalities.'

The Book of Enoch, trans. from Professor Dillmann's Ethiopic Text, R.H. Charles, ed., Oxford: Clarendon Press, 1893, p. 45

He further suggests elsewhere that:

1 Enoch will deepen our insights into and broaden our perspectives of intertestamental Jewish and early Christian theology. (p. 9)

The book of Enoch exercised a very important influence on the Christian and Jewish literature of the first three centuries A.D.

The Book of Enoch, trans. from Professor Dillmann's Ethiopic Text, R.H. Charles, ed., Oxford: Clarendon Press, 1893

According to a work by Professor Karl Baur:

The...writing which have been found at last in fragmentary form at...Qumran show the strong interest of the group in the so-called, apocalyptic literature....the themes of which are the great events which are to take place at the end of the world: the final victory over evil, the resurrection of the dead, the last judgment and the glory of the everlasting age of salvation. Fragments of works of this kind [are] already known, such as the Book of Jubilee, the Book of Enoch...

History of the Church, Vol.1, Karl Baur, New York: The Seabury Press, 1980, p. 6

Among the early Christians then, Enoch was understandably popular, although after the fourth century C.E. its influence declined.

In time, all complete manuscripts of this Hebrew - Aramaic work vanished.

It was not until the end of the eighteenth century that an Ethiopic translation was found in Abyssinia.

Understanding the Bible, Stephen L. Harris, London: Mayfield Publishing Co., 1980, p. 230

As *The New Standard Jewish Encyclopedia* pointed out: "the early Christians utilized the accepted views on Enoch to expound the immortality of Jesus."

7th edn. Geoffrey Wigoder, ed., New York: Facts On File, 1992, p. 307

1 Enoch was a pre-Christian text. The New Testament and the early Christian writers show that it was used by the first Christians.

The Lost Prophet, (The Book of Enoch and its influence on Christianity), Margaret Barker, Great Britain: SPCK, 1988, p. 105

As Professor Schiffman explains:

1 Enoch (the Ethiopic Enoch) is an apocalyptic book in which Enoch reports his vision of how God will punish the evildoers and grant eternal bliss to the righteous.

Enoch describes the angels and the heavenly retinue.

From Text to Tradition, Lawrence H. Schiffman, New Jersey: Ktav Publishing House, 1991, p. 127

CHAPTER X

ENOCH'S NEW TESTAMENT LEGACY

(THE INFLUENCE OF ENOCH ON THE NEW TESTAMENT)

EARLY CHRISTIAN WRITERS KNEW ALL ABOUT THE BOOK OF Enoch:

indeed, "nearly all the writers of the New Testament were familiar with it, and were more or less influenced by it in thought and diction,"

according to R. H. Charles, who notes that "it is quoted as a genuine production of Enoch by St. Jude, and as Scripture by St. Barnabas...

'With the earlier Fathers and Apologists it had all the weight of a canonical book.'

Its influence is apparent in no less than 128 places in the New Testament..."

Enoch the Prophet, Hugh Nibley, Salt Lake City, Utah: Deseret Book Company, 1986, p. 95

In the Chapter entitled, "The Influence of Enoch on the New Testament, R.H. Charles, a major scholarly resource on the Enoch books, declares that:

The influence of Enoch on the New Testament has been greater than that of all the other apocryphal and pseudepigraphal books taken together.

The Book of Enoch, trans. from Professor Dillmann's Ethiopic Text, R.H. Charles, ed., Oxford: Clarendon Press, 1893, p. 40-41

R.H. Charles provides a long list of passages in Enoch, including a number from the parables, which he believes exercised an influence on the New Testament. (The Book of Enoch, 2nd edn., pp. xcv-ciii)

New Testament Studies, "The Date of the Parables of Enoch," M.A. Knibb, Vol. 1979, p. 369

Dr. Norman Golb, the 1st holder of the Rosenberger Chair in Jewish History and Civilization at the University of Chicago, asserts that:

"The Aramaic book of Enoch, of which a fragment was included in the American exhibitions, very considerably influenced the idiom of the New Testament and patristic literature, more so in fact than any other writing of the Apocrypha..."

He footnotes the following: (See "Enoch (Ethiopic), Book of in J. Hastings (ed.) Dictionary of the Bible, 1 (Edinburgh, 1898, pp. 705-708 (Art. of R.H. Charles; J.T. Milik, *The Books of Enoch, Aramaic Fragments of Qumran Cave 4* (Oxford, 1976).

Who Wrote the Dead Sea Scrolls?, Norman Golb, New York: Scribner, 1995

The section entitled "Influence of Jubilees on the New Testament" from the work of Professor Dillmann as edited by R.H. Charles provides the following examples:

Luke xi 49; John xiv. 26; Acts vii. 15-16; Jub. x.8; I.12; xxxii. 25; xlvi. 9...

The Book of Enoch, Ethiopic Text, Clarendon Press, Oxford, 1893,

Charles' notes are rich in New Testament parallels which he took to be quotations from 2 Enoch...

The Anchor Bible Dictionary, Vol. 2, David Noel Freedman, ed., New York: Doubleday Co., 1992., p. 520

The book *Christian Legends* notes that:

The Book of the Secrets of Enoch (2 Enoch)...survives only in a Slavonic version, but the original was certainly pre-Christian.

George Every, New York: Peter Bedrick Books, 1987, p. 25

The impact of 1 Enoch influence on the New Testament can be seen in the following arrangement of the evidence:

a) A series of passages of the New Testament which either in phraseology or idea directly depend on or are illustrative of passages in Enoch

b) Doctrines in Enoch which had an undoubted share in molding the corresponding New Testament doctrines.

For example:

Acts of the Apostles. iii. 14. 'The Righteous One,' i.e. Christ. Cf. also vii. 52; xxii. 14.

Enoch. xxxviii. 2. 'The Righteous One' (i.e. the Messiah).

The Gospels. S. John ii. 16. The temple is called 'God's house,'...

Enoch lxxxix. 54. Temple - house of the Lord of the sheep.

S. Luke xiv. 2. 'Many mansions.'

Enoch. xxxix. 4. 'Mansions of the righteous.' Cf. xxxix. 7; xlviii. I, & c.

The Book of Enoch, trans. from Professor Dillmann's Ethiopic Text, edited by R. H. Charles, Oxford: Clarendon Press, 1893, p. 48

As Funk & Wagnalls states:

"Modern scholars consider the book of Enoch significant because many of its concepts and even its terminology, are strikingly similar to later eschatological concepts and apocalyptic books and passages in the New Testament." (p. 491-493)

Likewise, the Dead Sea Scrolls widely-recognized expert, R.H. Charles adds:

In fact the history of the development of the higher theology during the two centuries before the Christian era could not be written without the Book of Enoch.

The Book of Enoch or 1 Enoch, R. H. Charles, Oxford, Clarendon Press, 1912,

All the writers of the New Testament were familiar with it, and were more or less influenced by it in thought and diction. It is quoted as a genuine production of Enoch by S. Jude, and as Scripture by S. Barnabas.

The Book of Enoch, trans. from Professor Dillmann's Ethiopic Text, edited by R. H. Charles, Oxford: Clarendon Press,1893,

CHAPTER X

ENOCH'S INFLUENCE ON THE NEW TESTAMENT'S MESSIANIC FIGURE

THE GREAT SCHOLAR R. H. CHARLES SUPPLIES TWO IMPORTANT instances that illustrate Enoch's influence on the New Testament:
a) The nature of the Messianic kingdom and of the future life. The Kingdom - We shall only deal with one incident coming under this head; it is found in the three Synoptists: S. Matt. xxii. 23-33; S. Mark xii. 18-27; S. Luke xx. 27-36.b).
b)The Messiah.

The Messiah. - Messiah in the Similitudes are afterwards reproduced in the New Testament. These are 'Christ' or 'the Anointed One,' 'the Righteous One,' 'the Elect One,' and 'the Son of Man.'

The Book of Enoch, trans. from Professor Dillmann's Ethiopic Text, edited by R. H. Charles, Oxford: Clarendon, 1893, p. 50-51

As for the Teacher of Righteousness, this may have been a general title that was given to a succession of Messiahs. Before the discovery of the Dead Sea Scrolls, the earliest references known to the Messiah as "The Elect One" and "The Righteous One" occurred in The Book of Enoch-which Charles assigned to the early years of the first B.C. century...

The Dead Sea Scrolls 1947-1969, Edmund Wilson. New York: Oxford University Press. 1969, p. 67

Since the discovery of Qumran...a connection with the Book of Enoch has been greatly emphasized. In particular the figure of Enoch himself is held to be significantly close to the Teacher of Righteousness...

Encyclopedia Dictionary of Religion, Vol I, Paul Kevin Meagher, et al., eds - Corpus Publications, Washington DC, 1979, p. 1209

As M.E. Stone, an associate profesor of Armenian Studies, pointed out: "..Parables or Similitudes...centers first and foremost on the revelation of the Son of Man or the Elect One."

Jewish Writings of the Second Temple Period, Michael E. Stone, ed., Van Gorcum, Philadelphia: Assen Fortress Press, 1984, p. 401

MESSIAH

As William Guthrie says: "The figure of the Messiah which Jesus adapted to his creative purpose, cannot be imagined by a modern without a perusal of the book of Enoch which is its classic and most entrancing glorification."

Professor of Biblical Studies at Tel Aviv University Yehoshua M. Grintz declared that:

The Book Of Enoch had tremendous influence.

From it, or at any rate, through it the Manual of Discipline received the solar calendar and it also served as an exemplar of the composition of the burgeoning apocalyptic literary genre. From it, too, comes the concept of preexistent Messiah, which influenced early Christianity and prepared the way for belief in the divinity of Jesus.

Encyclopedia Judaica:, David Flusser, ed., Jerusalem, Israel: Keter Publishing House, 1971, p. 795

To quote from The Universal Jewish Encyclopedia, Vol. 4:

Chaps. 37 to 71 are the Book of the Messiah: it contains similar reports of a visionary trip. ..the eternal bliss of the pious. The Messiah is also called the "son of man" as in Dan 7:13 - the chosen one, the perfectly just man, who takes his position next to God, the Ancient of Days (Dan 7:13)...(Isaac Landman, ed., N.Y., 1941, p. 132)

The principal figure in these scenes is a transcendent heavenly figure whom God has designated...as "the Chosen One" (his primary title), "the Righteous One," "that son of man," and "God's Anointed One." See SON OF MAN.

As these designations indicate, the descriptions of this figure are the fruit of speculations on the Biblical texts about "one like a son of man" (Daniel 7), the Deutero-Isaianic servant of the

Lord (esp. Isaiah 42, 49, 52-53), and the Davidic king (Psalm 2 and Isaiah 11).

The Anchor Bible Dictionary, Vol. 2, David Noel Freedman, ed., New York: Doubleday Co., 1992, p. 512

Professor F.L. Cross of Oxford Univerity asserts that:

The passages on 'the Son of Man' in the Parables or Similitudes (chs.37-71) have been widely held to have influenced the New Testament writings; and of the New Testament titles, such as 'the Righteous One' and 'the Elect One' have been said to have appeared here first as Messianic designations.

The Oxford Dictionary of the Christian Church, New York: Oxford University Press, 1974, p. 459

Duke University's W.D. Davies and Chancellor L. Finkelstein stress the fact that:

"There is no other book in Judaism in which th Son of Man is credited with such a position and such dignity as in the Similitudes of Enoch." (*The Cambridge History of Judaism*, p. 427)

In fact, without Enoch modern Christians would have little idea of what a Messiah would look like.

CHAPTER XI

"SEMITIC" PEOPLE OF EUROPE

ACCORDING TO WEBSTER'S NEW WORLD DICTIONARY: "A SEMITE IS conventionally defined as 'a member of any of the people whose language is Semitic...The adjective Semitic is defined as '... designating or of a major group of languages of southwestern Asia and northern Africa, related to the Hamitic languages...Webster's New World Dictionary also informs us that the prefix, 'semi - (L., akin to Gr. hemi-, Sans.sami-,AS.sam) means half, as in semidiameter.' "

Webster's New World Dictionary:

> Thus, both of the words Semite and Hamite (the later from the Greek "Hemite") could refer to peoples who were Black, but a mulatto-type mixture of Black and white and combinations thereof, hence "semi-" or "hemi-" half Black and half white...

> The Isis Papers, Dr. Francies Cress Welsing, Third World Press, Chicago, 1991, p. 223

Dr. Cheikh Anta Diop presents this point:

> "The Jewish people, that is, the first branch called Semitic, descendants of Isaac seem to have been the product of that crossbreeding. That is why a Latin historian wrote that the Jews are of Negro origin." (The African Origin of Civilization)

Dr. Welsing adds the following examples of famous "Semitic" personalities:

> It is significant to this discussion that Karl Marx (1818-1883), another Semite of the Jewish religion, had such dark skin that his children called him "The Moor," meaning of course, "the Black." (p. 224)

Another Semite of the Jewish religion who was identified as "a Black" was Albert Einstein. Albert Einstein (1879-1955), the great Nobel prize physicist, as documented by Robert Clark's *Einstein: The Life and Times* was once described as "1.76 meters tall...broad shouldered, with a slight stoop. ..His complexion is swarthy..." (*Webster's New World Dictionary* defines the word "swarthy" as "having a dark skin; dusky, dark, SYN. see dusky.") (p. 225)

Freud even went further in his last work, *Moses and Monotheism*, written in part while fleeing from the Nazis, to describe the founder of the Jewish religion, Moses, as an Egyptian - meaning of course, a Black man. (p. 226)

A related point was made by Dr. Charles S. Finch III who states that:

This brings us to the imposing figure of Moses, the human centerpiece of the whole Exodus. Sigmund Freud in *Moses and Monotheism* proposed that the original Moses was in fact an Egyptian priest who...was influenced by the ideas and example of Akhenaten, who lived at least 100 years earlier.

Echoes of the Darkland, Charles S. Finch III, Decatur, Georgia: Khenti, Inc., 1991, p. 141

Futhermore, Moses married, Zipporah, his first wife, a black woman, from Midia, an Ethiopian, the daughter of Jetro and got his first (black) son, Gershom. (Exodus 2:21-22)

This Black Jesus, Dr. Etiese T. Mkpa Abasika, 1993, p. 65

But as Professor Charles B. Copher pointed out:

It was upon the basis of the rabbinical interpretation rather than the Bible itself that Cecil B. DeMille in the movie "The Ten Commandments" could portray Moses' wife as White. (See Henry S. Noerdlinger, *Moses and Egypt*, University of Southern California Press, Los Angeles, 1956, p. 70)

Black Biblical Studies, Chicago, Ill.: Black Light Fellowship, 1993, p. 59

Writes Bishop Alfred G. Dunston, Jr.:

The preceding chapter analyzed the statistics of the Exodus population and the possible indications involved in the phrase, "the mixed multitude." It was concluded that many people in the Exodus population must have been black native-stock Egyptians, and it was also thought that the Cushite was not uncommon among them.

The Black Man in the Old Testament, New Jersey: Africa World Press, Inc., 1992, p. 76

Dr. C. Finch quotes the following classical writers:

Strabo: "This region [Judae] lies toward the north; and it is inhabited in general, as is each place in particular, by mixed stocks of people from Aegyptian and Arabian and Phoenician tribes...

But though the inhabitants are mixed up thus, the most prevalent of the accredited reports in regard to the temple at Jerusalem represents the ancestors of the present Judaens, as they are called, as Aegyptians."

Celsus: "The Jews were a tribe of Egyptians who revolted from the established religion."

Diodorus:...the nation of the Colchians on the Pontus, and that of Jews lying between Syria and Arabia, were also settled by certain expatriates from Egypt.

This explains the traditional circumcision of male children practiced among these races, an age-old custom imported from Egypt."

Echoes of the Darkland, Charles S. Finch III, Decatur, Georgia: Khenti, Inc., 1991, p. 173

Herodotus echoes the same observation:

"There can be no doubt that the Colchians are an Egyptian race...My own conjectures were founded first in the fact that they are BLACK-SKINNED and have WOOLLY HAIR, which certainly amounts to but little since several other nations are so too, but further and more especially on the circumstance that the Colchians, the Egyptians and the Ethiopians are the only nations who have practiced circumcision from the earliest time."

HERODOTUS HISTORIES, Book III, Chap. 104

Remember, as the Bible says, "And Moses was learned in all the wisdom of the Egyptian..."(ACTS 7:22)

Says Professor C.B. Copher: "Harry L. Shapiro in his 'Biological History of the Jewish People,' (*Race and Science*, pp. 114ff.) admits of an Israelite Palestinian population suggestive of 'negroid affinities.' "

Black Biblical Studies, Charles B. Copher, Black Light Fellowship, Chicago, Ill., 1993, p. 128-9

Elsewhere in the same work, Professor Copher concludes that: "And today one need not wonder at the fact that present population of Israel is as mixed in color as are the Black people in the United States of North America. (*Black Biblical Studies*, p. 14)

"What are we to conclude when people as late as 70 A.D. looked at Jews and believed them to have been descendants of Ethiopians? The Greek term "Ethiopian" means "black" or literally "burnt-faced," and the only way to decide that a person or a people were Ethiopians would be by sight identification.

The Abington Commentary concludes its discussion of Exodus 12:38 by saying:

'The mixed company must have included Egyptian and other co-laborers, how may have intermarried with them and now sought with them this way to freedom."

When all the available facts are examined, we know beyond doubt that the black presence was one of the dominant elements in the original native Egyptian population, and furthermore we know that the Cushite (Ethiopian) formed a large part in the Egyptian population of Israel's day.

In truth, it must be admitted that Moses perhaps led more black people out of Egypt than those of other colors. we understand with little wonder why the Judaic lawgiver decreed, "Thou shalt not abhor an Egyptian 'because thou was a stranger in his land.' (Deuteronomy 23:7) "

The Black Man in the Old Testament, Bishop Alfred G. Dunston, Jr., Africa World Press, Inc., New Jersey, 1992, p. 73

A very recent observation was made by Brenda L. Webber of *Emerge* ("Is Jesus Black"?, *April 1995*, p. 31) about the likely racial identity of the people in the Bible:

There are certain accepted facts in Black Biblical scholarship that appear repeatedly in writings and discussions: The people of Egypt were dark-skinned; Egypt is in North Africa, not today's "Middle East" ; Blacks traditionally have been described as descendants of Ham (Genesis 10), and that the Israelites mixed with the descendants of Ham.

"The earliest Jews were in all probability, Negroes. Abraham, their ancestor, is said to have come from Chaldea and the ancient Chaldeans were black," so declares J. A. Rogers, (SEX AND RACE, Vol. I).

According to Profesor Charles B. Copher:

"In dealing with Ham's descendants, Joseph singles out Cush in his *Antiquities of the Jews* and writes: 'time has not at all hurt the name of Cush; for the Ethiopians...are even at this day, both by themselves and by all men in Asia called Cushites. [Flavius Josephus, *Antiquities of the Jews*, 6.2, trans., Willian Whiston in the *Works of Flavius Josephus*, S.S. Scranton Co., Hartford, Conn., 1903, p. 40]

Black Biblical Studies, Charles B. Copher, Black Light Fellowship, Chicago, Ill., 1993, p. 101

Sir Higgins, in his other scholarly masterpiece, *The Celtic Druids*, goes on to say:

"Mr. Maurice labors hard to prove, that a great nation of Cuthites or Cushites overran Asia. By Cushites are always meant Blacks or Ethiopians.

Dr. Welsing presents her views on how the original Hebrews acquired a lighter hue:

In the diaspora of the Semites of the Jewish religion after the Babylonian exile 2,000 or so years ago, Semites left Africa and went to Europe. With continuing genetic admixture with the European (white population), operating under the definition that a Jew is "anyone whose mother is a Jew," it was possible, if enough white males had sexual intercourse with a sufficient number of Semitic or colored women, for the once Black population of Semites to become progressively lighter and lighter...All offspring from these white males and Semitic women of the Jewish religion then would become Jews.

The Isis Papers, Dr. Frances Cress Welsing, Third World Press, Chicago, 1991, p. 224

Jews long have discussed the problem of defining Jewry. A race? There are Chinese Jews, Black-skinned Ethiopian Jews, and Mexican Indian Jews.

The World's Great Religions, Henry R. Luce, ed., New York: Time Inc., 1957, p. 133

The findings of physical anthropology show that, contrary to the popular view, there is no Jewish race...The Hebrews of the Old Testament period were already a racially mixed population as shown by occasional references in the Bible (e.g. Deut. xxvi, 5:S. of Sol. 1,5,6; I Sam xci,12; Ezek. xvi 3) and by contemporary representation of Hebrews on Egyptian, Assyrian and other monuments.

Encyclopedia Britannica Vol. 8, Chicago, Ill., William Benton Publ., 1973, p. 1054

A well known modern Jewish writer offers a similar view:

An important part of any valid definition is what a Jew is not. To begin with, the Jews are not a race....There are dark Jews and blond, tall Jews and short; there are blue-eyed, brown-eyed, and hazel-eyed Jews as well as those whose eyes are jet black. Though most Jews are of the white or Caucasian race, there are black African Jews from Ethiopia and African-American Jews in the United States; until recently, there were Chinese Jews in Kai-Fung-Fu and there still are Jewish communities in various places on the subcontinent of India.

What is a Jew?, Rabbi Morris N. Kertzer, Revised by Rabbi Lawrence Hoffman, Collier Books, New York: Macmillan Publishing Company, 1993

The *Encyclopedia Britannica* echoes a related ethnic perspective:

The Chinese Jews of K'ai feng...looked like Chinese; the Ethiopian Jews - the so-called Falasha like the non-Jewish Ethiopians have black skin...both Yemenite Jews and Yemenite Muslims have dark...complexion...The only race to which the Jews have not achieved a high degree of assimilation is the Nordic: a smaller percentage of Jews exhibits the Nordic physical features than is the case among the gentiles of the locality. In other words, there are relatively more light-skinned, blond, blue-eyed, long-headed, tall individuals among, say German gentiles than among German Jews.

Dr. Frances Cress Welsing suggests that the lighter skin Jew came about because: "Over 2,000 years or 100 generations, the population that was once Black became significantly lightened.

The Isis Papers, Third World Press, Chicago, 1991, p. 224

Carl Conrad Nichols, a brilliant self-taught scholar, argues that through conquest (Persians, Greeks and Romans); through assimilation (white conquerors mixing with the conquered Black Hebrews) and through migration (the subsequent lighter to whiter Hebrews traveling north to present day Europe) all help to create what is known as your modern day white Jew (see Mr. Nichols' lecture tapes distributed by Transatlantic Productions). He suggests that the term "Jew" belongs more appropriately to Europeans and Hebrews to those who are black or of African ancestry (Edenic).

About the same time that the European academy coined the term Semitic, it also created the geographical designation called the Middle East - all in an effort to avoid talking about Africa! This academic racism sought to de-Africanize both the sacred story of the Bible and Western civilization.

The Original Africa Heritage Study Bible, Hope Cain Felder, ed., Nashville: Dr. James Peebles, Winston-Derek Publishers, 1993, p. xv

In like manner, Dr. Finch reminds us:

The Semites are conventionally held to be a branch of the Caucasian race and the term "Semitic" is regularly invoked whenever antiquarians wish to prove that civilization began in

Mesopotamia. It is easy enough to decode the intent behind this approach; it is a way of saying that civilization was created by the Caucasian race. One can readily succumb to this facile way of thinking because the contemporary Semitic group of Western Asia more or less approximates to the Caucasian type and it is easy to suppose that this has always been the case. As we shall see, though, the case was very different in antiquity.

Echoes of the Darkland, Charles S. Finch III, Decatur, Georgia: Khenti, Inc., 1991, p. 131

CHAPTER XII

THE AFRICAN ORIGINS OF THE HEBREW

MESOPOTAMIA NOT THE FIRST CIVILIZATION

IN A LETTER PUBLISHED BY THE *NEW YORK TIMES* ENTITLED "History Didn't Begin In Mesopotamia," we hear from a Professor of Cornell University William B. Branch who writes:

To the Editor:

"To Endangered List in Gulf, Add Archeology" (front page, Sept. 16) asserts that ancient Mesopotamia-which spanned the territory encompassing much of present-day Iraq-"produced the first writing and earliest experiments in agriculture." You also credit the valley of the Tigris and Euphrates rivers in Iraq as "the place where historical time began."

Early writing systems have long been known to have developed in the Nile Valley...and in other parts of Southwest Asia before writing's codification as cuneiform in Mesopotamia by the early Sumerians, who were designated in later Assyria Babylonian inscriptions as the blackheads or black-faced people. Sir Henry Rawlinson is said to have traced the Sumerians back to Egypt and Ethiopia....scholars have since postulated the development of agriculture even earlier-up to 9,000 or 10,00 B.C.-in East Africa, where it is believed humankind itself first walked the earth.

I, too, was taught in school that history (and civilization) began at the juncture of the Tigris and Euphrates, and was taught nothing about the great civilizations Africans and Asians built long before the emergence of Europe. I was unaware that Africans and Asians are not "minorities" , but together with other people of color comprise close to four-fifths of the world's population.

Your misinformation strikes me as a prime example of the need for a sweeping curriculum overhaul, such as has been proposed for New York State.

William B. Branch Ithaca, N.Y. Oct. 5, 1990 The writer is a professor of African studies at Cornell University.

Further, there are many Biblical students who hold to the traditional view that humanity and civilization began in Asia's Mesopotamia, in contrast to those who believe that it all began in Asia, in Egypt's Nile Valley. Nevertheless, whatever geo-Biblical view one adopts the historically and otherwise verifiable fact remains that the roots of humanity and civilization are Black = whether in Asia or Africa. In Asia we have the indigenous "Blackheads" of Sumer, while in Africa we have the indigenous Cushites and Egyptians.

The Black Presence in the Bible, Rev. Walter Arthur McCray, Vol. 2, Black Light Fellowship, Chicago, Illinois, 1990, p. 2

There are many powerful voices on this subject; among the first was:

"Herodotus, who visited this region in the Fifth Century, B.C., mentions the dark skins of the people. He calls them Ethiopians but says their hair was straighter than those of the Western Ethiopians who he says, had woolly hair. The Elamites, however, seemed rather to have belonged to the more Negroid stock of the west as their hair as seen on the monuments is, short and woolly."

J. A. Rogers, *Sex and Race*, Vol. I

A point which was not lost on Dr. Finch who explains:

From what we know about the early migrations of Africans out of the continent to populate the rest of the Old World, there is nothing strange in this aboriginal presence in Western Asia.

Western Asia is, after all, geographically adjacent to Africa and therefore a logical conduit through which Africans could migrate.

The first cultures of Western Asia, especially those in the Fertile Crescent, arose out of the aboriginal black population...(Weiss R, "Many Faces of a Gene Mapping Project," Science News (13), 10 14/89)

Echoes of the Darkland, Charles S. Finch III, Decatur, Georgia: Khenti, Inc., 1991, p. 254

Moreover, Tacitus (80 A.D.) says that

'many Romans of his time believed that *the Jews originated in Ethiopia...*" (SEX AND RACE, Vol. I)

See also: THE JEW, M. Fishberg, pp. 117, 147-8

A contemporary illustration of the racial identity of the Hebrews is given in the *New York Times*, Friday, March 4, 1955:

Falasha Jews From Ethiopia Studying in Israel

Their Tribe Practices Judaism According to Law of Moses by Harry Gilroy Special to The New York Times

"-Twelve young Falasha Jews, who might be taken as living proof of the legend that today's Ethiopians descend from Solomon and the Queen of Sheba are studying at this children's village.

They come from a tribe, numbering 50,000, scattered over Ethiopia. The tribe is called Falasha, which in the Ambharic tongue means 'stranger'.

Its members practice Judaism according to the law of Moses, but have no tradition about later feasts such as Hanukkah and Purim. They never left Ethiopia."

Albert B. Cleage, Jr., author of *Black Christian Nationalism: New Directions for the Black Church*, lists Biblical evidence showing that:

"THE HEBREWS WERE DARK-SKINNED AFRICAN PEOPLE ACCORDING TO THE BIBLICAL SOURCES:

Our skins were Black... (Lam 5:10)

My skin is Black... (Job 30:30)

They are Black... (Jer. 14:2)

His hair was like wool... (Rev. 1:14)

Look not upon me because I am Black....(Solomon Songs 1:6)

His feet were like brass.... (Rev. 1:15)"

This is how the *New York Times* described the Falasha (Ethiopian Jews) in their March 2, 1984 editorial section:

EXODUS FOR A TWICE-LOST TRIBE

"Ethiopia is both a country and a living museum. Christian since the fourth century, its people speak 70 languages and 200 dialects. Ethiopia also boasts, or should boast, an ancient Jewish Community called the Falashas. A saner world would celebrate this human link to an epic past - - a lost tribe that has kept its identity for more than 2,000 years in a remote corner of Africa...this dwindling community of 20,000 black Jews..."

A special to *The New York Times* (December 10, 1984) also talks about these Black so-called "Falasha" Jews

Airlift to Israel Is Reported Taking Thousands of Jews From Ethiopia

"The operation may involve about half of the 25,000 to 30,000 black Jews who have lived for many centuries in northwest Ethiopia in the region of Gondar.

'Almost all the black Jews' are 'commonly called Falashas from the Ethiopian word for immigrants, or Beth Israel, meaning House of Israel, as they call themselves.' "

Moreover, aside from Professor ben-Jochannan's work on the subject of BLACK HEBREWS, there are others who have expressed similar opinions, J. A. Rogers, for one, writes:

"THE FALASHAS, OR BLACK JEWS OF ETHIOPIA ARE PROBABLY VERY ANCIENT. THEY CLAIM LINEAL DESCENT FROM ABRAHAM, ISAAC AND JACOB, CALL THEMSELVES BETA-ISRAEL (THE CHOSEN PEOPLE) AND OBSERVE THE PASSOVER." (*SEX AND RACE*, VOL. I)

Dr. Charle S. Finch in a section entitled "African Origins of the Early Hebrews: Quotations from Classical Writers" cites the following ancient writer:

Josephus: "[Ragmus] had two sons, the one of who, Judadas, settled the Judadeans, a nation of Western Ethiopians, and left them his name..."

Note: Although the word Jew is given, Hebrew would be the more accurate historical designation.

Charles S. Finch of Morehouse College remarked that:

The Hebrew story begins around 2000-1900 B.C.E. when the shepherd Abram migrates from his father's lands in Chaldea, through southern Canaan, and into Egypt during a pre-Hebrew stage of history...

Echoes of the Darkland, Charles S. Finch III, Decatur, Georgia: Khenti, Inc., 1991, p. 136

He further adds:

Celsus, Plutarch, Tacitus, Eusebius, and Diodorus all recorded the received tradition that the original Hebrews were a group of Ethiopians and Egyptians who were forced to leave Egypt and migrate to Canaan.

Thus when we echo the assertions of scholars of the caliber of Diop and Massey by affirming that the historical Semites, including the original Hebrews, evolved out of the African world and were originally Black-skinned, we are insisting only on facts known and attested to by the ancient authorities who wrote on the subject.

Manetho's history, the only surviving one from an identifiable Egyptian historian, corroborates this impression.

Thus we must reiterate: if Jacob's clan was not black when it entered Egypt, it certainly was when its descendants departed in the group and led by Moses-Osarsiph.

To the extent that there were any literate persons among them, apart from Osarsiph himself, their written language and literature would have been Egyptian, at a time when the Hebrew language didn't even exist. (p. 141)

To quote Dr. Churchward in his book The Origin and Evolution of Religion:

Manetho states that Moses received his priestly education and learned all the wisdom of the Egyptians in the city of Heliopolis...the Biblical City of On...Manetho also state, that Moses was one of the priests...(London: George Allen & Unwin Ltd., 1924, p. 291)

As J. A. Rogers, (SEX AND RACE, Vol. I), pointed out:

"Only seventy Jews went to Egypt, but according to the Bible, 600,000 men left it, which must have meant an additional two or three million women and children. Thus, Jewish culture was Egyptian culture.

For example, the Egyptians did not and still do not eat pork."

The peerless Egyptologist Dr. Cheikh Anta Diop reflects the same viewpoint:

Those who would become the Jews entered Egypt numbering 70 rough, fearful shepherds, chased from Palestine by famine and attracted by that earthly paradise, the Nile Valley.

The African Origin of Civilization: Myth or Reality, Conn., Lawrence A Hill. Co., 1974, p. 5

Later on he footnotes the following:

Genesis, XV, 13. If the Biblical version is even slightly accurate, how could the Jewish people be free of Negro blood?

In 400 years it grew from 70 to 600,000 individuals in the midst of a Negro nation that dominated it throughout that period.

If the Negroid traits of Jews are less pronounced today, this is very likely due to their crossbreeding with European elements since their dispersion.

At present it seems almost certain that Moses was an Egyptian, therefore a Negro. (p. 279)

To sum up the evidence. it would be more historically accurate to say that Hebrew means someone of African descent (black) and Jewish means someone of European descent (white).

CHAPTER XIII

"In The Beginning".... We Were There

IN VOLUMES 1 AND 2 OF THE *BOOK OF THE BEGINNINGS*, GERALD Massey launches forth his position on where we may find the origin of civilization:

So far as the records of language and mythology can offer us guidance, there is nothing beyond Egypt and Ethiopia but Africa..."

Thus the world renowned American Orientalist, James H. Breasted, discloses that:

"Our moral heritage, therefore derives from a wider human past enormously older than the Hebrews, and it has come to us rather THROUGH THE HEBREWS THAN FROM THEM."

THE DAWN OF CONSCIENCE, New York, 1933 p. XV,

As a matter of fact, "there was NO HEBREW written language until 850 BC. when the Jewish scribes (Hasidim) translated the original manuscripts, from Egyptian and Gecez to Hebrew," as Carl C. Nichols, a Biblical scholar puts it.

Indeed, it is quite interesting and somewhat puzzling as to how Charleston Heston in the movie the 10 COMMANDMENTS comes down from Mount Sinai with 2 stone tablets containing the 10 COMMANDMENTS in ancient Hebrew, when the language did not exist until ~200 years later. Another observation made by Mr. C. C. Nichols.

Using dates as reference points, 1250 BCE (Abraham enters Egypt) could be considered the benchmark date for Jewish history. Everything before that date is pre-Jewish (before authentic Jewish history); everything after it until 538 B.C. (the Persian Conquest of Babylonia) would be within Jewish history. One can use that date to compare how old or how young a particular idea or nation is based on Western Civilization's frame of references regarding its religions. For example, the date of 3000 BC is clearly a time before the Jewish people became a nation. (See Palmer and Colton, *A Modern History*). Or, if you use the figure around 1500 BC as Diop did in dating the arrival of Europeans into Egypt in his book *Civilization or Barbarism*. That too is pre-Jewish meaning it is before the history of the Jews as a religion, a people and a nation.

Thus Professor Breasted reminds us that:

The Ethiopians were the first to give religious thought and aspiration to the world.

"A voluminous note, in which standard authorities seems to prove that this statement is substantially correct, and that we are in reality indebted to the ancient Ethiopians, to the fervid imagination of the persecuted and despised negro, for the various religious systems now so highly revered by the different branches of both the Semitic and Aryan races. This fact, which is so frequently referred to in Mr. Volney's writings..."

Count Volney, *The Ruins of Empire*, Publisher's Preface

Centuries before Europe's conversion to Christianity - centuries in which Celtic, Germans and Slavic peoples saw the natural world as magical, with trees, birds and thunder possessing ominous power - **Africa gave birth to the world's first Christian state**....So why is the Christian legend of Ethiopia so little known in the West?...perhaps because the Ethiopian ('burnt faces' in the Greek language that named them) are black, and European cultures continued to identify Christianity as a Western religion.

"Burnt by the Sun," *American Visions*, Vol.10, No., Washington D.C. American Visions Communications, December/January, 1996, p. 14-5

Bamber Gascoigne who wrote the book, *The Christians*, (which also appeared as a television program) speaks of Ethiopia this way:

"There is only one country in the world today, which has been Christian almost from the start, and in which one can still find monks living with something of the early simplicity: Ethiopia.

Until 1974 Ethiopia was still essentially its own small Christian empire, with a tradition longer than any, Christianity had penetrated its mountain vastness as early as 340 A.D.

The imperial title 'Lion of Judah' is one of the phrases used for Christ himself in Revelation, and Haile Selassie - - the name which Ras Tafari chose for himself in 1920 means 'Might of the Trinity'."

When the King James translators completed the translation in 1611...they knew by calling the slaves Negroes this would give bearing to the white Christian world that the people they were enslaving were Christians well before Europe knew about the Risen Christ.

The Original Africa Heritage Study Bible, Hope Cain Felder, ed., Nashville: Dr. James Peebles, Winston-Derek Publishers, 1993, p. xv

Put more directly by Father Martin de Porres, Walsh, O.P. in the book The Ancient Black Christians "...**ETHIOPIA, A BLACK COUNTRY, IS THE OLDEST CHRISTIAN COUNTRY IN THE WORLD!**" (p. iii)

Therefore it should not come as a surprise that our main source of information has been the Ethiopic version of Enoch which was discovered by James Bruce, a Scottish explorer. He set out on his travels in June 1768, and landed in Ethiopia in September 1769, after many adventures. He describes in his journals how he found THE ANCIENT CHRISTIAN CIVILIZATION OF ETHIOPIA.

The Lost Prophet, (The Book of Enoch and its influence on Christianity), Margaret Barker, Great Britain: SPCK, 1988, p. 8

The author of Anacalypsis, G. Higgins provides us with a scene from Genesis written on the walls of an Ethiopian temple, which also supplies another link to the Bible and its African origins:

"One of the greatest African Ethiopian temples was located at Abu Simbel, or Ipsambul, in Nubia.

When an English Traveler named Wilson visited this temple, he saw sculptured on its walls the story of the Fall of Man as told in Genesis.

Adam and Eve were shown in the Garden of Eden as well as the tempting serpent and the fatal tree.

Commenting on this fact, Godfrey Higgins asked:

'How is the fact of the mythos of the second book of Genesis being found in Nubia, probably a thousand miles above Heliopolia, to be accounted for?' [Anacalypsis, Vol. I, p. 403]

African Presence in Early Asia, "Krishna and Buddha of India: Black Gods of Asia, "John G. Jackson, p. 106

A *History of Civilization* proclaimed that "Christianity...after two thousand years, is still the religion professed by the overwhelming majority of men and women in the western world. All these, it must be noted, came to us westerners not directly, but filtered through and in part transformed by...Hebrews...

Crane Brinton, John B. Christopher Robert Lee Wolff, vol. 1, Prentice Hall, New Jersey, 1967, p. 20

However, the author of *The Conquest of Civilization* made the following revelation: "But literature remained the only art the Hebrews possessed. They had no painting, sculpture, or architecture. "(Breasted, James, Harper & Bros., New York and London, 1946, p. 239)

Therefore, before we give all the credit to the Hebrews, let us remember the words of Professor Breasted, a leading Egyptologist, who added this historical insight concerning the cultural achievements of the Hebrews and its dependence on Egyptian civilization:

"The ripe social and moral development of mankind in the Nile Valley which is 3000 years older than that of the Hebrews contributed essentially to the formation of the Hebrew literature."

THE DAWN OF CONSCIENCE, p. XV, New York, 1933

Therefore, as Count C. F. Volney once wrote in his book *Ruins of Empire*:

"ALL RELIGIONS ORIGINATED IN AFRICA."

Likewise, Dr. Albert Churchward declared in his classic *The Signs and Symbols of Primordial Man*:

"THERE IS EVERYTHING TO PROVE THAT ALL RELIGIONS HAD THEIR ORIGIN IN ANCIENT EYGPT."

Dr. Diop, the foremost contemporary authority on African history and culture, concludes:

"Universal knowledge runs from the Nile Valley toward the rest of the world...As a result, no thought, no ideology is foreign to Africa which was the land of their birth."

The African Origin of Civilization, Lawrence Hill & Co., Conn., 1974,

For example, the book *Ancient Egypt in Light of Modern Discoveries*, in a similar vein of thought, stated that "the oldest places of culture in the Nile valley...believed that originally there was but one God 'which was from the beginning...the Father of Beginnings...the Nameless One...whose names are numberless...the One God to whom there is so Second...the Father of the gods,'~ the mysterious invisible Creator..."

Charles H.S., Davis, Camden, M. Cobern, Introduction by Rev. C. Winslow, of the Egypt Exploration Foundation, Meridian, Conn.: Biblia Publishing Co., 1892, p. 272

Professors Davis and Cobern add:

De Rouge, Mariette, Chabas, Devfria, Pierrot, Renouf, Brugsch and almost all other Egyptologists have held that the earliest monuments show unmistakable signs that the primitive religion of the Nile valley was a monotheism.

According to H.V.F. Winstone author of *Uncovering the Ancient World*:

De Rouge was writing before the discoveries of the coffin texts which found their way to the Louvre and the British Museum from about 1876.

De Rouge's view nonetheless received a warm welcome in some theological quarters as showing that the God of Judah and Christianity was an integral part of human consciousness from the earliest recorded times...

The Egyptian God, the `One' or the `One One', of the very earliest texts, was certainly singular: the God of the heavens from whom light, warmth and the good things of life derived...It is true that the metaphor of light is at the heart of most religions, and is central to the Talmudic texts.

New York: Facts On File Publications, 1986, p. 219

Martin Bernal, a professor at Cornel University, explains:

Emmanuel de Rouge and Heinrich Brugsch, the leaders of the second wave of Egyptology in the 1860s and 70s, both followed Champollion, and the Hermitic and Platonic tradition behind him, in believing that the pure Egyptian religion was sublime and essentially monotheist, as de Rouge said: 'one idea predominates, that of a single primeval God; everywhere and always is One Substance, self-existent and an unapproachable God.'

Black Athena, Vol. I., Bernal, Martin, Rutgers New Brunswick, New Jersey: University Press, 1987, p. 258

According to that Professor Cheikh Anta Diop:

Ra achieves creation through the word (Islam and Judeo-Christian religions), the *logos* (Heraclitus), the spirit (the objective idealism of Hegel)...In fact, Ra is in the history of religious thought, the first God, autogenous (who was not created, who has neither father nor mother).

Civilization or Barbarism, New York: Lawrence Hill Books, 1981, p. 312

Similarly, Professor M. A. Murray of University College, London, disclosed that:

The temples of Egypt still stand as a witness to that firm belief in God which can be traced back to the most primitive inhabitants of the Nile Valley. At Luxor the worship of the Almighty Creator has continued without a break for thirty-five centuries on the same spot. The name by which the Deity was known has changed with the passing of time; but whether known as Amon, Christ, or Allah, the feeling that prompts the worship of God is unchanged and the place is as sacred as it was fifteen hundred years before Christ.

The Splendour That Was Egypt. Philosophical Library, New York, 1957, p. xvii-xix

Even St. Augustine one of the church's Founding Fathers says that:

"What is now called the **Christian religion** has existed **among** the **Ancients** and was not absent from the **beginning** of the **human race**...(Retract 1, 13)

James Bonwick author of *Egyptian Belief and Modern Thought* cites a passage that reflects a similarity in monotheistic thought between the ancient Egyptians and the Hebrews:

All those who live on earth, come to thee. - Thou art their God, to the exclusion of all others. - Beings and non-beings depend on thee. - Beloved by all who see him. - Every one glorifies his goodness. - Mild is his love for us. - His tenderness surrounds our souls."

In the above extracts most readers cannot fail to recognize the lofty conception of a First God, a Providence, and a pure and Personal Deity. The Hebrew prophets spoke of Jehovah in similar terms.

To quote from the book *Uncovering the Ancient World*:

There was much excitement in Europe when these compilations began to emerge from burial tombs along the entire length of the Egyptian Nile. Here, as the American Egyptologist Breasted put it, was the `dawn of conscience', the right of every man to his own soul, to his own judgment day. De Rouge, in his introduction to a hieratic version of the Book of the Dead, saw an absolute connection between the cults of the Nile Valley and the religion of the Hebrews. In what amounted to a paraphrase of Newton's *Principia* he declared that the Egyptians believed in one supreme, eternal and almighty God, who created the world and everything in it, and endowed man with an immortal soul. (H.V.F. Winstone, Facts On File Publications, New York, 1986, p. 218)

There is, however, no doubt whatever that in the earliest phases of Egyptian religion known to us there emerges a God Almighty, whose presence fills the whole region of the skies and whose eyes shine like the sun and the moon; this god of heaven is called 'the Great', 'the Lord of All', and 'He who is';

Egypt Architecture, Sculpture and Painting, Kurt Lange & Max Hirmer, London: Phaidon Press, Ltd., 1956, p. 118

Adds Professor James Henry Breasted: [the] Nile-dweller...caught a noble vision of social values and unselfish character which had never before dawned on the world...He who knows the story of the transition from the prehistoric hunters of the Nile jungle to the sovereigns and statesmen, the architects, engineers, and craftsmen, the sages and social prophets of a great organised society, which wrought these monumental wonders along the Nile at a time when all Europe was still living in Stone Age barbarism...

The Dawn of Conscience, New York: Charles Scribner's Sons, 1935, p. 12

R. A. Schwaller de Lubicz, the author of *Her Bak* and several books on Egyptian religion writes:

About 3000 B.C. the Pyramid Texts were already speaking with authority of the constitution of man, his survival of death, and his relation to the life of the cosmos. (*The Opening of the Way*, New York: Inner Traditions International, 1981)

The Egyptians could think in terms of abstract religion. The proof comes from a text generally called Memphite Theology, which dates back to the 3rd millennium. The Theology describes a cosmogony according to which Ptah, the local god of Memphis, and his emanation Atum, were the primal beings. Ptah created the world in his heart, the seat of his mind, and actualized it through his tongue, the act of speech. This...looks remarkably like the Platonic and Christian logos, the 'Word' which 'already was, The Word dwelt with God, and what God was, The Word was, The Word then was with God at the beginning, and through him all things came to be...'

The Healing Gods of Ancient Civilizations, Walter Addison Jayne, New Haven, Yale University, 1925, p. 140

For a knowledgeable scholar like Professor John A. Wilson of the University of Chicago the evidence is clear:

"What we have in the Memphite Theology is of the greatest importance. It is a search for the First Principle, the intelligence underlying the universe...But we must remember that the Memphite Theology lies two thousand years before the Greeks or Hebrews. Its insistence that there was a creative and controlling intelligence, which fashioned the phenomena of nature and which provided, from the beginning, rule and rationale, was a high peak..."

The Culture of Ancient Egypt: Chicago and London, The University of Chicago Press, 1951, p. 60

Monotheism. with all its abstraction, already existed in Egypt, which had borrowed it from the Meroitic Sudan, the Ethiopia of the Ancients...'the Supreme Deity, viewed in the purest of monotheistic visions as the 'only generator in the sky and on earth who was not engendered...the only living god in truth...' "(*Archeologie de l'Afrique Noire*, D.P. de Pedrals, Paris: Payot, 1950, p. 37

The African Origin of Civilization: Myth or Reality, Cheikh Anta Diop, Conn.: Lawrence A Hill. Co., 1974, p. 6

"What the average educated man of late antiquity thought he knew we might perhaps best summarize by quoting from the fourth-century Roman historian Ammianus Marcellinus:

"If one wishes to investigate with attentive mind the many publications on the knowledge of the divine...he will find that learning of this kind has spread abroad from Egypt through the whole world. There, for the first time, long before other men, they discovered the cradles...of the various religions, and now carefully guard the first beginnings of worship, stored up in secret writings. (Ammianus xxii. 20ff. The translation is that of J.C. Rolfe, Loeb Classical Library vol ii, pp. 306f.)"

The Legacy of Egypt, John R. Harris, ed., London: Oxford University Press, 1971, p. 140-41

Today popular Christianity too easily assumes that modern ideas about race are traceable to the Bible or that there is not a significant Black presence in the Bible...Centuries of European and Euro-American scholarship along with a "save the heathen Blacks" missionary approach to Africa have created these impressions.

The Original Africa Heritage Study Bible, Hope Cain Felder, ed., Nashville: Dr. James Peebles, Winston-Derek Publishers, 1993, p. vii

But the words of J.A. Rogers are clear and direct in this matter. He simply writes that:

"The Bible really **originated in ancient Egypt, where the population,** according to Herodotus and Aristotle, **was Black.** Here the Jews received almost all of their early culture." (*100 Amazing Facts About The Negro*)

Professor Cyrus H. Gordon in his article, *"Ancient Israel and Egypt,"* puts it this way:

"Many Egyptian customs, adopted by the Hebrews and recorded in the Bible, became part of Western civilization."

Dr. Cheikh Anta Diop in his monumental classic *Civilization or Barbarism* lists other religious connections from the Egyptian priesthood:

God servants can approach him only when they are free of any physical blemish; therefore twice each day and twice each night, they must perform their ablutions...Royal baptisms done within lustral water.

Christian baptism (John the Baptist and the water of the Jordan River,) the Catholic priest's tonsure, and the Muslims' ablutions find their distant origin here.

Eudoxus of Cnidus was shaven before being initiated by the Egyptian priests...Fasting and prohibition form eating certain foods are no less revealing of the Egyptian legacy to the later Religions, Judaism, Christianity, Islam: pork, fish, wine, etc., are forbidden to the priests...

Civilization or Barbarism, Cheikh Anta Diop, New York: Lawrence Hill Books, 1981, p. 334

Adds Dr. Diop:

and we know that certain Biblical Passages are practically copies of Egyptian moral texts." (*African Origin Of Civilization: Myth or Reality*, 1974)

To take but two examples among many, we have the following:

The 10 COMMANDMENTS originally came from the 42 NEGATIVE CONFESSIONS OF BLACK EGYPTIANS. NEGATIVE CONFESSIONS (4100 BC)

From the BOOK OF THE DEAD and PAPYRUS OF ANI

1.   I have not committed theft.

2.   I have not slain man or woman.

TEN COMMANDMENTS (700 BC)

1. Thou shalt not steal

2. Thou shalt not kill.

SOURCE: Tutankhamen's African Roots, Haley, et al., overlooked by Yosef A. A. ben-Jochannan

As the Associate Curator of the Brooklyn Museum's Egyptian and Classical Art Department, Robert Bianchi points out:

In many respects, *these sentiments echo the Ten Commandments* and place the ancient Egyptians much closer to the Judeo-Christian ethos than is generally admitted."

A similar view is given by Professor Breasted in the classic *Dawn of Conscience:*

"All old Testament scholars of any weight or standing now recognize the fact that this whole section of about a chapter and a half of the Book of Proverbs, is largely drawn verbatim from the Wisdom of Amenenope; that is the Hebrew version is practically a literal translation from the Egyptian.

It is likewise obvious that...in the Hebrew law, in Job, as we have already noticed in Samuel and Jeremiah, Amenenope's wisdom is the source of ideas, figures, moral standards, and especially certain warm and humane spirit of kindness."

For example:

"SOLOMON'S PROVERBS

~Beware of robbing the poor...

~Consider these **thirty chapters**...

AMENENOPE

~Rob not the poor for he is poor...

~Have I not written for thee **thirty sayings**."

BLACK MAN OF THE NILE AND HIS FAMILY, Yusef A. A. ben-Jochannan

James Bonwick, author of *Egyptian Belief and Modern Thought*, says that the Egyptian Book of the Dead is "by far the most ancient of all holy books."

Even THE ARK OF THE COVENANT comes from Egypt according to Yusef A. A. ben-Jochannan and Dr. Albert Churchward:

"The Ark of the Covenant, built and set up by Moses in the wilderness, according to the Sacred volume - and which has not been seen - is precisely similar in all measurements to the 'Stone Chest' still to be seen in the King's Chamber of the Great Pyramid. (BLACK MAN OF THE NILE AND HIS FAMILY)

According to Cornell University's Professor Martin Bernal:

If Egyptian religion were monotheist, it could be seen as the basis or origin of Christianity. In the late 19th century, however, the racial question was more salient. If Egyptian religion were monotheist, it would impinge on the Aryo-Semitic monopoly of civilization."

Black Athena, Vol. I., Bernal, Martin, Rutgers University Press, New Brunswick, New Jersey, 1987, p. 258

Later, he adds:

I think it is fair to say that this essentially racist attitude of skepticism about and scorn for, Egyptian achievements was predominant in Egyptology throughout the high tide of imperialism between 1880 and 1950 ." (p. 263)

According to Dr. Churchward, Dr. Kuhn, Professors ben-Jochannan, John G. Jackson and Gerald Massey four of the fundamental beliefs of Christianity can be found originally on the walls of the Egyptians, as Dr. Albert Churchward illustrates:

The story outlined in the canonical Gospels can be traced to "The Annunciation, Conception, Birth and Adoration of the Child" of the Ancient Egyptians.

The story of Annunciation, the miraculous Conception...the Birth and the Adoration had already been engraved in stone and represented in four consecutive scenes upon the innermost walls of the holy of the holies...in the Temple of Luxor, which was built by Amen-hetep III, 1700, or 1800 B.C.

The Origin and Evolution of Religion, London: Unwin Bros., Ltd., 1924, rep. 1986 Heath Research, p. 368

As The Original Africa Heritage Study Bible states:

Africa, her people, nations, cultures, must be acknowledged as making primary direct contributions to the development of Christianity.

Hope Cain Felder, ed., Nashville: Dr. James Peebles, Winston-Derek Publishers, 1993, p. v

CHAPTER XIV

THE COMMON BLACK ORIGINS OF THE ETHIOPIANS, EGYPTIANS, NUBIANS AND KUSHITES.

"PROFESSOR ROSELLINI, THROUGHOUT HIS 'MONUMENTI' accepts and continues the doctrine, of the descent of civilization from Ethiopia and the African origin of the Egyptians.

Champollion Figeac, in his *'Egypte Ancienne'*, (Paris 1840) supports the same theory which his illustrious brother sets forth in the sketch of Egyptian history...(published in his letters from Egypt and Nubia) wherein, he derives the ancient Egyptians according to the Grecian authorities, from Ethiopia and considers them to belong to...an African race..."

Ancient Egypt, George R. Gliddon, p. 58

It is important here to review the words of a dominant figure in Egyptology, Professor Adolph Erman, who suggests that:

"The inhabitants of Libya, Egypt, and Ethiopia have probably belonged to the same race since prehistoric times in physical structure they are still Africans..."

Life in Ancient Egypt. H.M. Tirard, trans., Benjamin Blomdale, New York, 1969, p. 32

The "Father of (European) History," Herodotus, states:

"The Colchians, Ethiopians, and Egyptians have thick lips, broad nose, woolly hair, and they are burnt of skin."

As Bishop Alfred G. Dunston, Jr., points out:

As intelligent as he was, it is positively unthinkable that Herodotus would have made an extended visit to the land of people visibly of different colors, and then have mistakenly inferred that they had black skins...

The Black Man in the Old Testament, Africa World Press, Inc., New Jersey, 1992, p. 31

"According to Homer and Herodotus, the inhabitants of the following territories were Ethiopians:

1.   The Sudan
2.   Egypt
3.   Arabia
4.   Palestine
S.   Western Asia
6.   India"

A HISTORY OF ETHIOPIA, Sir E. A. Wallis Budge, Vol. I, pp. 1-2

Professor Emil Naumann used music to demonstrate how the Ethiopians and the Egyptians were originally related:

"We will first deal with the Ethiopians, as they are the nearest neighbors of the Egyptians, and further because it is historically affirmed that the latter originally migrated from Ethiopia. Indeed, the music of the Ethiopians offers strong internal evidence in support of this assertion.

It is first to be noticed that the Ethiopians have a number of instruments in common with the Egyptians...their songs are also to be found in Ethiopia. But the most important fact establishing a musical connection between the two nations seems to be the marked resemblance that the songs already alluded to - sung to this day in Abyssinia - bear a great number of melodies still prevalent in Egypt. The similarity consists in the common employment of the tetra chord."

The History of Music, Emil Naumann, trans. F. Praegen, ed. Rev. Sir F.A. Gore Ouseley, Mus. Doc. (Late professor of music in the University of Oxford), London: Cassell and Company Ltd., 1902, pp. 53-4

In like fashion, John D. Baldwin wrote:

"Diodorus Siculus adds to his statement that the laws, customs, religious observances, and letters of the ancient Egyptians closely resembles those of the Ethiopians, 'the colony still observing the customs of their ancestors.' "

The classical writer Diodorus of Sicily once wrote:

The Ethiopians say that the Egyptians are one of their colonies which was brought into Egypt by Osiris...They add that from them, as from their authors and ancestors, the Egyptians get most of their laws. (*Universal History*, Abbe Terrasson, Paris, 1758, p. 341)

This is why in Chancellor Williams' book *Destruction of Black Civilization*, Egypt is called "Ethiopia's Oldest Daughter."

Professor Gaston Maspero, a prominent Egyptologist, reveals the consensus regarding the racial identity of the ancient Egyptians:

"By the almost unanimous testimony of ancient historians they belonged to an African race (read: Black) which first settled in Ethiopia..." (THE DAWN OF CIVILIZATION, London, 1984)

According to Dr. C.B. Copher: St. Augustine refers to the Ethiopians as black in his commentary on the Psalms.

Black Biblical Studies, Charles B. Copher, Chicago, Ill.: Black Light Fellowship, 1993, p. 106

Even Aristotle says that the Egyptians were "very Black" and the Ethiopians "woolly haired." (Physiognomy, Chap. VI).

For example, "the ancient Greek historian Herodotus in a passage comparing the Colchians to the ancient Egyptians argued that the Colchians were similar to the Egyptians in that '...they had in common, their black pigmentation and their crinkly hair.' "

General History of Africa II (Ancient Civilizations of Africa). ed., G. Mokhtar (vol.II), 1981, p. 68

The well-known modern philosopher Bertrand Russell reflects the same racial reality in a different way when he cites the words of the Greek philosopher Xenophanes who "said that 'The Ethiopians make their gods black and snug-nosed; the Thracians say theirs have blue eyes and red hair.' "

A History of Western Philosophy, Bertrand Russell, New York: Touchstone Book, Simon & Schuster, 1972, p. 40

Similarly, British historian Basil Davidson declared:

"That the Ancient Egyptians were black (again, in any variant you may prefer) -- or, as I myself think it more useful to say, were African -- is a belief which has been in Europe since about 1830..."

"The Ancient World and Africa: whose roots?," *Race and Class.*, Vol. XXIX, Autumn 1987, Number 2, p. 2

Professor of Governmental Studies at Cornell University and the author of *Black Athena* came straight to the point in the September 23, 1991 issue of *Newsweek*:

"Says Bernal...few Egyptians could have bought a cup of coffee in America's Deep South in 1954..."

Even a detractor like Mary Lefkowitz, professor in the Humanities at Wellesley College, had to concede that:

It is probably fair to say that if a person from Memphis, Egypt, in 1930 B.C. turned up in Memphis, Tennessee, in A. D. 1930, he would have had to sit at the back of the bus.

"Not Out of Africa," Chronicles, September 1995, p. 18

The ancient Greek writer and historian Herodotus wrote in his *The Histories*, Book II that the Egyptians "are black-skinned and woolly hair..." (London: Everyman's Library, J.M. Dent & Sons Ltd., 1992, p. 169)

According to the unanimous testimony of the Ancients, first the Ethiopians and then the Egyptians created and raised to an extraordinary stage of development all the elements of civilization, while other peoples...were still deep in barbarism.

The African Origin of Civilization: Myth or Reality, Cheikh Anta Diop, Conn.: Lawrence A Hill. Co., 1974, p. 230

As Rev. Walter Arthur McCray reminds us:

The student of the Scripture well understands that Egypt, Africa, as a great Black nation, played a most important role in connection with the Israelite people. Matter of fact, Egypt, Africa formed the contextual civilization which for hundreds of years affected the development of the Israelite cultural experience....A numerical picture may be helpful. Throughout the Revised Standards Version "Egypt" appears 617 times, "Egypt's" 3 times, "Egyptians" 24 times, "Egyptian's" 3 times and "Egyptians" 103 times.

The Black Presence in the Bible, Vol. 2, Chicago, Illinois: Black Light Fellowship, p. 97

However, according to some scholars, the Black Egyptians were not black; they were white Hamitic people. Moreover, Egypt is not in Africa. It is in the "Middle East" or in Europe.

It is called the power of definition. You define what a thing is and what it is not; what is legitimate and what is not; what is important and what is not; what is valuable and what is not.

Power lets you do this whether it is right or wrong.

White supremacy may not have a logic, but it does have a purpose. White supremacist must be the first in everything that proves superiority be it in civilization, the arts, the sciences, or religion. It must have the control and ruthless power in all things sacred or profane. Its goal is to exploit, oppress, hinder and obstruct all growth, progress, success and development of the so-called "inferior" people. It weakens the spirit and contaminates the mind.

With the power of definition, it can even define black as white and put a whole country on another continent. It follows the "tribal imperative" of white supremacy.

CHAPTER XV

THE POWER OF DEFINITION

BLACK NOT BLACK

REISNER UNEARTHED A CIVILIZATION OF BLACK FOLK IN Ethiopia, but hastened to declare that they were not Negroes! Reisner was born in sight of Negro slavery in America and never forgot it. Flora Shaw wrote of the blackest men of the Sudan and their brilliant civilization, but warned her readers that they were not Negroes! So here in Ethiopia, "Land of the Blacks," country of "Burnt Faces," we are continually faced with the silly paradox that these black folk were not Negroes.

The World and Africa., W.E.B Dubois, New York: International Publishers, 1965, p. 118

The legendary W.E.B Dubois, then asked the question: What then are Negroes? Who are Africans? Why has the whole history of Ethiopia been neglected or ascribed to white "Hamites"? And why does every historian and encyclopedist, whenever he writes of the civilization of the upper Nile, feel compelled to reiterate that these black people were "not Negroes"?

Professor George A. Kersnor, head of the Harvard-Boston expedition to the Egyptian Sudan, returned to America early in 1923 and, after describing the genius of the Ethiopians and their high culture during the period of 750 B.C. to 350 A.D. in middle Africa, he declared the Ethiopians were not African Negroes. He described them as dark colored races...showing a mixture of black blood. Imagine a dark colored man in middle Africa being anything else but a Negro. Some white men, whether they be professors or what not, certainly have a wide stretch of imagination...

Amy J. Garvey, *The Philosophy and Opinions of Marcus Garvey.* The Majority Press, Mass., 1986, p. 19

In response to a testimony by Count Volney, "Champollion-Figeac, brother of Champollion the Younger, was to reply in the following terms: 'The two physical traits of black skin and kinky hair are not enough to stamp a race as negro and Volney's conclusion as to the Negro origin of the ancient population of Egypt is glaringly forced and inadmissible.' (J.J. Champollion-Figeac, 1839, p. 26-7."

UNESCO (International Scientific Committee for the Drafting of a General History of Africa). *General History of Africa II (Ancient Civilizations of Africa).* ed., G. Mokhtar (Vol. II), Heineman Educational Books Ltd., London, 1981, p. 40

Likewise, the Summary of the introductory papers from the Symposium on the peopling of ancient Egypt at UNESCO included the following statement:

The people who lived in ancient Egypt were 'white' even though their pigmentation was dark, or even black, as early as the predynasty onwards. (Heineman Educational Books Ltd., London, 1981, p. 59)

In a similar line of "thought" Lady Lugard suggests that:

The Haussa and the Songhay are other races which, though black, are absolutely distinct from the pure negro type.

A Tropical Dependency, (originally published in 1832, by James Nisbet & Co., Ltd., in 1906), ECA Associates, Chesapeake, New York, 1992,

To which German Professor A.H.L. Heeren adds:

To the south of Dongola is...a very remarkable race. They are of a very dark brown, or rather black colour, but by no means Negroes."

Historical Researches into the Politics, Intercourse, and Trade of the Carthaginians, Ethiopians, and Egyptians, Vol. I., (originally published in 1832, by D.A. Talboys, Oxford), rep., Va., ECA Associates, 1991. p. 306

So, too, the author of *European Civilization* Edward Eyre expressed the idea that the Nubians were not Black:

On her south frontier Egypt was in continuous hostile contact with the Nubians (not Negroes).

London: Oxford University Press, 1935, p. 459

Professor Diop is one of the many objective voices who would point out the obvious contradiction of making black white when he says:

What we cannot understand, however, is how it has been possible to make a white race of Kemit: Hamite, black, ebony, etc. (even in Egyptian). Obviously, according to the needs of the cause, Ham is cursed, blackened, and made into the ancestor of the Negroes. This is what happens whenever one refers to contemporary social relations. On the other hand, he is whitened whenever one seeks the origin of civilization, because there he is inhabiting the first civilized country in the world.

The African Origin of Civilization: Myth or Reality, Cheikh Anta Diop, Conn.: Lawrence A Hill. Co., 1974, p. 9

As it was recorded in the magazine of the Library of Congress, *Civilization*, entitled "Understanding Afrocentrism" by Gerald Early, director of Afro-American Studies Program at Washington University, St. Louis, who cites a friend as saying:

"if you have one-thirty-second portion of black blood, a mere drop of black blood, then you are black, no matter what your skin color. But when it comes to the ancient Egyptians, it doesn't matter if they have a drop of black blood, and we know that they had at least one-thirty-second portion of African blood. It doesn't matter how much African blood they have, they are still white."

By the same token, Bishop Alfred G. Dunston, Jr. revealed that:

Until very recently, most of the historians and writers have conveyed to the world the idea that the earliest Egyptians were white, or at least near-white, and any blackness found among them was imported with slavery.

The Black Man in the Old Testament, New Jersey: Africa World Press, Inc., 1992, p. 27

Professor John Henrik Clarke maintains that:

Europeans...wanted to prove that everything good in African history was brought in from the outside. The Hamites are supposed to be "black white people" . Western historians move the so-called Hamites around Africa as they see fit in order to prove that the rest of Africa has no history worthy of its name.

Introduction to African Civilization, John G. Jackson Introduction by John Henrik Clarke, University Books, NY, 1970, p. 6

Until the late eighteenth century, it was generally accepted that Hamites were black people. The extraordinary results of Napoleon Bonaparte's expedition to Egypt in 1798, however, became the historical impetus for Europeans to transform the Hamites into Caucasians.

Briefly stated, according to Edith Sanders, "The Hamitic hypothesis states that everything of value ever found in Africa was brought there by the Hamites, allegedly a branch of the Caucasian race." (Edith Sanders, "The Hamitic Hypothesis; Its Origin and Functions in Time Perspective," *Journal of African History* 10, No. 4 (1969), 532).

Charles G. Seligman (1873-1940) explained the civilizing role of the Hamites in Africa in the following manner: 'The civilizations of Africa are the civilizations of the Hamites...The incoming Hamites were pastoral 'Europeans'- arriving wave after wave - better armed as well as quicker witted than the dark agricultural Negroes" (Charles G. Seligman, *The Races of Africa* (New York: Henry Holt, 1930, p. 96)

Egypt, Child of Africa, Ivan Van Sertima, ed.,, Transaction Publishers, New Brunswick, 1995, p. 106

Dr. Charles B. Copher of Atlanta, Georgia reminds us that:

[The] new Hamite hypothesis or view...removes color from the criteria for determining racial identity, and regards black non-Negroids to be white - Caucasoid or Europid Blacks...*The Journal* of *The Interdenominational Theological Center,* vol.,. 3, no. 1 (Fall 1975):10)

The Black Presence in the Bible, Rev. Walter Arthur McCray, Vol. 2, Black Light Fellowship, Chicago, Illinois, 1990, p. 5

The French scholar Abbe Emile Amelineau reaches this conclusion:

It clearly follows from what has been stated earlier: Egyptian civilization is not of Asiatic, but of African origin, of Negroid origin, however paradoxical this may seem. We are not accustomed, in fact, to endow the Black or related races with too much intelligence, or even with enough intelligence to make the first discoveries necessary for civilization. Yet, there is not a single tribe inhabiting the African interior that has not possessed and does still possess at least one of those first discoveries.(*PROLEGOMENES A L'ETUDE DE LA RELIGION EGYPTIENNE* (Paris: ed., Leroux, 1916), p. 330.)

Professor Ivan Van Sertima in his book *They Came Before Columbus* quotes from E. Sanders (p. 109):

"A strange guilt troubled Count Volney. It was so natural to think of blacks as 'hewers of wood and drawers of water.' When did this curse begin? 'How we are astonished,' he later wrote, 'when we reflect that to the race of Negroes, at present our slaves, and the objects of our contempt, we owe our arts and sciences...'

Fifteen years later an expedition under Napoleon marched into Egypt. The scientists of that expedition were equally astonished and impressed., From what they saw they concluded, as the Greeks had done a thousand years before, that Egyptian civilization owed its inspiration to a black race." ("The Hamitic Hypothesis," *Journal of Africa History,* 5,2, 1974, p. 177)

EGYPT NOT IN AFRICA

The Rev. Wyatt Tee Walker once wrote:

I have just returned from another of more than a dozen visits to Egypt with a tour group of sixty persons. One of our guides came to me quizzically on the second day and remarked that a tour member had inquired. 'Is Egypt in Africa?" Any American over forty might have that same mind-set given the slant of Eurocentric geography and social studies texts of the United States.

Egypt, Child of Africa, Ivan Van Sertima, ed.,, Transaction Publishers, New Brunswick, 1995, p. 249

A similar view is made by Professor Cain Hope Felder:

The Eurocentric view creates a Middle East, a non-Black Egypt, even a non-Black Ethiopia, in any case, more so in antiquity than even today, Egypt was intimately (culturally, linguistically, and racially) a part of black Africa.

Troubling Biblical Waters, Orbis Book, New York, 1994, p. 13

Randall C. Bailey, an associate professor of Old Testament and Hebrew and chairman of Bible Studies at Atlanta's Interdenominational Theological Center, says, 'Sometimes the methods used to deny the presence of Africans within the text have been subtle. Other times they have been not so subtle.'

Baily suggests turning to Biblical maps, where one is likely to find very little of Africa. The key to the map may even be placed in the space where Africa is, he adds, 'which conveys to the reader that this is wasted space, unimportant'...Books have even located Cush, ancient Ethiopia, outside of Africa. Ethiopia is mentioned in the Scriptures more than 50 times, and Egypt more than 600 times giving poignancy to Bailey's argument. "

Emerge, "Is Jesus Black"?, Vol. 6, No.6, Brenda L. Webber, April 1995, p. 31

Likewise, in the same article "Is Jesus Black"? it reads:

"Americans have been misguided in their understanding of the geography of the Scriptures, largely because Europeans were cast in the starring role as the people who gave us the Bible. A true picture of the regions' geography was further hampered when the approximately 105 mile Suez Canal was built between 1859 and 1869, separating Asia from Africa. Subsequently, this region was renamed the Middle East." (p. 30)

However, in *The Ancient History of the East*, a book written by the English scholar Philip Smith in London in 1881, it emphasized this fact:

"No people have bequeathed to us so many memorials of its form, complexion and physiognomy as the Egyptians...If we were left to form an opinion on the subject by the description of the Egyptians left by the Greek writers we should conclude that they were, if not Negroes, at least closely akin to the Negro race. "

The Rev. Adam Clayton Powell, Sr., pastor of the Abysinnian Baptist Church in New York City and father of the famed Congressman, gave his opinion following an early 1920's visit to Egypt and Jerusalem.

"No colored man can go to Egypt and study the past and present achievements of its people without being proud that he is a colored man, for the Egyptians are undoubtedly Colored People. The features of all the pictures that are in the tombs, pyramids and galleries of the old Egyptians are Negroid. "

Writes John Henrik Clarke in the Introduction to John G. Jackson's *Introduction to African Civilization*:

There are many physical varieties of African peoples. The complexions of Africans are mainly black and brown. Most of the light-skinned people in Africa today are latecomers or interlopers. They have little or no relationship to Africa's ancient history. The Egyptians are a distinct African people. (New York: University Books, 1970, p. 6)

"A generation ago the idea of constructing a history of Africa on the same lines as a history of Europe, Asia, or the Americas would have seemed to almost all Western scholars an undertaking at once eccentric and impracticable. Africa, in the cliché of the age, was the continent without a history - or rather a continent whose "history" only began when it was drawn into the orbit of 'civilization' by the coming of the Europeans."

Africa to 1875, Robin Hallet, Ann Arbor: The University of Michigan Press, 1970, introduction

As the British historian Basil, Davidson noted:

It is a denial, in short, that belongs to the rise of modern European imperialism, and has to be explained in terms of the 'new racism', together with and was consistently nourished by that imperialism. I say 'new racism' because it followed and further expanded the older racism which spread around Europe after the Atlantic slave trade had reached its high point of 'take off' in about 1630.

Race and Class, Vol. XXIX, Autumn 1987, Number 2. "The Ancient world and Africa: Whose Roots?"

Professor Martin Bernal of Cornell University concludes:

That racism became an obsession in northern Europe. Starting in Britain and France, but then spreading throughout northern Europe. And the origin of that, I think is pretty clearly, slavery. The enslavement of millions of Africans and their maltreatment. And the need to justify that slavery by dehumanizing the victims. You couldn't behave so badly to men...So you have to dehumanize the people you are behaving badly to. I think that's the essential - it's a complicated and subtle thing. But that is the core, the crux of the issue.

Like It Is with Gil Noble (October 30, 1988

Dr. James Peebles explains:

Probably the greatest act that crystallized the justification of European slave trading was the Catholic priest Bartholomo de las Casas' writing in his encyclical to the papacy that these people (the Africans) were without souls and suitable for the torturous work in the Americas. The result was *carte blanche* exploitation justified and sanctioned by the Western Church, marking the very beginning of color prejudice.

The Original Africa Heritage Study Bible, Hope Cain Felder, ed.,, Nashville: Dr. James Peebles, Winston-Derek Publishers, 1993, p. 3

According to the book *New Dimensions in African History*, by Dr. Yosef A., ben-Jochannan and Dr. John Henrik Clarke:

In approaching this subject, the first thing you need to know is that for thousands of years before the existence of Europe, what we know as Africa was the world. Our greatest contribution to the world was civilization itself and the concept of family structure... (Trenton, New Jersey: African World Press, Inc., 1991, p. 97)

Dr. James Peebles wrote these words in the preface to *The Original Africa Heritage Study Bible:*

Throughout the world today, the view that almost all biblical characters are Caucasian has become standard...Such presumptions are only now being challenged by the importance of the Egyptian and Ethiopian civilization in the shaping of the biblical world. Thus, today, there is a critical need to examine not only how this narrow and distorted view emerged in Western history, but also how the Bible specifically treats Africa and Blacks. (Hope Cain Felder, ed., Nashville: Winston-Derek Publishers, 1993, p. xii)

It is important to note that the stage of civilization was already set and over when the European arrived. They were basically watching very old and very ancient reruns of Ethiopian (Kush) and Egyptian (Kmt) civilizations when they came to the African continent.

CHAPTER XVI

THE FOUNDERS OF CIVILIZATION

"Let princes come out of Egypt and let Ethiopia hasten to stretch forth her hand to God!" (Psalms 68:31)

It would scientifically follow that the first people in the Bible would have African (Ethiopian) origins since they [Black People] created the first civilizations.

In Volumes 1 and 2 of the BOOK OF THE BEGINNINGS, Gerald Massey launches forth his position on where we may find the origin of civilization:

"...has now to be sought for in Africa the birthplace of the black race, the land of the oldest known human types...

ETHIOPIA AND EGYPT PRODUCED THE EARLIEST CIVILIZATION IN THE WORLD..."

Thus, Diodorus was the first European to focus attention on the Ethiopian claim that tropical Africa was the cradle land of the world's earliest civilization, the original Eden of the human race.

Introduction to African Civilization, John G. Jackson Introduction by John Henrik Clarke, University Books, NY, 1970, p. 6

The distinguished historian Count Constantin F. Volney maintains that "there are A Race of Men now rejected for their Black Skin and Woolly Hair Founded on the study of The Laws of Nature those civil and religious systems...Which Still Govern the Universe."

RUINS OF EMPIRE, 1789, Preface of 1st Edition

To which C.F. Volney adds in another work:

"This Race of Blacks is the very one to which We owe our Arts and Sciences, and even the Use of the Spoken Word..."

Journey in Syria and Egypt, Paris, 1787, pp. 74-75

The scholar Geoffrey Higgins in his search for the beginning of nations could come to no other conclusion based on the facts he had uncovered except the one in which he expressed in the following words:

"We have found the black complexion or something relating to it whenever we have approached the origin of nations.

Anacalypsis, Vol. I, p. 286

The eminent scholar Gerald Massey confirms this when he says that:

"The most reasonable view on the evolutionary theory...is that the black race is the most ancient and that Africa is the primordial home." (*A Book of the Beginnings*, Vol. II)

An European scholar by the name of Professor B. Lumpkin adds

We must go back to the beginnings of the human race for the beginnings of science, because wherever there are humans, there is, already, the chemistry of fire. Wherever there are humans, there is mathematics, because every language has number words, and the concepts of logic are needed for mathematics - the words "and" , "or." (Karl Menger, lecture on *History of Mathematics*, I.I.T. 1970). Since Africa is widely believed to be the birth place of the human race, it follows that Africa was the birthplace of mathematics and science.

Egypt, Child of Africa, Ivan Van Sertima, ed., Transaction Publishers, New Brunswick, 1995, p. 324

"For thousands of years, the Nile Valley was the Main Street of the civilized world." says Professor Lumpkin.

Speaking about "the advocates of the African origin of civilization," American Egyptologist George Gliddon concludeds that:

"...the advocates of the African origin of the Egyptians cling to the superior antiquity of the pyramids at Meroe, as a proof of the origin of civilization in Ethiopia, and its consequent descent into Egypt..."

Ancient Egypt, George R. Gliddon, The New World, Nos. 68-69, Park Benjamin, ed., J. Winchester, Publish., New York, April, 1843, p. 59

In his essay, "On the Ethnic Affinities of the Races of Western Asia," Professor George Rawlinson states:

"the uniform voice of primitive antiquity, which spoke of the Ethiopians as a single race, dwelling along the shores of the Southern Ocean from India to the Pillars of Hercules."

HERODOTUS, Vol. I, Book I, Appendix, Essay XI, Section-5

The classical historian Strabo wrote:

"I assert that the ancient Greeks, in the same way as they classed all the northern nations with which they were familiar as Scythians, etc., so, I affirm, they designated as Ethiopia the whole of the southern countries toward the ocean."

Strabo adds that "if moderns have confined the appellation Ethiopians to those only who dwell near Egypt, this must not be allowed to interfere with the meaning of the ancients."

Bishop Alfred G. Dunston, Jr., echoes the same viewpoint:

The TERM "ETHIOPIA" (or Ethiopian) is used almost from the beginning to the end of the Holy Bible, and its usage continues to mislead millions of people who think that the Ethiopia of today and the Ethiopia of the Bible are the same; but such is not the case at all.

The Black Man in the Old Testament, New Jersey: Africa World Press, Inc., 1992, p. 13

A Book of the Beginnings is a work written by that eminent scholar, G. Massey who advanced that:

"In Kam or Kush, the black race of the Aethiopic center, was the primeval parentage. The name was continued by Kam in Egypt, Kush, Mizraim, Phut and Canaan represent the four branches in four different directions."

Pursuing a simlar line of thought, the renown historian C. Rawlinson in his *Origins of Nations* concludes:

"The author of Genesis unites together as members of the same ethnic family the Egyptians, the Ethiopians, the Southern Arabians, and the primitive inhabitants of Babylon."

Thus *The Dead Sea Scriptures* cites the Biblical reference in Genesis which indicates that: "the sons of Ham were Cush (Ethiopic) and

Egypt and Put (Somalialand?) and Canaan. "(3rd ed., (English translation), New York: Anchor books, Doubleday, 1976, p. 362)

The eminent Egyptologist Gaston Maspero in his book *The Dawn of Civilization* puts it this way:

> the Bible states that Mesraim, son of Ham, brother of Chus (Kush) the Ethiopian, and of Canaan...settle with his children on the banks of the Nile." (London, 1894)

The celebrated scholar General Sir Henry Rawlinson's findings were presented by his brother Canon Rawlinson as follows:

> "A laborious study of the primitive language of Chaldea, led him (Sir Henry Rawlinson) to the conviction that the dominant race in Babylonia at the earliest time to which the monuments reached back was Kushite or Ethiopian." (George Rawlinson, THE ORIGIN OF NATIONS)

One of the leading 18th century advocates of early Ethiopian diffusions into Asia, John Baldwin once wrote:

> "It is now admitted that a people of the Cushite or Ethiopian race, sometimes called Hamites, were the first civilizers and builders throughout western Asia, and they are traced, by the remains of their language, their architecture, and the influence of their civilization, on both shores of the Mediterranean, in eastern Africa and the Nile Valley, in Hindustan, and in the islands of the Indian Seas."

PRE-HISTORIC NATIONS, New York: Harper & Bros., 1872

Many experts like to say that everything comes from the Greeks who they proclaim as the "Fathers of Civilization" .

But the Greeks are, in terms of civilization and religion, relatively late arrivals to the stage of civilization and origins.

As we have seen Ethiopia stands at the very threshold of civilization. Comparing just one primary ingredient to civilization, namely, religion, we would see Greece's infancy and lack of origins.

The same could also be said of language. Why then would any-one claim that the Greek manuscripts are older than the Ethiopic ones is anyone guess. Perhaps there is some hidden agenda. It may be one of "blind" supremacy mixed with unrealistic wishful thinking.

CHAPTER XVII

THE RUDE AND BARBAROUS
EARLY HISTORY OF THE GREEKS

A HISTORY OF WORLD SOCIETIES STATES THAT:
Greece was not so blessed as Mesopotamia or Egypt with fertile soil or other natural resources. Its physical geography consisted of many mountains, small and scattered coastal plains and river valleys, and the ever-present sea.

John P. Mc Kay, Bennett D. Hill, John Buckler, volume I: to 1715, Boston: Houghton Mifflin Company, 1987

The Oxford History of the Classical World agrees:
the land of Greece is mountainous, broken up into a multitude of separate small plains, river valleys, and islands...with jealous hostility and intermittent war the rule between neighboring cities, is clearly connected with the terrain.

John Boardman, Jasper Griffin, Oswyn Murray, Eds., Oxford:Oxford University Press, 1987, p. 2

Greece in ancient times was never nation; it never had a capital, a government or a single ruling element. The typical Greek-speaking sovereign state was a tribe cultivating an area of land separated from the next cultivable area by a range of rocky hills or mountains.

The Greeks, (from the BBC television series by Christopher Burstall and Kenneth Dover) Kenneth Dover, British Broadcasting Corporation, London, 1980, p. viii

Professor Cyril E. Robinson tells us that:
We saw how when the Greeks first entered Greece one group passed into Epirus and remained there in rude isolation...the Dorians in Epirus remained as primitive and uncultured as they

had been when they dwelt in the northern plains. (*A History of Greece*, New York, 1983, p. 25)

According to the author of *The Loom of HIstory*, Herbert J. Muller:

The modern Western world, it is often said, was born in the Greek cities of Ionia toward the close of the eighth century B.C...(Harper and Bros. N.Y. 1958)

And yet, "J. Brunet" as quoted by Herbert Muller "wrote in his *Early Greek Philosophy*" that Ionia was a country without a past..." there was no traditional background there at all." (*The Loom of History*, 1958)

And Greece settles down into a Dark Age of 300 years, dark both because its history is wrapped in obscurity and because no light of art or culture seems to have shone upon it.

A *History of Greece.*, Cyril E. Robinson, Methuen Educational, 9th Edition, London, New York, 1983, p. 25

A similar point is made in the book, *The Rise of the West* by William H. McNeil.

The Greeks of the Dark Age were rude and barbarous.

Professor at the University of Chicago James H. Breasted says the same:

Long after 1000 B.C. the life of the Greeks continued to be rude and even barbarous... (*Conquest of Civilization*, p. 281)

To which Professor Jean Hatzfeld adds:

By that time, however, signs of internal decay were evident and the process was hastened by the invasion of the Dorians, a people who were Greek but who were culturally impoverished and unacquainted with the art of writing.

History of Ancient Greece, E.H., Goddard trans., New York: W.W. Norton & Company, p. 27

According to tradition, about 1200 B.C. the cities were attacked by an invading horde of more primitive Greeks known as Dorians. They were illiterate, and though they possessed weapons of iron, their knowledge of the arts and crafts was no more than rudimentary. They burned the palace at Mycenae and sacked a number of the others.

World Civilizations, Edward Burns and Phillip Ralph, New York: W.W.Norton & Co.,p. 177

GREEKS HAD NO ANCIENT RELIGIOUS HISTORY

In the first place, it is not even easy to talk about "'Greek religion' since the Greeks had no uniform faith or creed....The Greeks had no sacred books, such as the Bible, and Greek religion was often a matter more of ritual than of belief.

Nor did cults impose an ethical code of conduct. Greeks did not have to follow any particular rule of life, practice certain virtues, or even live decent lives in order to participate.

Unlike the Egyptians and Hebrews, the Greeks lacked a priesthood as the modern world understands the term. I

n Greece priests and priestesses existed to care for temples and sacred property and to conduct the proper rituals, but not to make religious rules or doctrines, much less to enforce them. In short, there existed in Greece no central ecclesiastical authority and no organized creed."

A History of World Societies, John P. Mc Kay, Bennett D. Hill, John Buckler, volume I: to 1715, Boston: Houghton Mifflin Company, 1987

As Professor C. E. Robinson simply says:

"The Greeks were not, a deeply religious race."

A History of Greece, London, Methuen Educational, 9th Edition, 1983, p. 160

CHAPTER XVIII

BLACK MADONNA IN EUROPE AND THE EGYPTIAN
ORIGINS OF GREEK CIVILIZATION

THE CONTINUAL AFRICAN INFLUENCE ON THE MAJOR RELIGIONS of the Western world can be found in many instances. Not the least of these is concerning European worship of a Black woman and her child commonly referred to as the Black Madonna.

Says Bonwick in his book *Egyptian Beliefs*:

"We may be surprised that...EUROPE HAS BLACK MADONNAS...At the same time it is odd that the *Virgin Mary copies* most honored should not only be Black, but *have a decided Isis cast of features*. And elsewhere he declares: 'The Black Osiris? with *a decided Ethiopian appearance* was a mystery as was the Black Isis.' "("The Rosicrucians," p. 134.)

A similar view is taken by T. W. Doane:

"The Egyptian Isis was also worshipped in Italy many centuries before the Christian era and all images of her with the Infant, Horus, in her arms have been adopted as we shall presently see by the Christians even though they represent her and *the child as black as an Ethiopian...*" ("Bible Myths," Chap. XVIII, New York, 1882.)

Frank Snowden, *Blacks in Antiquity*, also touches on the African origin of Isis when he states that:

"A substantial *Ethiopian influence* on Isis worship in *Greece* and in *Italy* is strongly suggested, if not proved, by *the tradition of Ethiopian association with* the cult, by *the Blacks* depicted in Isis ritual..."

THE EGYPTIAN ORIGINS OF GREEK PHILOSOPHY

As we will see, it would *not* have been a problem for the Greeks to worship a Black Madonna and child because the Greeks had always looked up to the ancient Black Egyptians as their teachers. They were proud to sit at the feet of these highly civilized Africans to obtain enlightenment and knowledge.

Needless to say, what many try to overlook or ignore is that the Greeks originated from very humble and barbaric beginnings according to the scholars of history.

Therefore it should come as no surprise as Professor Serge Sauneron, the former Director of the French Oriental Archaeological Institute in Cairo, in his book *The Priests of Ancient Egypt* (Grove Press: distributed by Random House) would point out this fact:

"In going through the ancient Greek Texts, one cannot escape the idea that in the eyes of these old authors,

EGYPT WAS THE CRADLE OF ALL KNOWLEDGE AND ALL WISDOM.

What They Never Told You In History Class, Indus Khamit-Kush, New York: Luxorr Publications, 1983, p. 240

The book *The Legacy of Egypt* makes a similar point:

"Greek authors point to Egypt as the source of their philosophy.

Thales, Solon, Pythagoras, Democritus of Abdera, and Plato are all asserted to have visited Egypt and to have sat at the feet of Egyptian priests...Of Pythagoras it is even related that he had been initiated into ancient Egyptian literature by the high priest Sonchis. "(S.R.K. Granville, ed., Oxford University Press, London, 1942, p. 64-5)

Professor Margaret A. Murray of University College, London wrote:

EGYPT WAS TO THE GREEK THE EMBODIMENT OF ALL WISDOM AND KNOWLEDGE.

The Splendour That Was Egypt, Philosophical Library, New York, 1957, p. xvcc

The well-known French engineer, geographer, and archaeologist E.F. Jomard was quoted by John Anthony West, author of *The Serpent in the Sky* as stating that "'the GREEKS themselves, almost without exception, HAILED EGYPT AS THE SOURCE OF KNOWLEDGE AND WISDOM. '"

The Traveler's Key to Ancient Egypt., New York: Alfred A. Knopf, 1985, p. 87

British Professor Basil Davidson, a well-known authority in the field of history, makes the same point regarding the fact the Greeks themselves proclaimed Egypt as the source of their civilization and knowledge:

"To begin with, there is the evidence of what the Greeks themselves thought...The Greeks all agreed upon the cultural supremacy of Pharaonic civilization, and the ways in which they wrote about this clearly show that they would have thought it absurd to advance a contrary opinion...For the Greeks of the Classical Age, Egypt was where one went to learn history." (*" The ancient world and Africa: whose roots?"* Race & Class, vol. xxix, Autumn 1987, Number 2, p. 5-6)

Professor M. Bernal of Cornell University in citing the work of Professor James Henry Breasted's *Memphite Theology* states how Breasted reached a similar conclusion as to the Egyptian origins of Greek philosophy recorded by the Greek themselves. He admitted as much in these words:

Thus the Greek tradition of the origin of their philosophy In Egypt, undoubtedly contains more of the truth than has in recent years been conceded"

Black Athena, Vol. I.,Rutgers University Press, New Brunswick, New Jersey, 1987, p. 264

The founder of the Department of Egyptology at University College (London) reminds us that the Greeks themselves admitted that "they owed the first elements of civilization and those greatest of all gifts, the alphabet and the art of writing, to the wisdom of the Egyptians. "

Pharaohs, Fellahs and Explorers, Amelia B. Edwards, Harper & Bros., New York, 1891, p. 167

Writes the pre-eminent Senegalese scholar Cheikh Anta Diop:

"...the Greeks (Pythagoras, Plato, Oenopides, etc.), were initiated to different degrees in Egypt, which was then the intellectual center of the world."

Civilization or Barbarism, New York: Lawrence Hill Books, 1981, p. 322

English historian Winwood Reade records the same:

"Egypt from the earliest times had been the university of Greece." (*Martyrdom of Man.* Watts & Co., London, 1934)

Professor George G. M. James clearly illustrates in his book:

"STOLEN LEGACY"

That the Greeks were NOT the authors of "Greek philosophy," but the people of North African commonly called the Egyptians.

The French scholar Amelineau expresses a similar view:

"I saw at the time, and very clearly too, that the most renowned systems of Greece, namely those of Plato and Aristotle, have Egypt for their cradle...I see no reason why ancient Greece would keep the honor of ideas that she borrowed from Egypt." (Amelineau: Prolegomenes Introduction, pp. 8 and 9)

Cheikh Anta Diop, Black Nations and Cultures

Like Amelineau, Professor Martin Bernal discloses the fact that "Herodotus, after relating his eyewitness account informing us that the Egyptians were blacks then demonstrated...that Greece borrowed from Egypt all the elements of civilization...and that Egypt was the cradle of civilization."

Black Athena, Vol. I., Rutgers University Press, New Brunswick, New Jersey, 1987, p. 5

Dr. Diop follows the same line of thought as to the Greeks borrowing and employing Egyptian wisdom into their civilization when he wrote that:

The Greeks who were initiated in Egypt appropriated everything they learned once they went back to their country.

Civilization or Barbarism, Cheikh Anta Diop, New York: Lawrence Hill Books, 1981, p. 322

Nevertheless, most European scholars believe that the "Greeks...laid the foundations of European civilization."

Encyclopedia Britannica, Vol. 8, William Bention, Chicago, 1965, p. 853

Thus "GREECE has traditionally been looked upon as the CRADLE of WESTERN CIVILIZATION."

Archaeology, Michael Carter, Brandford Press Lid.

However, "Plato says the Egyptians looked upon the Greeks as children, too young and innocent to be the creators of great things. The Greeks had no pyramids, no kings as splendid as the Pharaohs..."

The Splendor of Greece, Robert Payne, Harper and Row, New York, 1960, p. 9

In fact, it is Professors R. R. Palmer and J. Colton who point out that: "while the pharaohs were building the first pyramids, Europeans were creating nothing more distinguished than huge garbage heaps."

To which they further add:
HALF OF RECORDED HISTORY HAD PASSED BEFORE ANYONE IN EUROPE COULD READ OR WRITE...[In contrast]...the priests of Egypt began to keep written records between 4000 and 3000 B.C..."

A History of the Modern World, 3rd edn. Alfred A. Knopf, New York, 1964, p. 3

"The researches of Dr. Alan Gardiner, ("The Nature and Development of the Ancient Egyptian Hieroglyphic Writing," *Journal of*

Egyptian Archaeology, Vol. II, Part II, April, 1915), make it abundantly clear that:

the art of WRITING was...INVENTED in Egypt...and spread from Egypt at an early date to Western Asia and the Mediterranean...n7 "

n7Dr. G. Elliot Smith The Influence of Ancient Civilization in the East and in America.

Professors Edward McNall Burns and, Philip Lee Ralph declared that:

"The EGYPTIANS must be credited with the INVENTION of the principle of the ALPHABET. "The Phoenicians merely copied this principle, based their own system of writing upon it, and diffused the idea among neighboring nations."

World Civilizations, 5th ed., New York: W.W. Norton & Co., pp. 21-22
Egypt had a school of architecture and sculpture, a recorded literature, religious ceremonies, mathematics, astronomy, and music, when the inhabitants of Europe were dwelling in caves, and ages before the race of Hebrews became a nation...The alphabet, if it were constructed in Phoenicia, was conceived in Egypt, or developed from Egyptian characters.

Ancient Egypt in Light of Modern Discoveries., Charles H.S. Davis, Camden M. Cobern, Conn.: Biblia Publishing Co., Meridian, 1892, preface.

Dr. Willis N. Huggins in his book INTRODUCTION TO AFRICAN CIVILIZATION wrote these words in the 1930's:

"before there was any 'Glory that was Greece' or 'Grandeur that was Rome,' the Monarchs of Egypt were creating Empires, building pyramids, fashioning colossi, using measurements to the billionth of an inch..."

The Missing Pages of "His-story," Indus Khamit-Kush, New York: D&J Publications, 1993, p. 15

Drawing from one of the great figures in Egyptology, John D. Baldwin quotes Professor Lepsius who said:

"Under the fourth dynasty, when the two great pyramids were built, the nation seems to have approached the highest glory of that wonderful development of intelligence and power to which after the flight of nearly 6000 years, the ruins still bear witness, and to which they will continue to bear witness for ages to come." (*Pre-Historic Nations*, Harper & Brothers, New York, 1898, p. 29)

As the author of *A History of Egypt* would proclaim:

Egypt stood forth before the world of the ancient East manifestly the first of powers and the leader of the human race.

James Baikie, New York: The Macmillan Company, 1929, p. 103

"Plato relates that when Solon visited Egypt, the priests of Sais said to him, 'O Solon, Solon! you Greeks, you are nothing but children ; there is not one old man among you in all Greece!' To have opened the way along which for 2500 years so many nations have followed in her train is for all time Egypt's crowning glory."

Outlines of Ancient Egyptian History, Auguste Mariette, trans. & ed., Mary Brodrick, New York: Charles Scribner's Sons, 1892, p. xxxi

Notes Professor Bernal of Cornell University:

Classical authority for the image of Greeks as children came from Plato's Timaios...Plato reports an aged Egyptian priest as telling Solon: 'You Greeks are always children: there is no such thing as an old Greek...You are always young in soul, every one of you. For...you possess not a single belief that is ancient...

Black Athena, Vol. I., Bernal, Martin, Rutgers University Press, New Brunswick, New Jersey, 1987, pp. 209-10

Champollion, the founder and 'Father' of Egyptology, and famous translator of the Rosetta Stone, in speaking about his expedition into Egypt made the following comparison between ancient black Egyptian and his white European counterpart:

"In contrast with this we may cite another ruin where were found twelve human figures representing four races of men-three of each race-ranged according to their respective claims to preference.

The Egyptians were first, and were clothed in white, the product of their own loom; while last in the procession, and lowest in scale came the European race, with a delicate white skin, blue eyes, flaxen or reddish beard, and *clothed in bullock's hides, with the hair still upon them!*

Here is an antiquity not dreamed of by our classics, when such barbarians were Europe's only representatives at the learned and refined court of the Pharaohs."

R.W. Haskins, ARTS, SCIENCES, and CIVILIZATION, Anterior to Greece and Rome. p. 21

To which Bishop William Montgomery Brown concludes:

"For the first two or three thousand years of civilization, there was not a civilized white man on the earth...It was southern colored people...who gave the northern white people civilization."

THE BANKRUPTCY OF CHRISTIAN SUPERNATURALISM, Vol. II, p. 192

Similarly, Cheikh Anta Diop supplies a revealing examination of the first contact the ancient Black Egyptians had with the inhabitants of Europe:

"...about the year 1500 B.C., the Western region of the Nile delta was invaded by *Indo-Europeans*, tall, blond, blue-eyed, their bodies covered by tattoos and *clothed in animal skins.*

This is how they are described in documents found by Champollion at Biban-el-Molouk.

'...lastly (and I am ashamed to say so, since *our own race* is the last and *most savage* of the series)...' "[Champollion le Jeune, Lettres, (Coll. l'Univers, 1839), pp. 30-31]

The Cultural Unity of Black Africa. (trans. 1963), Third World Press, Chicago, 1963, p. 62-63

The same fact is recorded by Dr. Victor Robinson in his book *The Story of Medicine*:

"Egyptian sculptors...depicted skin-clad savages-these were Europeans. Centuries passed, and sunburnt barbarians, blue-eyed and red of hair, peered into the valley of the Nile..." (Albert & Charles Boni, New York, 1936, p. 28)

The Missing Pages of "His-story," Indus Khamit-Kush, New York: D&J Publications, 1993, p. 63

"How low the savage European must have looked to the Nile Valley African looking north from his pyramid of Cheops?" says Professor Dorsey in his book WHY WE BEHAVE LIKE HUMAN BEINGS.

As the historians Palmer and Colton declared: "Europeans were by no means the pioneers of human civilization. "

A History of the Modern World, 3rd edn. Alfred A. Knopf, New York, 1964, p. 3

"They [Egyptians] were pioneers. They laid the foundations of mathematics and science, and in the early period of their history they made astonishing progress in the practical applications of their knowledge, centuries before the Greeks...Thales and others...athirst for wonders...came to Egypt. "

The Legacy of Egypt., S.R.K. Granville, (ed.), Oxford University Press, London, 1942, p. 177-8

James Baikie, the author of *A History of Egypt*, suggests that:

"The Land of Egypt, the home of that wonderful ancient culture...might almost seem to have been created and set apart by nature for the home and the nursery of the arts and crafts in which its people were destined to be the pioneers of the human race." (The Macmillan Company, New York, 1929, p. 3)

Dr. Walter Addison Jayne points out:

"The ancient Egyptians were a people of superior attainments...and were...pioneers and leaders in the arts of civilization."

The Healing Gods of Ancient Civilizations., New Haven: Yale University, 1925, p. 4

The Ancient Egyptians gave the world the first major civilization in history. Like the Nile which cradled its growth, the surprising ideas of these remarkable people flowed out to the world around them. In this early period, some 6,000 years ago, two other civilizations were stirring: the Sumerian in the valleys of the Tigris and Euphrates, and the Chinese on the yellow river. Of these, now only the Chinese remains but in antiquity neither the Chinese nor the Sumerians reached the level achieved by the people of the Nile Valley or affected western civilization so much.

The Wisdom of the Ancient Egyptians, William Macquitty, New York: New Direction Books, 1978, p. 3

"The genealogy which connects European with Egyptian civilization is direct and certain. From Egypt it came to Greece, from Greece to Rome, from Rome to the remote nations of the West, by whom it has been carried throughout the globe.

Ancient Egypt: Its Antiquities, Religion, and History, Rev. George Trevor, Boston: American Tract Society, p. 18

The historian Sheldon Cheney, author of *A World History of Art*, tells us that:

"[When] Northern Africa...[was]...giving the first impulse to the current of art, Europe still lay in Stone Age savagery and obscurity. Our forefathers there were 'prehistoric,' without written language, without metals, without communal organization..." (The Viking Press, New York, 1952, p. 35)

"Albert Hyma who was knighted by the Dutch Queen Wilhelmina for his work in Dutch history [made] the following statement in his *Ancient History*:

'IT IS CLEAR TO ALL HISTORIANS THAT EUROPE WAS ORIGINALLY BARBAROUS...'

(CHICAGO: UNIVERSITY OF CHICAGO PRESS, 1963, P. 99)

Kemet, Afrocentricity and Knowledge, Molefi Kete Asante, Trenton, New Jersey: Africa World, Press, Inc., p. 63

According to the historians R.R. Palmer and Joel Colton in their massive book, *A History of the Modern World* wrote:

"THERE WAS REALLY NO EUROPE IN ANCIENT TIMES."

In the words of Dr. Yosef A. ben-Jochannan and Dr. John Henrik Clarke:

"It is hard for you to imagine that there was a time when not only did Europeans not exist, there was a time when the word did not exist."

New Dimensions in African History, African World Press, Inc., New Jersey, 1991, p. 99

The author of   *Pharaohs, Fellahs and Explorers*   expresses a related point:

"We are accustomed to think of the days of Plato and Pericles, of Horace and the Caesars, as 'ancient times.' But Egypt was old and outworn when Athens and Rome were founded...the Pyramids were already hoary with antiquity when Abraham journeyed into the land of Egypt..."

Amelia B. Edwards, Harper & Bros., New York, 1891,

When Abraham visited Egypt he saw a great monarchy, the inhabitants of which had already been long enjoying all the advantages of a settled government and established laws."

Ancient Egypt in Light of Modern Discoveries., Charles H.S. Davis, Camden M. Cobern, Introduction by Rev. C. Winslow, of the Egypt Exploration Foundation, Biblia Publishing Co., Meridian, Conn., 1892, p. 1

Two thousand years before Jewish...these people lived, thought, wrote in full development. At the hour when Abraham is seen at the summit of history...this Egyptian race has already grown old...for twenty centuries its cities have been prospering in the shade of pyramids...' "

Thebes, Jean Capart, and Marcelle Werbrouck, The Dial Press, New York, 1926, p. 352

Egypt was the land of Abraham, 'the friend of God' of Joseph, who was honored with the highest office in the gift of the Pharaohs, and of Moses the great law giver who was 'learned in all the wisdom of the Egyptians.' The influence of Egyptian ideas upon Israel has a profound interest for the whole Christian world. The Jordan sweetens the waters of every stream of Christendom..." (*Ancient Egypt in Light of Modern Discoveries*, Charles H.S. Davis, Camden M. Cobern, 1892, preface)

The Missing Pages of "His-story," Indus Khamit-Kush, New York: D&J Publications, 1993, p. 1

As Professor John A. Wilson of the University of Chicago once wrote:

It seems probable that the Pyramids, which have already borne inanimate witness to the existence of their creators for nearly five thousand years, will survive for hundreds of thousands of years to come. It is not inconceivable that they may outlast man himself and that, in a world where there are no longer human minds to read their message, they will continue to testify;

'BEFORE ABRAHAM WAS, I AM.'

(*A Study of History*, Oxford Press, 1947 p. 30) "

The Culture of Ancient Egypt., The University of Chicago Press, Chicago and London, 1951, p. 310

The source of almost all human endeavors from civilization to religion to the arts & sciences can be found at the mouth of the Nile which uttered, by the permission of the Supreme Creator, all things into existence.

There you will find the "origin of things." Or, as Gerald Massey so aptly puts it in his classic two volume work: "The Beginnings."

National Geographic (May 1985) supplies the reader with a clear illustration that shows where the sources of the Nile would be. Naturally, of course, in the heart of Africa:

The National Geographic reporter Caputo adds: "My destination was the source of the Nile...deep in the heart of Africa.' "

Professor ben-Jochannan in his *Black Man of the Nile and His Family* confirms this fact when he quotes the "Egyptians", who said:

"We came from the beginning of the Nile where God Hapi dwells, at the foothills of the mountain of the moon". (Kiliminjaro/Rwensori)

Source: Hunefer-Papyrus

NOTEWELL: This area (the mountain Kiliminjaro) is around the African countries: Kenya, (The heart of Africa) Tansania, Rwanda, Burundi, Uganda and the Sudan (Nubia).

CHAPTER XIX

RELIGIOUS GENESIS OF RACISM

WHAT IS SO IMPORTANT ABOUT ESTABLISHING THE AFRICAN origins of the Ethiopians and Egyptians and their subsequent development of the first civilizations? There are several reasons. First, to help remove from our subconscious minds the belief that we have contributed nothing toward the development of mankind and civilization.

DR. DIOP DRAWS OUR ATTENTION TO THE FACT THAT IT IS THE AFRICAN GENIUS, THE INTELLECTUAL (MENTAL) GENIUS OF THE BLACK MAN AND WOMAN THAT IS AT THE ROOT OF EGYPTIAN CIVILIZATION. THUS, HE REFERS TO "THE ONENESS OF EGYPTIAN AND BLACK CULTURE AND CONCLUDES: "BECAUSE OF THIS ESSENTIAL IDENTITY OF GENIUS, CULTURE, AND RACE, TODAY ALL NEGROES CAN LEGITIMATELY TRACE THEIR CULTURE TO ANCIENT EGYPT AND BUILD A MODERN CULTURE ON THAT FOUNDATION"

LIKE DIOP, "'PAUL MASSON-OURSEL EMPHASIZES THE NEGRO CHARACTER OF EGYPTIAN PHILOSOPHY:

By accepting it [that philosophy] the intellectualism born of Socrates, Aristotle, Euclid, and Archimedes, conformed to the Negro mentality that the Egyptologist perceives as a backdrop for the refinements of a civilization at which he marvels...Venturing to express what should be a cliché - the African aspect of the Egyptian mind- we can use it to account for more than one of its cultural traits.' "

The *African Origin of Civilization: Myth or Reality*, Cheikh Anta Diop, Conn.: Lawrence A Hill. Co., 1974, pp. 139-40

Secondly, to help remove from our subconscious minds the "curse of Ham" as it originated in the Babylonian Talmud. This is how the Bible was used to make us feel comfortable with worshipping white images as God since our own image was cursed and historically "inferior ."

THIRDLY, TO HELP EXPOSE WHITE SUPREMACY AS IT EXISTS IN THE BIBLE IN ORDER TO JUSTIFY OUR ENSLAVEMENT AND "INFERIOR" STATUS IN THIS COUNTRY AND THROUGHOUT THE WORLD.

THE BABYLONIAN TALMUD

Now, I cannot beget the fourth son whose children I would have ordered to serve you and your brothers! Therefore, it must be Canaan, your first born, whom they enslave. And since you have disabled me...doing ugly things in Blackness of night, Canaan's children shall be born ugly and Black! Moreover, because you twisted your head around to see my nakedness, your grandchildren's hair shall be twisted into kinks, and their eyes red'; again because your lips jested at my misfortune, theirs shall swell; and because you neglected my nakedness, they shall go naked, *and their male members shall be shamefully elongated! Men of this race are called Negroes, their forefather Canaan commanded them to live by theft and fornication, to be banded together in hatred of their masters and never to tell the truth.*

We the *Black Jew*, Vol. I &II, Yosef A. A. ben-Jochannan, Md.: Black Classic Press, 1983,

Professor Emeritus of the Old Testament, Charles B. Copher cites two additional offshoots of this so-called "curse of Ham" as translated in the Midrash Rabbah-Genesis:

R. Hun said in R. Joseph' name (Noah declared), 'you have prevented me from begetting a fourth son, therefore your seed will be ugly and dark-skinned." R. Hiyya said: 'Ham and the dog copulated in the Ark, therefore Ham came forth black-skinned while the dog publicly exposes its copulation' [See *Midrash Rabbah, Genesis*, eds., Rabbi Dr. H. Freedman and Maurice Simon, foreword by Rabbi Dr. Isidore Epstein (London: The Soncino Press, 1939) chap. xxxvi, 7-8, 293].

Black Biblical Studies, Charles B. Copher, Chicago, Ill.: Black Light Fellowship, 1993, p. 103

The other excerpt comes from the book *Hebrew Myths* by Robert Graves and Raphael Patai who "relate the passage in Sanhedrein 108a to other sources such as *Tanhuma Noah* 13, 15," and reproduced the same narrative:

'Moreover, because you twisted your head around to see my nakedness, your grandchildren's hair shall be twisted into kinks, and their eyes, red; again, because your lips jested at my misfortune, theirs shall swell; and because you neglected my nakedness, they shall go naked, and their male members shall be shamefully elongated. Men of this race are called Negroes,'. (Greenwich House, New York, 1983, p. 121)

Clause Wauthier reports that as early as 1870, at the first Vatican Council, a group of missionary bishops produced a document asking the Pope to release the Negro race from the curse which, it seems, comes from Ham (*The Literature & Thought of Modern Africa*, p. 209).

Black Biblical Studies, Charles B. Copher, Black Light Fellowship, Chicago, Ill., 1993, p. 118

Says Professor Tony Martin of Wellesley College:

Black Biblical scholarship has given comfort to African-American religious communities that have become disconnected with European images and Biblical interpretations that suggest Blacks contributed little to the Biblical narrative, that they come from a cursed race (Genesis 9:25-27) and that they were destined in the Scriptures to be the slaves of other nations. In Genesis 10 are the descendants of Noah's sons. These scriptures, and others, were used as justification, first for the enslavement of Blacks in America, and then for the legalization of racial segregation and discrimination.

The more important version of the myth, however, ingeniously ties in the origins of blackness - and of other, real and imagined Negroid traits - with Noah's Curse itself. (*The Jewish Onslaught*, The Majority Press, Dover, MA, 1993)

And still today many of the Biblical passages that were employed to justify slavery are used to relate the Black man to, and keep him in, an inferior position within American society.

Black Biblical Studies, Charles B. Copher, Black Light Fellowship, Chicago, Ill., 1993

If you think that Black intellectuals are spared from the "curse" guess again.

According to Dr. Raymond Winbush, director of the Johnson Black Cultural Center at Vanderbilt University in Nashville:

If you're a Black professor, you're still considered inferior.

To which he adds:

Research done by Black professors tends to be in line with Black history. Producing research in reference to Black people is not considered important on white campuses.

Research on a superior people is obviously more important than one done on inferior one, if you believe the not so subtle message.

CHAPTER XX

"SCIENTIFIC" RACISM, THE RACISM OF SILENCE (THE FURHMAN CONNECTION)

THE DAILY CHALLENGE DID A VERY INFORMATIVE AND REVEALING editorial on racism. Excerpts from it read as follows:

"Science has been distorted in the service of racism. Scientific racism is a fact.

The beginning of 'scientific racism' in America occurred in 1797, when the 'Father of American psychiatry' , Dr. Benjamin Rush declared that 'Blacks were black because they suffered from a rare disease called 'Negritude'. Rush did not believe God created the Negro Black or was Black by nature. He also believed that the only evidence of a 'cure' was when the skin color turned white.

Segregation stemmed directly from the 'scientific findings' of Rush in America and other psychiatrists in Europe. Rush cautioned whites that 'whites should not intermarry with them, for this would tend to infect posterity with the 'disorder'...' Using disease as the reason for sexual segregation, Rush medically initiated a pervasive discrimination against African Americans.

Through the use of science Dr. Benjamin Rush not only stigmatized the Negro as scientifically inferior, his attitude toward the Negro fostered an idea that has become a fundamental principle of institutionalized psychiatry, namely that 'a patient does not know and cannot protect his own best interests. He needs a medical man to do it for him.'

In 1851 Samuel A. Cartwright, a Louisiana physician, published an essay in which he claimed to have discovered two mental diseases peculiar to Blacks, 'Drapetomania' and 'Dysaesthesia Aethopis' , which he believed justified their enslavement.

Drapetes means a runaway slave and mania means 'mad' or 'crazy' . Dr. Cartwright diagnosed that the uncontrollable urge for slaves to run away was caused by Drapetomania and that the 'treatment' for this disease was 'whipping the devil out of them' .

The diagnosable signs of 'Dysaesthesia Aethopis' were disobedience, answering disrespectfully and refusing to work. The treatment was to put the person to some form of hard labor. This cure sent 'vitalized blood to the brain to give liberty to the mind.'

A census 'proved' that Blacks living in the 'unnatural conditions of freedom' in the North were more prone to 'insanity and idiocy' . A specialist in mental disorders, Dr. Edward Jarvis, accepted the census at 'face value' and used this to propound that slavery protected Negroes from 'some of the liabilities and dangers of self-direction.' It was later discovered that the census was a fraud, and even Jarvis himself condemned it.

But pro-slavery people eagerly seized upon the census figures as 'scientific confirmation' of the Black man's inferiority. 'Here,' said one pro-slavery proponent, 'is proof of the necessity of slavery. The African is incapable of self-care and sinks into lunacy under the burden of freedom. It is mercy to give him the guardianship and protection from mental death.'

Coming into the twentieth century, the famous psychoanalyst, Carl Jung, asked, 'What is more contagious than to live side by side with a rather primitive people ?' In the book 'Racism and Psychiatry,' Dr. Alexander Thomas wrote, 'Jung saw the influence of 'the childishness of the Negro,' not all of it unfavorable, he conceded, in everything from the swaying of American hips to the 'inimitable Rooseveltian laugh.'

Black mental-health workers say the trouble is that virtually all the progress the U.S. has made toward racial fairness has been in one direction. To be accepted by whites, blacks have to become more like them, white many whiles have not changed their attitudes at all. Study after study has shown that the majority of whites, for all the commitment to equality they espouse, still consider blacks to be inferior, undesirable and dangerous. 'Even though race relations have changed for the better, people maintain their old stereotypes, 'says Powell-Hopson. 'The same racial dynamics occur in an integrated environment has occurred in an segregation; it's just more covert.' "

These stereotypical views and "superior" beliefs of the white supremacist are defended in the white psyche through various mental "defense mechanisms" used to justify racism and to deny that injustices exist based on skin color.

Harvard University's Gordan W. Allport's classic The Nature of Prejudice talks about the "mechanism of denial" [as] the tendency for the ego to defend itself when conflict threatens to upset its equilibrium. The strategy of denial is a quick reflex against disturbing thoughts." p. 502

The Nature of Prejudice, 25th ed., Gordan W. Allport, Addison-Wesley Publishing Co., Mass., 1954, p. 502

Further, Allport outlines several of these mechanisms as follows:
"A common escape from feelings of guilt is to assert that there is no reason to have them. A familiar justification for discrimination against the Negroes is, 'They are happier by themselves." p. 379

Likewise, in defining projection the basic idea is that "there is guilt somewhere, yes, but it is not my guilt." p. 380

He defines projection "as the tendency to attribute falsely to other people motives or traits that are our own, or that in some way explain or justify our own. p. 382

Essence magazine (October 1995) says that "the legacy of slavery is alive and well in America. But like an abuser in a dysfunctional family who refuses to admit that he has committed the abuse, America denies its pervasive racism." (p. 103)

Unfortuantely as the work Egypt, Child of Africa ponts out: "the most progressive European thinkers are unable to move beyond the imprisonment of Eurocentric thinking."

Ivan Van Sertima, ed., Transaction Publishers, New Brunswick, 1995, p. 202

Clearly, many of those of European decsent are too addicted to the destructive drug of white supremacy that does not serve their own best interest since it definitely leads to other kinds of abuse commonly found among their own family members. Which is why you have so much child and spousal abuse. Because if a person is a "hell-raiser" in the world, when he comes home he is not going to be a saint.

In fact, the root of alcoholism within the white community can be traced directly to white supremacy. To perform the demonic acts of white supremacy, an individual has to intoxicate himself so that he can "desensitize" and anesthetize his own conscience from the monstrous deeds he is about to do in the name of this satanic myth. To de-humanize other human beings is ungodly and makes oneself in the same proportion less of a human being.

Treating Black people as 3/5 of a human being is constantly acted out today among certain White people. In fact, it is less than that fraction since we did not have 60% of our numbers represented in Congress or in business or in most social, political and economic elements of this society in any real opportunistic way.

Some people are still attacking the intelligence and worth of Black people as human beings. If you doubt it, ask Mr. Fuhrman of the O. J. Simpson trial how he views us.

The global implicastions can be seen when one recalls how a prominent Japanese Minister said that Blacks were lowering the intellectual level of America.

Then we have Rutgers University president Francis Lawrence telling faculty members that "disadvantaged" students do not have "that genetic hereditary backgrounds to have HIGHER AVERAGE " IN STANDARDIZED TESTS.

However, *Los Angles Times'* Carol Tavris calls our attention to the fact that:

Early in this century H. H. Goddard, a leading educator, gave IQ tests to immigrants, including the non-English speaking, as they arrived at Ellis Island. The results: 83% of the Jews, 80% of the Hungarians, 79% of the Italians and 87% of the Russians scored a "feebleminded." Goddard concluded that low intelligence, which he linked to poor character, is inherited, and that "undesirable" should be kept out of the country or at least prevent them from having children."

Harvard University Professor K. Anthony Appiah makes this logical extension concerning the IQ question:

We'd have to start investigating the genetic differences between different parts of the White population. We'd start to see whether the 19th-century hypothesis that the Irish are stupid can be empirically verified. And we'd have to see whether we can find statistical evidence of the relative superiority of the Nordic over the Mediterranean type.

Emerge, "Dumb Questions About Black IQ," Harriet A Washington, p. 32

"That racism became an obsession in northern Europe. Starting in Britain and France, but then spreading throughout northern Europe. And the origin of that, I think is pretty clearly, slavery. The enslavement of millions of Africans and their maltreatment. And the need to justify that slavery by dehumanizing the victims. You couldn't behave so badly to men...So you have to dehumanize the people you are behaving badly to. I think that's the essential - it's a complicated and subtle thing. But that is the core, the crux of the issue.

Like It Is with Gil Noble (October 30, 1988

It will be seen that when we classify Mankind by color, the only primary race that has not made a creative contribution to any civilization is the Black Race.

Historian Arnold Toynbee, A STUDY OF HISTORY, 1934

If a race has no history...it stands in danger of being exterminated."

Historian Carter G. Woodson

"Whites are more intelligent than Negroes; intelligence is over-whelmingly the result of genetic inheritance rather than environmental influence. . ."

"Race and Intelligence: The findings of A. R. Jensen" by J. Cass

On the problems of black people, Jensen fretted about "...the genetic enslavement of a substantial segment of our population."

New York Times Book Review, June 9, 1985, Prof. Leon J. Kamin, Princeton University

National Review magazine reported Professor W. Shockley of Stanford University of saying that:

"Since Negro intelligence is naturally ... low... let's give blacks cash incentives not to breed."

"Lesser Breeds, Dec. 7, 1973

Nobel Prize winner William Shockley also suggested:

"A voluntary sterilization program for people of low intelligence."

In the Name of Eugenics, Professor Daniel Kevles, California Institute of Technology

Francis H. C. Crick, a Nobel Prize winner for solving the mystery of DNA discussed eugenics and genetics at a symposium of biological scientists. The British geneticist explained:

"I do not see why people should have the right to have children .... if one did have a licensing scheme the first child might be admitted on rather easy terms. If the parents were genetically unfavorable, they might be allowed to have only one child . . . . that seems to me the sort of practical problem that is raised by our new knowledge of biology."

Professor Daniel J. Kevles Science Historian at California Institute of Technology, In the Name of Eugenics, Alfred A. Knopf, 1985

J. Phillipe Rushton, author of *Race, Intelligence and Behavior*, explained that Blacks were more likely to get AIDS because they are genetically programmed to be sexually promiscuous.

Emerge "Murray's 'Bell Curve' Rings of Racism," Harriet A. Washington, December/January 1995, p. 22

Thirty years later, the tradition of ignorance continues. The most recent example is the book *The Bell Curve* by Charles Murray and the late Richard Herrnstein.

These so-called "scholars" wrote a book that attempts to prove whites are intellectually superior to Blacks.

Unfortunately, professors Murray and Herrnstein come from a pantheon of "closet" racists the likes of Rushton, Jensen and Shockley, who chose to disregard historical truth over their version of "history" and "science."

One wonders how these "superior" intellects could have conveniently overlooked the historical contribution of African People. A careful reading of history shows without a doubt that the accomplishments of Black People are second to none.

If these "all-knowing" intellects had the advantage of studying an unbiased view of history, they would have learned that Blacks were *the* Original Intellectuals and Teachers of Humanity.

The superior germ-stuff of the great white race is completely discredited {Joseph McCabe}by the fact that our ancestors remained in the wings, pure barbarians, during the two thousand years when the dark men of the Mediterranean race were constructing civilization, and that our white race, first in the Greeks and then in the Teutons, devastated civilization for centuries. Until about 700 B.C. the philosophers of the world would have said that white men seemed incapable of civilization . By the year 1,000 Europe was reduced to a condition which, if were not Europeans, we should frankly call barbarism... [*The New Science and the Story of Evolution*, pp. 292-98, b y Joseph McCabe]

Introduction to African Civilization, John G. Jackson, Introduction by John Henrik Clarke, University Books, NY, 1970, p. 190

As Ruth Benedict and Gene Weltfish once remarked:

"If you had to depend on the Inventive Genius of the Ancient Europeans, you'd be living on crab apples and hazel nuts..." ("*The Races of Mankind*")

Over a half century ago, the French intellectual Jacques Weulersse wrote the following:

"At a time when all Europe was only savagery...Africa already possessed an antique civilization in the valley of the Nile; it had populous cities...great public works, sciences, and arts..." (*L'Afrique Noire*)

The English scholar Joseph McCabe reminds us that:

The accident of the predominance of white men in modern times should not give us supercilious ideas about color, or persuade us to listen to superficial theories about the innate superiority of the white-skinned man. Four thousand years ago, when civilization was already one or two thousand years old, white men were just a bunch of semi-savages on the outskirts of the civilized world. (*Life Among the Many Peoples of the Earth*)

CHAPTER XXI

WHITE SUPREMACIST QUOTES

HOWEVER, THE FOLLOWING QUOTES GIVE A GOOD INDICATION of how widespread white "scientific" and "religious" racism is despite historical evidence to the contrary, and how many modern day white supremacist views can be seen to have branched off from the so-called "curse of Ham."

I am apt to suspect the Negroes to be naturally inferior to the White. There never was a civilized nation of any other complexion than white, nor even any individual eminent either in action or speculation. No ingenious manufacturers amongst them, no arts, no sciences.

Philosopher David Hume, ESSAYS AND TREATISES ON SEVERAL SUBJECTS, Vol. I, London: 1753

Never yet could I find that a black had uttered a thought above the level of plain narration...never saw an elementary tract or painting or sculpture.

U.S. President: Thomas Jefferson

I have no purpose to introduce political and social equality between the white and black races...There is a physical difference between the two which, in my judgment, will probably forever forbid their living together upon the footing of a perfect equality; and inasmuch as it becomes a necessity that there must be a difference, I am in favor of the race to which I belong having the superior position.

U.S. President: Abraham Lincoln, Debate with Stephen Douglas, 1858

He agreed with Wister that the blacks "as a race and as a mass... are together inferior to the whites..."

U.S. President: Theodore Roosevelt, Letter to Novelist Owen Wister, 1906

(I have) a strong feeling of repugnance when I think of the negro being made our political equal and I would be glad it they could be colonized, sent to heaven, or got rid of any decent way..

U.S. President: James A. Garfield, Letter to Jacob D. Cox, July 26, 1865

According to both his brothers, John and Donald, (*New York Times*, Thursday, June 4, 1981)

America's blacks could only marginally benefit from federal programs because 'blacks are genetically inferior to whites.'

Belief expressed by Richard Nixon according to one of his top advisors, John D. Ehrlichman, *New York Times*, Friday, December 11, 1981

". . . blacks are genetically less intelligent than whites."

Belief expressed by Ernest W. Lefever nominee by President Reagan for Assistant Secretary of State for Humanitarian Affairs.

Talking to me about Desdemona, he assured me, with a most serious expression of sincere disgust, that he considered all her misfortunes as a very just judgment upon her for having married a *nigger*.

U.S. President: John Quincy Adams, statement made to a Miss Kemble in a conversation about the Shakespearean character "Othello" as reported by Mr. James Parton in his article on "Antipathy to the Negro."

[a] dark skin color [is] linked to moral and mental inferiority

Benjamin Franklin: Belief reported by Martin Bernal, Black Athena, 1987

I got a wire from the Reverend Doctor King in New York. He was getting ready to get the Nobel Prize ~ he was the last one in the world who should ever have received it... I held him in complete contempt because of the things he had said and because of his conduct. (He) said he never criticized the FBI. I said, "Mr. King" I never called him reverend - "Stop right there . You're lying."

FBI Director: J. Edgar Hoover, Director of the federal Bureau of Investigations. Statement made in 1964

I can't understand it. I can't understand it I never did think Martin Luther King was a good American, anyhow.

U.S. Vice- President: Spiro T. Agnew. remark to an aide following riots after assassination of Dr. King.

It is now entirely clear to me that, as his cranial structure and hair type prove, Lassalle is descended from the Negroes who joined Moses' flight from Egypt (that is, assuming his mother, or his paternal grandmother did not cross with a nigger). Now this union of Jewry and Germanism with the negro-like basic substance must necessarily result in a remarkable product. The officiousness of the fellow is also nigger-like.

Karl Marx, Letter to Friedrich Engels, 1862

I believe in white supremacy until the blacks are educated to a point of responsibility. I don't believe in giving authority and positions of leadership and judgment to irresponsible people.

Actor John Wayne, Interview in PLAYBOY, May 1971

Africa has No Rich Nature for Education to Cultivate

Explorer Richard Burton, as quoted by John Corry, New York Times, 1985

I can summarize my attitude about employing more negroes very simply - I think it (integration, open housing and jobs) is a wonderful idea for somebody else, somewhere else, I feel the negroes have already made enough progress to last the next 100 years...

Billionaire Howard Hughes, Memorandum to Roger Maheu, April 1968

At a banquet given in Paris on the 19th of May, 1879, in commemoration of the abolition of slavery, M. Victor Hugo said: "In the nineteenth century, the white man has made the Negro a man, and, in the twentieth century, Europe will make Africa a world."

... but there are some things inborn in you...My father was once stabbed by a Negro.

Actress Farrah Fawcett-Majors, Regarding her admitted prejudice against blacks that she was trying to overcome. *NATIONAL ENQUIRER,* Aug. 2, 1977

Stephen, if it weren't for you wretched Britishers, we wouldn't have any Negroes in this country anyway; we wouldn't have this mess.

Evangelist Billy Graham, To Stephen Olford, 1940

Hegel called Africa: the land where men are children

German philosopher Hegel as quoted by John Corry, New York Times, March 1985

The round eyes of the Negroes, their flat noses, thick lips, ear of different shape,. the wool of their heads, the measure of their intelligence, place between them and the other species prodigious differences.

French Philosopher: Voltaire Essai sur les Moseurs, 1829

"...where of white or flesh-color in England being one, the child can demonstrate to you that *a negro is not a man,* because white color was once of the constant simple ideas of the complex idea he calls man; and therefore he can demonstrate, the principle,. It is impossible for the same thing to be and not to be, that a negro is not a man."

English philosopher John Locke, An Essay Concerning Human Understanding, p. 1

Those creatures are all over black and with a flat nose can scarcely be pitied. It is hardly to be believed that God, who is a wise Being, should place a soul especially a good soul in such a black, ugly body. It is so natural to look upon color as the criterion of human nature...

French philosopher Baron de Montesquieu, Spirit of Laws, 1748

"The color of the Negroes, as above observed, afford a strong presumption of their being a different species from the Whites; and I once thought that the presumption was supported by inferiority of understanding of the former....Abroad, they are miserable slaves, having no encouragement either to think or act..."

Scottish philosopher Lord Kames, *Sketches of the History of Man*

We come among the Africans as members of a superior race and servants of a Government that desires to elevate the more degraded portions of the human family.

Doctor Dr. Livingstone, of the famous statement "Dr. Livingstone, I presume," Elspeth Husley Livingstone, 1974

The Negro is a child, and with children nothing can be done without the use of authority. With regard to the Negroes then, I have coined the formula: I am your brother, it is true, but your elder brother.

Missionary Albert Schweitzer M.D., *ON THE EDGE OF PRIMEVAL FOREST*, 1961

No rational man, cognizant of the facts, believes that the average Negro is the equal ... of the average white man.

Biologist Thomas Huxley, Emancipation, Black and White, 1865

Having demonstrated that the Negro and the Caucasian are widely different in characteristics, due to a deficiency in the Negro brain, a deficiency that is hereditary... we are forced to conclude that it is useless to try to elevate the Negro by education or otherwise.

Doctor Dr. Robert Bennett Bean, "Some Racial Peculiarities of the Negro Brain," *American Journal of Anatomy*, Sept. 1906

The negroid streak creeps northward to defile the Nordic race. Already the Italians have the souls of blackamoors. Raise the bars of immigration and permit only Scandinavians, Teutons, Anglo-Saxons and Celts to enter ... I believe at last in the white man's burden. We (Nordics) are as far above the modern French-men as he is above the Negro.

author: F. Scott Fitzgerald in a letter dated 1921

The essence of Polygenist thinking about race was preserved in Darwinian framework "the fundamental Ante-bellum Concept" was the persistence of Negro inferiority through all recorded history.

author: George Stocking, The Black Image in White Mind, 1971

The African race is greatly inferior to the Caucasian in general intellectual

journalist: John Weiss, Life and correspondence of Theodore Parker, New York 1864

The permanent, natural inferiority of the Negro was the true and only defense of slavery

journalist: Edward A. Pollard, The Lost Cause Regained 1868

The states and people that favor this equality and amalgamation of the white and black races, God will exterminate...A man cannot commit so great an offense against his race, against his country, against his God... as to give his daughter in marriage to a negro - a beast...

publisher: Buckner H. Payne, The Negro: What is His Ethnological Status, 1867

G. Cuvier in his *Animal Kingdom* wrote:

"The Caucasian, to which we ourselves belong, is chiefly distinguished by the beautiful form of the head, which approximates to a perfect oval... From this variety have sprung the most civilized nations, and such as have most generally exercised dominion over the rest of mankind.

The Negro race is confined to the south of Mount Atlas. Its characteristics are black, woolly hair, and flattish nose . . . In the prominence of the lower part of the face and the thickness of the lips, its [characteristics] manifestly approaches to the monkey tribe. The hordes of which this variety is composed have always remained in a state of complete barbarism."

Quoted in General Studies, Project on Africa

Caucasian variety. I have taken the name of this variety from Mount Caucasus, both because its neighborhood, and especially its southern slope, produces the most beautiful race of men, I mean the Georgian..."

anatomist and naturalist: Johann Friedrich Blumenbach, *On the Natural Variety of Mankind*, 1795

Many dramatists who never created a single African character referred to . . . the monsters of Africa ... or merely used the terms 'Moors,' 'Negro' or 'Ethiop' in the simile of blackness, cruelty, jealousy, lustfulness or some other quality commonly credited to Africans.

author: Eldred Jones, *Othello's Countryman*, Oxford University Press, London, 1965,

According to Reuter, the blacks were

"without ancestral pride ... even a tradition of historic unity or racial achievements ... the whole record of the race was one of servile or barbaric status."

author: E. B. Reuter, American Race Problem, T. Y. Cromwell, N.Y., 1970,

Who can doubt that the Caucasoids and Mongoloids are the only two races that have made any significant contribution to civilization?

author: Richard Lynn, in Mankind Quarterly, 1991,

The Negro race...is marked by black complexion, crisped or woolly hair...a flat nose. The projection of the lower parts of the face, and the thick lips, evidently approximate it to the monkey tribe: the hordes of which it consists have always remained in the most complete state of barbarism.

professor: G. Culvier (1831), quoted by P. Curtin, Imperialism: The Documentary History of Western Civilization, 1971,

Perhaps in the future there will be some African history to teach. But at the present there is not; there is only the history of Europeans in Africa. The rest is darkness...and darkness is not the subject of history.

historian: Professor Hugh Trevor-Roper

Until the very recent penetration of Europe the greater part of the (African) continent was without the wheel, the plough or the transport animal; without stone houses or clothes except skins; without writing and so without history.

scholar: Margery Perham,

This statement by a Columbia University professor is very typical: "Over the past 5,00 years," he noted, "the history of black Africa is blank. The black African had no written language

A black skin means membership in a race of men which has never created a civilization of any kind. There is something natural in the subordination of an inferior race even to the point of enslavement of the inferior race...

scholar: John Burgess, respected as the dean of academics *The Slant of the Pen (Racism in Children's* books). Edited by Roy Preiswerk

all things point to the fact that the Negro as a race is reverting to barbarism with the inordinate criminality and degradation of that state. It seems, moreover, that he is doomed at no distant day to ultimate extinction.

professor: Dr. Paul B. Barringer, Chairmen University of Virginia, Prediction made at a conference in 1970

God has put in every white man's hand a whip to flog the black man.

historian: Thomas Carlye, upon meeting Emerson in 1848. See his "Nigger Question" written in 1849

The cause of humanity would be far more beneficial by the continuance of the (African slave) trade and servitude regulated and reformed, than by the total destruction of both or either.

political theorist: Edmund Burke, Works 1866

Professor R. B. Carttell "... concludes that savages, including the whole Negro race, should on account of their low mentality and unpleasant nature, be painlessly exterminated."

The sentiments of a contemporary scientist, Professor R. B. Carttell, transmitted by Lord Raglan, *The Origin Of Civilization*

The black variety is the lowest and lies at the bottom of the ladder. The animal character lent to its basic form imposes its destiny from the moment of conception...If its faculties for thinking are mediocre or even nonexistent...It is precisely in the greed for sensation that the most striking mark of its inferiority is found.

scholar: J.A. Gobineau

If Africa was the cradle of mankind, it was only an indifferent kindergarten. Europe and Asia were our principal schools.

professor: Charleton Coon, THE ORIGIN OF RACES, UNIVERSITY OF PENNSYLVANIA

Almost all civilized peoples belong to the white race. The people of other races have remained savage or barbarian, like the men of prehistoric times.

professor: Charles Seignobos, History Of Ancient Civilization, University Of Paris

It is European techniques, European examples, European ideas which have shaken the non-European world out of its past ~ out of barbarism in Africa . . .

scholar: Hugh Trevor-Roper, *The Rise of Christian Europe* (Thames & Hudson, London, 1966)

The negro is not the equal of the white man

congressman: representative, James Brook of the New York, from a speech delivered in December 18, 1867

We may concede it as a matter of fact that (the Negro race) is inferior...

congressman: Owen Lovejoy, 1860

And who is the negro that he should dispute this demand? A race that never yet founded a government or built a state that did not soon lapse into barbarism, a race that never yet made a single step towards civilization, except under the fostering care and guidance of the white man; a race into whose care was committed one of the three great continents, and who has made it, ever since the remotest times, a land of utter darkness, until today the nations of Europe, in the onward march of irresistible civilization are dividing his heritage, the greatest of the continents among themselves...

congressman: Thomas W. Hardwick of Georgia, address to the US House of Representatives in 1904 demanding the disenfranchisement of the black people.

Everybody likes to go to Geneva. I used to do it for the Law of the Sea conferences and you'd find these potentates from down in Africa, you know, rather than eating each other, they'd just come up and get a good square meal in Geneva.

senator: Ernest F. Hollings, reported in the *New York Times*, December 15, 1993

There is nothing in the gradual diminution and destruction of a savage or inferior race in contact with a more civilized and powerful which is mysterious.... The first gifts of civilization are naturally fatal to a barbarous people ...

philanthropist: Charles Loring Brace. The Races of the Old World: A Manual of Ethnology, New York 1870

It's not that the dedication is less. In fact, it's greater. They lack the intellectual capacity to succeed, and it's taking them down the tubes ... one of the best things (slave traders) did for you was to drag your ancestors over here in chains.

chairman: William K. Coors, Adolph Coors Brewing Co., reportedly told a group of minority business owners attending a seminar, (Jet Magazine April 19, 1984)

I don't believe it's prejudice . I truly believe that they may not have some of the necessities to be, let's say, a field manager,. or perhaps a general manager....why are black men, or black people, not good swimmers? Because they don't have the buoyancy? "

> vice-president of player personnel for the Los Angeles Dodgers: Al Campanis. Comment made on *Nightline*, April 6, 1987

Blacks have different muscles that react in different ways

> golf professional: Jack Nichlaus. comment offered to a reporter at *The Vancouver Province* in British Columbia, when asked why there was a lack of Black golfers.

I think people are afraid to speak out on the subject. White people have to have white heroes. I myself can't equate to black heroes. I'll be truthful. I respect them, but I need white people. It's in me - and I think the Cavaliers have too many blacks.

> owner of the Cleveland Cavaliers (Professional Basketball Team): Ted Stepien, *New York Times*, Monday, December 6, 1982

In the next couple of years, the black-owned businesses will disappear. They'll all be sold to the White companies...Black consumers buy quality products... too often their Black brothers didn't do them any good

> business executive: Irving Bottner, president of Revlon's professional product division, recently made in the October 13 issue of *Newsweek*

Four Greenwich high school seniors wrote in their yearbook: "kill ALL niggERS." As reported by Karen Freifeld in Greenwich, Conn. in June, 1995

Born in San Juan, Puerto Rico on January 24, 1874, Schomburg quickly learned the importance of having an awareness of one's cultural roots. Young Puerto Rican students in the literary club to which Arthur A. Schomburg belonged were assigned books about Latin American history and the history of Puerto Rico itself. When, however, Schomburg inquired about books about his own African past, his teacher told him that no such a thing as Black history existed! "

New National Black Moniter, July 8, 1982

The late Professor William Leo Hansberry was a distinguished Africanist. While a student at Harvard, Hansberry was a pupil of Professor George A. Reisner, an eminent Egyptologist. One day when Reisner told his class that the ancient Egyptians were white people, Hansberry questioned the validity of that opinion. He mentioned the fact that the Greek historian Herodotus, visited Egypt in the fifth century B.C. and described the people of that nation as being black skinned and curly haired. Of course the professor retorted by saying that he did not consider Herodotus to be an authority on that question. The student refused to be intimidated and reasonably replied that Herodotus was an eyewitness, and Reisner, thousands of years later, was not. Hansberry had hoped to study for a doctorate in Egyptology under Professor Reisner, but after the confrontation in class, this project never materialized.

The Golden Ages of Africa, John G. Jackson, Austin, TX: American Atheist Press, 1987, p. 2

In his book, Progress and Evolution of Man in Africa:

Dr. L.S.B. Leakey wrote that: "In every country that one visits and where is drawn into a conversation about Africa, the question is regularly asked by people who should know better - mostly everyone, " But what has Africa contributed to world progress?"

In the words of Toynbee: "The Black race has not helped to create any civilization, while the Polynesian white race has helped to create one civilization, the brown race, two, the yellow race, three, the red race and the Nordic white race, four apiece, the Alpine white race, nine and the Mediterranean white race, ten" (Arnold J. Toynbee. *A Study of History*, Vol 1, p. 234. London: Oxford University Press, 1946)

"Negro, Negress (Latin *niger*: black), man, woman with black skin. This is the name given especially to the inhabitants of certain countries in Africa...who form a race of black men inferior in intelligence to the white or Caucasian race. (*New Larousse Dictionary*, 1905, p. 516)

The African Origin of Civilization: Myth or Reality, Cheikh Anta Diop, Conn.: Lawrence A Hill. Co., 1974, p. 279

As *The Journal of Blacks in Higher Education* notes, "their loathsome thesis that blacks are an inferior subset of the human race is an ancient theme deeply embedded in the body of Western intellectual thought."

African Link, "The Bell Curve and Africa," Henry M. Codjoe, Vol. 6, No. 6, 1995, p. 13

Professor Frances Cress Welsing does a brilliant analysis of the global impact of white supremacy in her book the *Isis Papers* as well as in her classic the *Cress Theory of Color*.

A *Time* magazine's article (May 17,1993) reports on the contemporary expression of the so-called "curse" as James P. Comer, a Yale University psychiatrist, points out:

"there's still a lot that says that white is more beautiful power-ful than black, that white is good and black is bad..."

At the same time Bill Cosby was reported as saying that television pro-grams continued to portray African-Americans as "living cartoons...It's the same image most of the (television) writers and producers still have of us the funny minstrel. They think of us as living cartoons. And, for the most part, that's how they draw us."

Moreover, a CBS executive was allegedly reported in Detail maga-zine's February issue (1996) as having said that Blacks watch late night television because they don't have jobs and that they don't have a long enough attention span for serious televison.

As one can seen, Noah's so-called "curse" is conveniently em-ployed (and disguised) to prove our inferiority and our "cursed-ness" throughout the various segments of American society. We will always see white people as "better than" and "superior" to us unless it can be proven otherwise. God's people vs, the "cursed" people. A man who worships another man's image as God will forever live on his knees. Worshipping white image of the Su-preme Being brings about poverty in material blessings because we can not unite because our image of God is confused and alien to us.

Better to work for and support those who look like God than those who don't and are "cursed." If you accept the image of God from others, here is how they will also portray and think of you. Because an "inferiorize" ego is constantly overwhelmed by doubts in itself, and thus it remains mentally "destabilized" and "handicap" in terms of confidence and a willingness to be self-re-liant. It will consume rather than produce. It will prefer to work and build for others rather than for itself. The deadly "curse" brings poverty of mind and spirit. We should never forget the Willie Lynch letter on how to make and keep a slave.

HOW TO MAKE A SLAVE by Willie Lynch (1712 A.D.) from the *Million Man March* as quoted by Minister Louis Farrakhan

(THE WILLIE LYNCH GUIDE TO CONTROLLING BLACK SLAVES)

Gentlemen:

While Rome used chords of wood crosses for standing human bodies along its old highways in great numbers, you are here using the tree and a rope on occasions. I caught the whiff of a dead slave hanging from a tree a couple of miles back. You are not only losing valuable stock by hangings, you are having uprisings, slaves are running away, and your crops are sometimes left in the fields too long for maximum profit.

You suffer occasional fires, your animals are killed, gentlemen, you know what your problems are; I do not need to elaborate. I am not here to enumerate your problems. I am here to introduce you to methods of solving your problems. In my bag here, I have a Fool-Proof method for controlling your Black Slaves. I guarantee everyone of you that if installed correctly, it will control the slaves for 300 years. My method is simple, any member of your family or any overseer can use it.

I have outlined a number of differences among the slaves; and I take these differences and make them bigger! I use fear, distrust, and envy for control purposes. These methods have worked on my modest plantation in the West Indies and it will work throughout the South. Take this simple list of differences and think about them.

On the top of the list is "Age" but it is there only because it starts with "A," the second is "Color or Shade," there is size, sex, intelligence, size of a plantation, attitude of owners, whether the slaves live in a valley, on a hill, East, West, North or South, have fine or coarse hair, or is tall or short. Now that you have the list of differences, I shall give you an outline of action, but before that I shall assure you that Distrust is stronger than Trust and Envy is stronger than Adulation, Respect or Admiration.

The Black Slave, after receiving this indoctrination, shall carry it on and it will become self re-fueling, self-generating for hundreds of years, maybe thousands. Don't forget you must pitch the old black male vs. the young black male, and the young black male vs. the old black male.

You must use the dark skin slave vs. the light skin slave, and the light skin slave vs. the dark skin slave. You must use the female vs. the male, and the male vs. the female. You must also have your White servants and overseers distrust all Blacks, but it is necessary that your slaves trust and depend on us (slave owners). They must love, respect, and trust only us (slave owners). Gentlemen these kits are your keys to control, use them. Have your wives and children use them, never miss an opportunity. My plan is guaranteed, and the good thing about this plan is that if used intensely for one year, the slaves themselves will remain perpetually distrustful.

This speech by Willie Lynch, a West Indies plantation owner, was referred to by Minister Louis Farrakhan in a speech given at the Million Man March on October 16, 1995 in Washington, D.C.]

Nevertheless, the "curse" cannot be removed with mere wishful thinking or empty facts only historical truth can provide the real basis for our equality with any other people on the world stage of civilization. Or else we will continue to suffer the same kind of modern historical distortions and misconceptions that relentlessly assault us in our public and religious life.

If the Egyptians persecuted the Israelites as the Bible says, and if the Egyptians were Negroes, sons of Ham, as the same Bible says, we can no longer ignore the historical causes of the curse upon Ham - despite the legend of Noah's drunkenness. The curse entered Jewish literature considerably later than the period of persecution...

The African Origin of Civilization: Myth or Reality, Cheikh Anta Diop, Conn.: Lawrence A Hill. Co., 1974, p. 5

He continues:

It is not by chance that this curse on the father of Mesraim, Phut, Kush, and Canaan, fell only on Canaan, who dwelt in a land that the Jews have coveted throughout their history...In fact, we know that the Egyptians called their country Kemit, which means "black" in their language...Hence, it is natural to find Kam in Hebrew, meaning heat, black burned. (D.P. de Pedrals, Archeologie de l'Afrique Noire, Paris, Payot, 1950, p. 27. Here he is quoting Louis J. Morie.)

That being so, all apparent contradictions disappear and the logic of acts appear in all its nudity. The inhabitants of Egypt, symbolized by their black color, Kemit on Ham of the Bible, would be accursed in the literature of the people they had oppressed. We can see that this Biblical curse on Ham's offspring had an origin quite different from that generally given it today without the slightest historical foundation.

The Black Presence in the Bible, Rev. Walter Arthur McCray, Vol. 2, Black Light Fellowship, Chicago, Illinois, 1990, p. 5

Elsewhere, he summarizes the evidence:

So, the idea of the Eastern and Western Hamites is conceived - nothing more than a convenient invention to deprive Blacks of the moral advantage of Egyptian civilization and of other African civilizations.

The African Origin of Civilization: Myth or Reality, Cheikh Anta Diop, Conn.: Lawrence A Hill. Co., 1974, p. 9

By the standard American definition of those who classify themselves as white one cannot have one-thirty-second portion of black blood. This clearly disqualifies all the ancient Egyptians as white and makes them as black as your present day African American.

Consequently, the so-called mixed race theory still does not hold up since there are about 30 million African Americans of mixed blood in America today who are definitely viewed as Black and nothing else even if we chose to ignore the truth that the ancient Egyptian were clearly Black in color with woolly hair.

In fact, their own "father of history" Herodotus gives as an eye witness account attesting to the concrete historical reality that he saw them as a Black people. This is why without knowing your history, others will forever condemn you as an inferior and will chose to take your legacy from you.

Dr. Potter Holly once wrote, "The wonderful degree of civilization, to which the Egyptians attained, has led certain anthropologists who believe in the negro's innate inferiority...[to] assigned to a branch of the Aryan (Caucasian) family the Arts and Inventions of Ancient Egypt...but this is an hypothesis, one that conflicts with both sacred and profane history." (*God and the Negro*, p. 39).

This Black Jesus, Etiese T. M. Abasika, Dallas: Essence Research Enterprises, 1994, p. 60

In the words of that eminent scholar Chancellor Williams:

"the ancient Greek and Roman historians...did not seem to know what racism is--certainly not as it developed in modern white civilization. They...simply 'told it like it was'-- Pliny, Herodotus, Diodorus, Erastosthenes, Plutarch, et al., along with the Bible--all refute the interpretations of African history by modern Caucasians..."

The Destruction of Black Civilization, Chicago, Illinois: Third World Press, 1976, p. 92-93

Indeed, what can be done in selectively creating the origins of civilization can also be done to religion with the power of definition.

Temple University's Chairman of African Studies Molefi Asante revealed that "racism in Western thought, arrogantly claims for itself the mantle of "philosophy," the highest intellectual achievement of humanity; "The Asians don't have philosophy," Asante points out. "They have 'thoughts,' Africans have 'myths.' they do not have philosophy. That belongs to the Greeks.' "

Newsweek (September 23, 1991,) "Putting Africa at the Center," p. 44

But as Dr. Cheikh Anta Diop reminds us:

Egyptian "cosmogony" as summarized here is the one attested to by the text of the pyramids (2600 B.C.), so that we may stick to sure facts meaning, to the epoch when even the Greeks did not exist in history yet, and when the Chinese and the Hindu philosophies were meaningless.

Civilization or Barbarism, New York: Lawrence Hill Books, 1981, p. 310

Most modern researchers say "there's no real question that 19th-century academics were racist and anti-Semitic," as classicist Gregory Crane of Harvard University puts it...

Which is one of the main reasons why Professor Bernal of Cornell University wrote *Black Athena* to "lessen European cultural arrogance"...

Newsweek (September 23 1991) "Out of Egypt, Greece," p. 49

A well-known European historian from Britain, Professor Basil Davidson exposes the bare facts in his book, *African Civilization Revisited*:

None of this rather fruitless argument, as to the skin color of the Ancient Egyptians before the arrival of the Arabs in the seventh century A.D., would have arisen without the eruption of modern European racism during the 1830s. It became important to the racists, then and since, to deny Egypt's African identity, Egypt's black identity, so that they could deny to Africans any capacity to build a great civilization. We should dismiss all that. What one needs to hold in mind is the enormous value and direct relevance of the Pharaonic records to Africa's remote history. (p. 50)

"Those in the Nile Valley tradition say that the late Dr. Cheikh Anta Diop, a professor at the University of Dakar in Senegal, trained in history, linguistics and other disciplines, at a symposium convened in 1974 presented evidence that Egypt was a Black civilization that few could argue with.

'...the first inhabitants of the Nile valley belonged to the black race, as defined by the research findings currently accepted by

271

specialists in anthropology and prehistory,' a summary of the UNESCO symposium, held in Cairo, states. "Professor Diop considered that only psychological and educational factors prevented the truth of this from being accepted.."

Black Issues in Higher Education, February 28,1991, p. 14

A contemporary example of this mentality is demonstrated by John Leo, columnist for *US News & World Report*, who maintains that "Ancient Egypt was a black nation" is "an unlikely claim." (November 12, 1990).

However, Dr. Diop shows through "anthropology, iconography, melanin dosage tests, osteological measurements, blood groupings, the testimony of classical writers, self- descriptive Egyptian hieroglyphs, divine epithets, Biblical eyewitnesses, linguistics and various cultural data to support the fact that...THE EGYPTIANS WERE BLACK."

The English world renowned Egyptologist Wallis Budge conceded that "The Egyptians, [were] fundamentally an African people...." (*The Gods of the Egyptians*, London: Methuen, 1904, p. 143)

Dr. Charles B. Copher of Atlanta, Georgia, one of the premier scholars on the Black presence in the Bible, argues that:

Around 1800, and related to Napoleon's invasion of Egypt in 1798, there was born the New Hamite Myth. In its origins it was designed particularly to prove that, contrary to ancient writers such as Herodotus, the ancient Egyptians, were not Blacks/Negroes...

Black Biblical Studies, Charles B. Copher, Black Light Fellowship, Chicago, Ill., 1993, p. 122

Dr. Peggy McIntosh of Wellesley College in Massachusetts suggested on *ABC* television network that when teaching children "We talk about the birth of Western civilization. Just mention - 'And, incidentally, these Egyptians were African."

"Like It Is " August 10, 1990

Just as when Paul Robeson and more recently Larry Fishburne, played Shakespearse's "*Othello*" which showed that the original

Moors of Spain were Black, so, too, when Louis Gossett Jr. played Anwat Sadat in a television documentary entitled, "Sadat" clearly illustrates, in modern terms, the African [Black] origins of the Egyptians.

In fact, African/Eden was the source from which all people flowed. Recent scientific evidence illustrates that not only are the remains of the most ancient ancestors of man to be found in Africa/Eden, but also the oldest remains of what is called "modern man" have been discovered, not in Europe or China, but in Africa.

The Original Africa Heritage Study Bible, Hope Cain Felder, ed., Nashville: Dr. James Peebles, Winston-Derek Publishers, 1993, p. xi

Declares the author of Cradles of Civilization, Egypt:

it is no longer considered acceptable to explain the rise of Egyptian "dynastic" civilization as the result of the arrival of a "master race." Indeed, during the preceding millennium Egyptian society had remained remarkably stable.

Jamomir Malek, ed., Oklahoma: University of Oklahoma Press, 1993, p. 29

Dr. Cheikh Anta Diop, the foremost modern authority on African history, in his introduction to The African Origin of Civilization, Myth or Reality, sums up the evidence on page xiv:

The Ancient Egyptians were Blacks...that Black World is the very Initiator of...Western Civilization..."

The learned German Professor A.H.L. Heeren, says that:

"Except [for] the Egyptian, there is no aboriginal people of Africa with so many claims upon our attention as the Ethiopians; from the remotest times to the present, one of the most celebrated and yet most mysterious of nations. In the earliest traditions of nearly all the more civilized nations of antiquity, the name of this distant people is found." p. 290-291

Historical Researches into the Politics intercourse, and trade of the Carthaginians, Ethiopians, and Egyptians, Vol.1, 1832, rep. ECA Associates, 1991

He adds:

"The annals of the Egyptian priests were full of them; the nations of inner Asia, on the Euphrates and Tigris, have interwoven the fictions of the Ethiopian with their own traditions...at a period equally remote, they glimmer in Greek mythology." (p. 290-291)

Such was the antiquity of Ethiopia and its brothers Egypt, Nubia and Cush; the Nile Valley Clan; the Nile Valley Brotherhood; the Nile Valley Family, those ancient primeval Black Originators of almost everything.

Quite naturally, we have a seamless thread of flowing basic logic -- The 1st Man leads to the 1st Civilization leads to the 1st Religion and finally to the 1st Bible.

Thus, the Leakeys prove the "African Origins of Man."

Then Gerald Massey in his brilliant *Book of the Beginning* states that the origin of civilization: "...has now to be sought for in Africa...

ETHIOPIA AND EGYPT PRODUCED THE EARLIEST CIVILIZATION IN THE WORLD

In fact, he adds in the same work "that the **Black Race is the most ancient** and that Africa is the primordial home."

To which Geoffrey Higgins declared that we find a Black Man and Woman "whenever we have approached the **origin of nations**. "

Count Volney had to admit that the white Europeans owe their "Arts and Sciences, and even the Use of the Spoken Word..." to the Black Man.

Then finally the forgotten African Man of the Bible the Patriarch-Prophet, Enoch the Black Ethiopian, son of Jared, father of Methuselah, grandfather of Lemach, great-grandfather of Noah and great, great-grandfather of Shem, Ham and Japhet must lead us to the African Origins of the Bible.

With all this, we have come full circle.

CONCLUSION

It is up to us to bring Enoch the Ethiopian, our African ancestor back home to us.

Except for a very small minority of brave modern European scholars, most of the others clearly realize that if any white scholar hints at the possibility of African (read Black) origins they would immediately be ostracized, ridiculed, and dismissed.

Given this as a fact how does one argue with so-called "universal, objective, rational scholarship" of the western world that still asserts that Columbus founded the American continent already inhabited by millions of aboriginals, so-called "native Americans." Or, that Egypt, as some insist, is not an African country even though it comprises the right corner of the continent. Somehow it exists mystically and mysteriously in the "Middle East" or Europe.

Or that Black People are $\frac{3}{5}$ of a man, a subhuman, a jungle-bunny, a coon or a spade as Malcolm X used to say. One who has not made any significant contribution to mankind, if we listen to the likes of an Arnold Toynebee, or Hegel.

Keeping all of this in mind, what European scholar would investigate or seek anything that even remotely implies Black origins to ancient religious writings that helped form the foundations of Western civilization.

The fact that the most significant contributions to mankind started in Africa brings no disgrace or belittlement on others. Things had to begin somewhere, it just happened in this case to be Africa. Let us all accept reality and grow.

Regarding Enoch the Ethiopian we believe that there are several reasons to hold to his "African origins:

1) From Science: It has been proven that Man originated in Africa [see Chapter "African Origins of Man"]. And if Adam is the first Man according to Scripture then he must have been Black and if Enoch is his Seventh Seed then he, too, must have been

an African. According to many scholars, writing originated in Africa. Then Enoch who is purported to have "invented writing" must have come from that continent. [see previous Chapter reference]

2) From Geography: The continent of Africa extended into the region commonly referred to today as the "Middle East", all of its inhabitants at that time must have been dark skinned. [see Weens 1995; Budge 1902; Clarke & ben-Jochannan 1991; National Geographic 1985; maps, etc]

3) From Classical and contemporary writers: They attest through eye-witness accounts that term Ethiopic [Kushite] extended to the regions commonly recognized today as the place where the Bible and the people of the Bible originated from, in the so-called "Arabian Peninsula" or (Asia Minor). The people of this area are African (Black). [See Homer, Herodotus, Strabo, Ephorus, Budge 1902, Dunston 1992, McCray 1990, Felder 1994, Copher 1993, et. al.].

4) From ethnic origins and canonization. The very fact that 1 Enoch is referred to as Ethiopic Enoch, and that the Ethiopian Church is the only one today to view it as canon, points to an Ethiopian identification. In addition, it is complete only in Ethiopic, an ancient Ethiopian language. If the First Hebrews were Black then Enoch must certainly be numbered among the first since he is only seven generations from Adam. Therefore, he, too, must have been Black.[See the Chapter "Canonization of Enoch"]

The Biblical authorities say that the principal characters of the Bible are Black as was pointed out by many independent, critical thinking, scientific-minded scholars who dare to tell the historical truth.[See McCray 1990; Dunston 1992, Felder 1994, Peoples 1994, Copher 1993, et. al.]

Not only that but the very fact that Ethiopia is known to have the most ancient Hebrews; therefore, Enoch then must have been an Ethiopian as he comes near the beginning of Biblical history. [See Father Martin de Porres, The N.Y. Times, Gascoigne].

Futhermore, the original Ethiopians, Egyptians Nubian and Ku-shite people were African (Black) people. [See The Chapter "The Common Black Origins of the Ethiopians, Egyptians, Nubians and Kushites"]

5) From Chronological (time) considerations: Based on Enoch's antiquity as Adam's Seventh Seed, the only significant presence at that time and in that region was Black or African. [See Heeren 1892, Lugard 1905, Higgins 1836, Massey 1881, Volney 1795] Ethiopia's antiquity is well documented and by making Ethiopic Enoch a canonical work it points to the fact that this ancient country is recognizing one of its native sons. Ethiopians have in fact been heralded as "the oldest; the most sacred race" and "the most just of men" before other people and nations. Add to this fact, the antiquity and reputation of the Ethiopians as declared by ancient European writers [see Homer, Diodorus, Herodotus, et. al] could only logically and objectively point to an Enoch being an Ethiopian due to his Biblical placement in time i.e. "the seventh patriarch from creation."

6) From Biblical references: Like Revelations, (His feet were like brass (Rev.1:15; 1:14); Jer et. al [see the First Hebrews as Black] All points to the African origins of the main characters in the Bible. Enoch though mentioned only briefly is, to be sure, a main character.

7) Historical and linguistic perspectives: from an objective analysis and from a critical thinking historical perspective we have the following: If the First man is Black [See Chapter "In The Beginning...We Were There"], if the First Civilization is Black [See "Founders of Civilization"], if the First Religion is African [See "African Origins of Religion"], then if Enoch is among the first of men, "the seventh patriarch from creation" what else could he have been but an African. No matter what particular ethnic label some might bestow. Therefore, it follows that the First Bible would also be of Black (African) origins. And, that the principal characters in the Bible, like Enoch, would have to be dark skinned, and of African origins, if we can believe our eyes and

mental faculties. Linguistically speaking, the Bible itself was written in the beginning in Five African languages such as Gecez, Amharic, Aramaic, Egyptian, Phoenician-Hebrew.

Carl C. Nichols argued that if you trace the languages and chronological dates you will see that Ge'ez and Egyptian is the oldest language and when the Hebrews left Egypt they were all Black, and therefore speaking these two African languages. The Hebrew language comes basically from the Phoenician tongue (another African language) of the inhabitants of the area designated as Canaan (Black People again) mixed with a few words of Ge'ez-Egyptian and it was re-named Hebrew. [Nichols 1995, see also Epilogue]

The common ancestry of the Ethiopian and the people of ancient Egypt (KMT) supports the likelihood of a linguistic connection. Therefore, Enoch must have been an African since the book in which he appears was originally written in African languages; from African sources; by Africans and is mainly about African people.

If Africa gave to the Western world "the use of the spoken word" logic would lead one to conclude that it must have provided the first religious experience as well. [See Volney 1795, Breasted 1933, Winstone 1982, Diop 1974]

Thus, First Man is Black.

First Civilization is Black.

First Religions from Black People.

First Bible from Black People.

Needless to say, before someone switched the hour glass of history to empty, our cups were full of accomplishments and outstanding achievements. We must regain our "Eldership" among the Human Family again for humanity to strive and flourish.

What fair minded American would not agree with the words of the principal speaker of the Million Man March Minister Louis Farrakhan who said, "White Supremacy must die for humanity to live." Even Pope Paul VI has declared racism "white supremacy" a sin. Put another way, how many white supremacist do you think are in Heaven?

Absolute power corrupts absolutely, the myth of white surpremacy's power has corrupted the spirit of those of European descent. White supremacy has caused them to act in ways that as Frederick Douglas said, "would disgrace a race of savages."

The demonic brutality of slavery is well docuamented by Europeans themselves. If they are ever to be freed from a legacy of murder, kidnapping, theft, discrimination, prejudice and injustice, then they must become the greatest opponents of the debilitating disease known as racism (white supremacy). Mahatma Ghandi once said, " It has always been a mystery to me how men can feel themselves honored by the humiliation of their fellow beings."

Or else, They will forever be slaves to the Satanic forces of white supremacy that make one blind, deaf, and dumb. Blind to injustice and monstrous acts of human degradation. Deaf to the cries for fairness and equity. Dumb to speak out against racist acts and institutions and deny that it even exists. And unintelligent enough to think that the color of their skin makes them "better."

To erase the stain of blood worn by those of European descent for centuries, one of their generations must be bold enough to break the grip of evil that engulfs them in the form of white supremacy. It is a very old and a very new stain on the Caucasian race. Therefore it will take those who have the courage of their abolitionist and "underground railroad" ancestors - those who really risked their lives to confront their white brethren over the wickedness of white supremacy. From them they can draw the strength and courage to do what is right. It can be a "new beginning" for those whose tradition of exploitation and enslavement is ever present to have cleansing of truth and justice. This is their challenge and opportunity. Their *actions* will speak for them.

White supremacy is engaged in actively destroying white people themselves. Hitler and Neo-Nazism is but a present manifestation of this truth. White supremacists at all levels are slaves to the evil of white supremacy, slaves to their fears and insecurities that they cannot compete fairly with others without the unjust and unfair privileges and advantages of a white skin.

By poisoning the minds of others to make them feel inferior and inadequate, they have poisoned their own minds so much so that they are poisoning their own land, water and air in the name of money and the cause of white supremacy which makes them think that they will not have to deal with the consequences of their own actions. ' As a man soweth, so shall he reap. "

Is God a white supremacist, a racist? By the very definition of a Supreme Being this is not possible. Yet, there are those who are gambling that He is. Some people act as if the Supreme Being is stupid and blind to their real intent and motives, that somehow the Most High can be fooled, conned, hoodwinked as if an All-knowing, All-present, All-powerful Reality can be "had." Now, who is the real "fool" in this belief and practice.

As for those of African descent, only our ignorance and lack of correct living can today impede our progress today. We see ourselves as less and others as more. We think being smart is white and being athletic is black. The poison pill of white supremacy has diminished our self-worth and self-esteem. We want to be anything else but black. The pill of black inferiority with the active ingredients of white supremacy has caused various degrees of blindness, deafness, dumbness and self-hatred.

For example, we reject our African roots (self-hatred) and seek the alien, grafted, artificial roots of others. We can not see that the worship of a white image of God only causes further damage to our self-concept and self-esteem (blindness). We seem paralyzed to defend ourselves or protect our interests. We need a cure but will we take it. Time will tell.

Tom Powell a self-taught scholar of prodigious wisdom and insight once said to me, "Black People suffer from the disease of FREE." Mr. Powell calls it "an invisible monster sucking the life out of the community." YET, THE COSMOS OFFERS

NOTHING FOR FREE. Hard work is the essence of any worth-while accomplishment. To be righteous, to be good is hard work. The core of our problem and the most destructive disease you can catch is the "disease of FREE, that is, wanting something for nothing." You immediately step out of the harmony of nature and are destined for failure.

"The prisons are filled with people who have misunderstood the word FREE. A burglar wanted a car or money for FREE. A man might have killed someone because he wanted the pleasure of another man's woman for FREE. A drug addict wanted intense feelings of pleasure for FREE so he steals" says Mr. Powell.

Some people stayed ungrateful all their lives because they thought everything should come to them for FREE. Enoch understood that nothing in life is FREE; therefore, he lived a righteous life for "hundreds of years," and worked so hard for it that he could "walked with God" .

Freedom and independence is NOT FREE!

For example, the Million Man March is the call of the Divine to return to the Source. A plea to return to our divine rights by offering a committed, sincere heart to change our negative thoughts and behavior. To be more like Enoch, holy enough to "walk with God."

The Grand Legacy of Enoch is transcendent. He had a heart and spirit so pure and right that God "took him up," and he was changed from an earthly being to a heavenly angel.

Enoch was the master builder of righteousness. How appropriate it is that those who gave us our first experience with civilization would provide the first example of human potential and possibilities in Scripture.

Enoch is a symbol of human possibilities that with a "holy" way of living one can attain enough perfection to "walk with God," A righteous example is Enoch for he was called "blameless."

The Africans, and humanity in general, are truly "spiritual beings having a human experience, not human beings having a spiritual experience." This is a major facet of Africa's high spiritual tradition and way of life for thousands of years. How we all live this truth will determine in large measure our own spiritual destiny. Naturally, Enoch the Ethiopian, being a child of Mother Africa, lived his whole life reflecting this REALITY. His incredible spiritual achievements serve as a testimony and a lasting monument to this Truth.

Life is a classroom full of lessons to be learned towards perfecting the spirit. To reflect that which has been made in the image and likeness of the Divine. To learn the lessons is to possess fully what is called virtues or divine ways of living. The first building lesson is patience. Enoch "walked with God" for 300 years in righteousness, that is a long time being and doing what is right. But the rewards are also great, you can get to be "taken up into heaven."

From the *Holy Bible International Version* of Genesis chapter 5 we quote the following:

> When Enoch had lived 65 years, he became the father of Methuselah, Enoch walked with God 300 years and had other sons and daughters. Altogether, Enoch lived 365 years. Enoch walked with God; then he was no more because God took him away.

Zondervan Publishing House, Mich.: 1984, p. 4

His heart was in harmony with God's will; for 'can two walk together, except they be agreed?' Amos 3:3. And this holy walk was continued for three hundred years...Enoch's faith waxed the stronger, his love became more ardent, with the lapse of centuries.

Patriarchs and Prophets, Ellen G. White, California: Pacific Press Publishing Association, 1958, p. 85

The Divine laws of "difficulties at the beginning and gradual progress" are the ones which we all must submit to. Patience helps us to persevere and overcome all trials and tribulations. One of the rarest virtues to have in abundance is the Great One called Patience.

We must become so patien that Love pervades ALL, and the rooms of Humility, Selflessness, Kindness, Gentleness, Peace are like mansions unto themselves. "...in My Father's house there are many mansions,"

Idol worship was not meant merely to be objects. Idols were originally meant to mean things like selfishness, egotism, greed, lust, envy, self-righteousness, jealousy and all the other vices in this world. Worshipping sex, money, drugs and other vices as idols was the original intent of "idol worship."

The mind and heart can become "idols." That is vehicles and carriers of evil intent and motives to exploit, abuse and manipulate people. When we worship the dark side of our spirit, we can become "idol worshippers" if our true intent is some form of wickedness. No matter how cleverly it is disguised as something else.

Seek not short cuts to spiritual development, the path is long and winding. But perseverance and patience gets you through.

Whenever you feel you are still failing the grade ask yourself have you been studying your notes? Are you reviewing your material? Have you gone for tutoring, that is, taking *good* advice.

Let your Roots of Righteousness grow deep and strong so that can weather any storm of Adversity, with Joy and Tranquillity and Thankfulness.

Enoch is the first human testimony to wearing the righteous crown of glory and blessedness among men. Yet we can all wear that crown every day, if we so chose to serve God and our fellow man in righteousness.

Seek the Good, Chose the Good; and Live that which is Good. By viewing every test and challenge in life as an opportunity to grow, and not as a roadblock or hindrance. An opportunity to grow in patience, unselfishness, love, hard work etc. all that one calls virtuous living. Not as the exception but as the norm. This the African way of our ancient ancestors.

Which is why Enoch (and we) were made in His image and likeness of God meaning living with God-like Patience, God-like-goodness, God-like Justice God-like Humility etc.

Enoch was a man of strong and highly cultivated mind and extensive knowledge; he was honored with special revelations from God; yet being in constant communion with Heaven, with a sense of the divine greatness and perfection ever before him, he was one of the humblest of men.

Patriarchs and Prophets, Ellen G. White, California: Pacific Press Publishing Association, 1958, p. 85

And yet every time we seek to live righteously expect in that same instance to be tested and challenged regarding your sincerity.

The prime ingredient to growth is a mind set with a view towards change. A willingness to change all thoughts and behavior that are not in harmony with Truth and Justice.

Not being afraid of being imperfect while striving for the perfection of spirit which Enoch realized. Not being wedded to every opinion you have as if they were ordained by God. Be open to the possibility that you may not be right about everything. Humble yourself and see another's point of view. To really change is the real challenge in life. To avoid evil and seek Good. To live it rather than talk (or read) it.

We may sometimes fall short of our goals and expectations, but the Creator looks at our heart and sincere effort more than anything else. As long as we persevere and keep trying, we are blessed.

Talking and writing about being Good is the easy part, doing it becomes the place that separates the pretenders and "the true believers."

Constant renewal and positive reinforcement helps one to remain strong and committed. Music is a great comforter when it reflects the good and has uplifting words.

You can persevere because no tests or challenge last forever "for that too shall pass." Nothing stays the same. Think: "You are too bless to be stress!" Cling to that and it can help you stay the course as well as meditating, periodic fasting, prayer, good diet, exercise and righteous thoughts. Remember none of us have arrived; we are all just getting ready.

Be introspective, look inside yourself to weed out any decadent ideas. Uprooting all thoughts not rooted in truth no matter how comfortable you are with them and they with you.

Ideas that do not help one to further, to develop, to progress. Ideas of low gratification such as egotism, wanton sex, selfishness stifle all growth. You know that which we all serve so faithfully, but which does not serve our best interests. "Blessed is the man that walketh not in the counsel of the ungodly, nor standeth in the way of sinners, nor sitteth in tthe seat of the scornful. But his delight is in the law of the Lord. Psalm 1.

Changing by giving up the low to seek the High, possessing grateful spirits, the divine qualities of Thankfulness in such a way as to say to the Most High, "anyway You bless me, I'll be satisfied," Grateful for even the dust beneath your feet. A life lived beautifully with the angels of Gratitude and Appreciation. This is how Enoch must have lived.

For what is your purpose in this world? Have you come to praise that which is higher than the Highest, and Greater than the greatest, The Divine Supreme Essence of All that is or will ever be.

"If we could paint a portrait of our life's accomplishments, what would the Almighty see?

Create your own living portrait. Is your portrait filled with love, joy and thankfulness? Meditate on the portrait of Enoch and ask yourself. What words would he have uttered? What would have been his thoughts or actions of one who has "walked with God." We have examples of goodness (perfection). So let us begin to follow the path of righteous living. Let the colors of our portrait be filled with the spectrum of faith, hope, perseverance and Divine love. Let every stroke cast a reflection of patience and gratefulness. This portrait will be so colorful that it may only be viewed with divine eyes. Remember Enoch and his divine ways of living on Earth so that he could live a life that is everlasting. Live life with joy in our hearts and then we will truly experience a brighter tomorrow." (From Njeri, one who is striving to choose the correct paint brush.)

Remember the words of Psalm 52 which our ancestors lived and practiced before the invasions of aliens and their ways of living.

"O God. Thou art my God, early will I seek thee, my soul thirsts for thee, my flesh longeth for thee in a dry and thirsty land, where no water is, to see thy power and thy glory...because of thy loving kindness is better than life, my lips shall praise thee." (Ps.52)

Great men possess divine qualities and everyone of us have the potential for greatness. According to our African tradition what really counts is greatness in one's character, someone who is God-Conscious and God-focused on a daily basis. Enoch was a living example of this.

"Guide me by the light of Thy counsel, and let me ever find rest in Thee who art my Rock and my Redeemer."

If we possess the divine attribute of Sincerity and are committed to it, the Divine Supreme Being will move to assist us in ways we cannot even imagine both subtle and profound. "God is our refuge and strength, a very present help in trouble."

We are all "children of God" made in the image and likeness of the Most High. As Paul wrote to the Corinthians, "Do you not know that you are God's temple and that God's Spirit dwells in you?" (1 Cor 3:16)

Thus, there is something of the divine spirit in each of us. Therefore we should keep divine, holy thoughts as our constant companions because "...as a man thinketh so is he."

We can begin to follow Enoch's lead to seek perfection by righteous living and by forsaking the unrighteous..

We must become Temple builders as shown in the work of Enoch.

A more explicit expression of the divine Temple idea of those times appears in the pseudepigraphal Book of Enoch, that has certain affinities with the Dead Sea scrolls and Jubilees. In it Enoch speaks of the ultimate replacement of the 'old House'- the man-made Temple - by the God-made Temple, a 'new house greater and loftier that the first,' which would set 'up in place of the first'.

The Temple Scroll, Yigael Yadin, New York: Random House, 1985, p. 114

This new Temple must be built from within. All the old bricks of selfishness, greed, lust, killing, lying, cheating etc. from the "man-made Temple" must go to make way for the holy mortar of the "God-made Temple" built by the divine spirit of righteous living.

Enoch, like Christ, had a great concern for his fellow man and for social justice. He also revealed his African value system and ancestry in the "Beatitudes of Enoch" from 2 Enoch which "conclude with praise of a number of moral virtues:

6. Blessed is he who fears God and serves him. And you, my children, learn to bring gifts to the Lord, that he may enjoy life.

7. Blessed is he who judges a judgment justly to the widow and orphan, 8and helps everyone that is wronged, clothing the naked with garments and giving bread to the hungry.

10. Blessed is he who turns back for the changeable path ands walks along the straight path.

11. Blessed is he who sows the seeds of righteousness, for he shall reap sevenfold.

12. Blessed is he in whom is truth, that he may speak truth to his neighbor.

13. Blessed is he in whose mouth is mercy and gentleness.

14. Blessed is who understands the Lord's works and glorifies the Lord God."

Faith and Piety in Early Judaism, George W.E. Nickelsburg and Michael E. Stone, Philadelphia: Fortress Press, pp. 105-6

We all can be messengers of righteousness and servants of the Most High. By living a life of example, not talk but action, and actions done quietly without fanfare. This is our traditional African way. Before aliens taught us how to read from their books instead of living from our high examples and traditions.

We come from a high spiritual tradition that holds virtuous character as sacred and God-like. The man or woman who possess the divine attributes of patience, sincerity, unselfishness and goodness were honored and respected as were their families.

Africa's ancient high spiritual way of living reflects the best in the so-called major "western" religions.

In Africa, they say, "words are free." Meaning a man's greatness is measured by his actions and his example, not merely through his mouth. Some people "love their words," however, speaking or writing about greatness does not make one great.

Here is an ancient African example of how a person was supposed to act and how we praise the Most High through our way of living.

"This is from the Negative Confession in the 125th chapter of the most famous religious book of the ancient Egyptians -*The Book of the Dead*:

" 'Glory to thee, O thou Great God, thou Lord of truth and justice! says the dead man, when brought into the presence of the eternal judge. 'Lo! I have defrauded no man of his dues. I

288

have not oppressed the widow. I have not borne false witness. I have not been slothful. I have broken faith with no man. I have starved no man. I have slain no man. I have not enriched myself by unlawful gains. I have not given short measure of corn. I have not tampered with the scales... I have not turned away the food from the mouths of the fatherless. Lo! I am pure! I am pure!' "

Pharaohs, Fellahs and Explorers, Amelia B. Edwards, New York: Harper & Bros., 1891, pp. 232-3

Sounds familiar? It should. Because we are children of the Most High, we can ascend to our higher, more divine (Self), through sincere and persistent spiritual work.

In short, to live a saintly life like our shining example, Enoch. Like Christ, Enoch was, so that we could be.

...in the case of Enoch, God declares "that He is, and that He is a rewarder of them that diligently seek Him." Hebrews 11:6. He shows what He will do for those who keep His command-ments. Men were taught that it is possible to obey the law of God; that even while living in the midst of the sinful and cor-rupt, they were able by the grace of God, to resist temptation, and become pure and holy.

Patriarchs and Prophets, Ellen G. White, California: Pacific Press Publish-ing Association, 1958, p. 88

We can gather in "holy" fellowship "If my people come together in my name and humble themselves..." and see that there is something of us in each of our fellow human beings who walk along the path of divine light and righteousness.

As our Great Ancestor Enoch would said to the Most High: "Thy words are like a lamp unto my feet and a light unto my path."

EPILOGUE

THE STRUGGLE FOR AN ENGLISH PROTESTANT BIBLE
THE BATTLE OF LANGUAGES

*RACISM (WHITE SUPREMACY) CAN EVEN MANIFEST ITSELF against itself as in the case of the struggle for an English Protestant Bible, there was a war over languages wage between the northern and southern Europeans. It was over 'languages rights'. This conflict took over 2 centuries before it was concluded. The white Protestants fought that long to get a bible in their own language from their 'darker' southern brethren, the Greeks and Italians (Romans). Just as now, it has taken Black People over 3000 years to get its first modern Black Bible, the Africentric Bible.

The dark southern Europeans were the first to control Europe and the lighter Northern Europeans wrested control from them. Thus you had the light (whiter) North seizing power from the darker white from the South. European racism turned within itself, again based on skin color. This is still being practiced today in Euro-America. Southern and eastern Europeans are still not considered as superior as the white Anglo-Saxon, the German Teutonic, or even the blond-haired Scandinavian.

The northern European considers the southern European less white, more dark (more Black). Therefore, a threat to whites through "genetic annihilation." Today the northern European Teutonic, Aryan Nordic white consider themselves to be superior to the southern European Spanish, Italians, Greeks, Slavic, eastern European and Semites.

This is white supremacy played by whites against other whites.

Because the southern Europeans are closer to "Africa and Asia," they are likely to acquire their darker color through racial mixing with blacks or other non-whites, browns.

Its beliefs and practices laid the foundation for the best known white supremacist in history, Adolph Hitler and his Aryan superiority by casting other whites as non-Aryans, therefore, inferior. That was, Hitler's "gift" to Europe and fellow white supremacists, World War II and the Jewish Holocaust. Intelligent people must learn from history, or suffer the consequences. If not for moral reasons, then for plain, old common sense and enlightened self-interest, let's find another way to mutually co-exist if not in love, then in respect. The other alternatives can become very destructive.

The following is from an unpublished manuscript by Carl Conrad Nichols, historian and scholar. Printed with permission.

A SHORT HISTORY OF THE ENGLISH BIBLE BY CARL C. NICHOLS

THE AFRICAN-EDENIC ORIGIN AND DEVELOPMENT OF THEENGLISH LANGUAGE BIBLE

The origin of the English Bibles of today can be traced to a time when men, under the divine inspiration of God, first wrote the books of the Bible. This word of God was transmitted from generation to generation by handwritten copies and by word-of-mouth. As men began to realize how valuable these teachings were, attempts were made to collate these teachings into a single comprehensive book. Some of what we now know as the Old Testament (O.T.) was originally written in Egyptian and later translated into Hebrew and the New Testament (N.T.) in Greek and Aramaic-Syriac. Since no printing press existed until 1450 AD, all of the original compilations of the Bible were done by hand. The history and development of the English Bible can be divided into 3 sections; ancient versions in other languages, early English versions, and New English versions (since 1901). Brief descriptions of the significant versions in those time periods follows.

A Bible "Family Tree" diagram is also included at the start of this historical section.

Ancient Versions in other Languages

A. The Original Manuscripts (1250 BC - 150 AD) were written in 5 ancient African-Edenic languages. The Books of Genesis, Exodus, Leviticus, Numbers, Deuteronomy, Joshua and Job were originally written in Egyptian or Ge^cez-Amharic. The descendants of the Hebrews that conquered Canaan with Joshua adopted the Phoenician language circa 1000 BC and renamed it Hebrew. The rest of the O.T. and N.T. were written in Aramaic and Ge^cez. Everything then was first translated into Hebrew by the Holy Scribes circa 850 BC.

B. The Septuagint Version (285 BC) — This was a translation of the Old Testament Hebrew Scriptures into Greek. Probably done in Alexandria, Egypt.

C. The Samaritan Pentateuch (Ca. 250 BC) — A copy of the Hebrew text done in Samaritan characters. (The Torah)

D. The Dead Sea Scrolls (200 BC-68 AD) were discovered in 1947 in a series of caves in Jordan. They were deciphered and translated from Aramaic and Hebrew into English. Some of it (5 books) were written in the Original Languages ("Egyptian or Ethiopic"). (The 5 Lost Books are: 1. ENOCH, 2. JUBILEES, 3. LEVI, 4. SIRACH and 5. TOBIT.)

E. The Peshito or Syriac (330 AD) — A manuscript that contained the Greek Bible. It was purchased from, Russia in 1933 by Great Britain and is now housed in the British Museum. (The O.T. & N.T.)

F. The Codex Vaticanus (340 AD) — This manuscript is currently housed in the Vatican library in Rome. It originally contained the whole Bible, but parts have been lost. (The O.T. & N.T.)

G. The Vulgate (400 AD) — A Roman Catholic scholar in Bethlehem by the name of Jerome translated the entire Bible into Latin. This Bible became the standard in the Catholic church for well over 1,000 years. (First R.C. Bible)

Early English Versions

All of the earliest attempts at translating the Bible into English were fragmented. For example, Bishop Aldhelm of Sherbourne translated the Psalms into Old English around 709 A.D. Venerable Bede, a monk at Jarrow, translated a portion of the Gospel of John. By 900 AD all of the Gospels and most of the Old Testament had been translated into Old English.

1. John Wycliffe (1380) — John Wycliffe was the first to plan a complete English translation of the Bible from the Latin. His translation was based on the Latin Vulgate. He completed the New Testament prior to his death, and his friends completed the work after his death. (Incomplete)

PRINTING PRESS INVENTED-1450

2. William Tyndale (1525-1530) — Driven from England by persecution, William Tyndale, shared Wycliffe's desire to produce a Bible that common English-speaking people could understand. Using the Latin Vulgate and other ancient sources, Tyndale was able to translate the New testament and Pentateuch before he was martyred. (Incomplete)

3. Miles Coverdale (1535) — A friend of Tyndale's Coverdale was able to publish a complete Bible. It is generally believed Coverdale used Tyndale's work in producing his New Testament. This Bible was done to honor King Henry the VIII. (First Complete English Bible) (50% R.C. & 50% Protestant)

4. Matthews Bible (1537) — Despite the name, it is widely accepted that a friend of Tyndale, John Rogus, did most of the work on this Bible. Based largely on Tyndale's previous work, it also contains evidence of Coverdale's work as well. This might well be considered an updated Tyndale Bible. (60% Protestant)

5. The Great Bible (1539) — This Bible takes its name from its great physical size. Based on the Tyndale, Coverdale, and Matthews Bibles, it was used mainly in churches. Often chained to a reading desk in a church, people would come to listen as a minister read from the Great Bible. (70% Protestant)

6. The Geneva Bible (1560) — Produced in Geneva by scholars who had fled persecution in England under Queen Mary, this Bible was based not only on the Great Bible, but also on the other English translations of that day. Though very scholarly, it was a popular Bible because of its small size. (80% Protestant)

7. The Bishops Bible (1568) – This was a revision of the Great Bible and Geneva Bible done under the direction of the Archbishop of Canterbury during the reign of Elizabeth. (90% Protestant)

8. Douay-Rheims Bible (1582-1610) – The New Testament was published in Rheims in 1582 and the Old Testament in Douay in 1610. A revision of the Latin Vulgate, this has become the generally accepted English Version for the Roman Catholic Church. (First Complete Revised R.C. Bible)

9. King James Version, KJV (1611) – The most popular translation ever produced, this Bible was done during the reign and at the urging of King James the I of England. 47 scholars, divided into 6 groups, worked on this translation. Based largely on the Bishop's Bible, many Hebrew and Greek texts were also studied as well as all other available English translations, to insure the best results. By choosing men of many different theological and educational backgrounds, it was hoped individual prejudices of the translators could be minimized. Printed in a handy size and in clear type, the KJV was supposed to please clergy and congregation alike. Despite initial resistance, the KJV became and still is the largest selling translation of the Bible. (First Complete E.P. B. - 100%)

10. Revised Version (1881-1884) – Designed to be a revision of the KJV, the Revised Version, had the advantage of being able to access some of the ancient manuscripts. Although this revision was sponsored by the Church of England, many American scholars were invited to participate.

New English Versions (1901 to Present)

11. American Standard Version, ASV (1901) – This revision of the Revised Version incorporates many of the readings first suggested by the American members of the Revision committee of 1881-1885.

12. Complete Bible: An American Translation (1939) – Often referred to as the Goodspeed version, this translation was done by Edgar J. Goodspeed and J.M. Powis Smith. Using as many ancient texts as possible, Smith and Goodspeed produced a very readable and yet accurate translation. Also included in this translation was the Apocrypha.

13. Revised Standard Version, RSV (1952) – The National Council of Churches of Christ procured the copyright to the 1901 ASV Bible in the 1920's. Work began on a revision to the ASV, but

was abandoned in favor of an entirely new translation. Since many more Hebrew and Greek manuscripts were available to these scholars than were available in 1901, the RSV is considered to be much more accurate.

14. New Testament in Modern English (1958) — First published in 1958 and revised in 1973, this translation done by British writer J.B. Phillips is one of the best readings of the New Testament. It is published today by MacMillan Publishers of New York.

15. Berkley Version (1959) — This Modern English Version was done under the direction of Dr. Gerrit Verkuyl. Dr. Verkuyl translated the New Testament from the Greek, himself. The Old Testament was translated by a committee of 20 scholars with Dr. Verkuyl overseeing the project. Although this was a very good translation, it never has been widely accepted or used.

16. Amplified Bible (1965) — This Modern English Version was sponsored by the non-profit Lockman Foundation of California. Committees of Hebrew and Greek scholars tried to pay particular attention to the true translation of key words in the ancient texts. By bracketing explanatory words or phrases directly in the page for the other helps. A very popular Bible, the bracketing poses a problem for simple reading of the text. Currently this Bible is available in either KJV or in a parallel with other translations and is published by Zondervan Corporation of Grand Rapids, Michigan.

17. Jerusalem Bible (1966) — Basically a Roman Catholic translation, this Bible was originally a multivolume translation done in French at the Ecole Biblique et Archeologique in Jerusalem. Using all available sources including the Dead Sea Scrolls, this translation also included extensive scholarly notes. In the English translation, the original documents were again used with references made to the original French translation. The Jerusalem Bible also includes the Apocypha. Although the notes are strongly Roman Catholic, the translation itself is relatively non-sectarian. (Second Completed Revised R.C. Bible)

The Jerusalem Bible is published by Doubleday Publishers of Garden City, New York.

18. **New Testament: A New Translation** (1968-1969) — Translated by William Barclay in England, this translation is neither technical nor difficult. The problem with this Bible is the extensive views in the text. To properly use this translation, another Bible should be available for comparison.

19. **New English Bible, NEB** (1970) — A committee of scholars from the leading denominations of England, Scotland, Wales, and Ireland, cooperating with the Universities of Cambridge and Oxford, was to produce a new translation from the Hebrew and Greek. This Bible was to be used as an authoritative version along side the KJV. Due to the NEB's rather free use of the English language, many verses of scripture become almost paraphrases rather than translations. The Apocrypha is included in the NEB. Since the NEB often uses unfamiliar British expressions, this Bible has not received wide acceptance in America. The NEB is jointly published by Cambridge and Oxford University presses.

20. **New American Bible, NAB** (1970) — This Roman Catholic translation originally came directly from the Latin Vulgate. The Catholic Biblical Association of America compared this translation to the Hebrew and Greek manuscripts then available. The 3 volume Old Testament and single volume New Testament were then combined into a single volume. Although some Protestant translators helped on this project, this is still basically a Roman Catholic Bible. (Third Complete Revised R.C. Bible)

21. **New American Standard, NAS** (1971) — The Lockman Foundation of La Habra, California (see Amplified Bible) set out to produce the "most technically accurate translation of the Bible possible." Partially because of their dissatisfaction with the RSV's revision of the 1901 American Standard Version, the Lockman Foundation chose to use the best Greek and Hebrew texts available to revise to ASV. Though many conservative scholars consider this to be the most accurate translation available, because of

the NAS's desire for technical accuracy it is not the most readable of the modern translations.

22. Living Bible, LB (1974) – This is the work of one man, Kenneth N. Taylor. Not a translation in the true sense, Mr. Taylor set out to produce a paraphrase of the ASV Bible using the words and terms his children could readily understand. After founding Tyndale House Publishing, Mr. Taylor then expanded the availability of the LNB to include study Bibles and cassettes. The current Bible entitled "The Book" is essentially the LNB version.

23. Today's English Version, TEV (1976) – Often referred to as the "Good News Bible," this was a project sponsored by the American Bible Society to produce a Bible in English for people whose primary language is not English. Mr. Robert G. Bratcher did the work on the New Testament, and it was published in 1966. The Society then continued the work to include the Old Testament. Although particular attention was directed toward accuracy, the translators sometimes sacrificed this accuracy for readability. Due to the TEVs very up-to-date language and in many cases some modern pop art illustrations, it has become a popular edition for teenagers.

24. New International Version, NIV (1978) – The New York Bible Society sponsored this translation of the Bible. A committee was formed to search world-wide for Bible scholars from colleges, universities, and seminaries that would represent varied backgrounds and denominations. Each book of the Bible was assigned to a different team of scholars, who then used the best available Hebrew, Aramaic, and Greek texts to do the actual translation. Additional committees checked and re-checked the translations for accuracy as well as understandability. This combination of accuracy and readability has propelled the NIV to the number 2 spot in Bible sales behind the KJV. Zondervan Publishing of Grand Rapids, Michigan, owns the rights to the NIV Bible.

25. New King James Version, NKJV (1982) – Thomas Nelson Bible Publishers and the International Trust for Bible Studies co-sponsored this update of the 1611 KJV Bible. 119 scholars worked on this project to make the KJV version more accurate and readable and yet maintain the grace and beauty of the original KJV text. Generally, the translators used the best available texts in their work, but rather than assuming the oldest was the most accurate, they chose to use the texts found most often in the ancient writings. While not as popular as the old KJV or NIV versions, the NKJV consistently remains in the top 5 best selling Bible versions in the United States.

26. Revised English Bible, REB (1989) – Under the auspices of the Universities of Oxford and Cambridge, a committee of leading Bible scholars revised and updated the New English Bible. This was the first major revision of the New English Bible since its release in 1970. Particular attention was paid to archaic words, phrases, and sentence structure. This re-examination was done by referring to the most current manuscripts, commentaries, and exegesis.

27. New Revised Standard Version, (NRSV) 1990 – This Bible was released in late 1990 and culminated 15 years of work by a special committee of scholars. This committee was under the sponsorship of the Division of Education and Ministry of the National Council of Churches. The original Revised Standard Version and the New Revised Standard Version can trace their roots to the King James Version. While maintaining the tradition of the KJV the New Revised Standard Version aimed for accuracy rather than simply paraphrasing. It can then be considered a literal translation. The revision committee was chaired by Professor Bruce Metzger of the Princeton Theological Seminary. Mr. Metzger's instructions were to introduce only changes as "were warranted on the basis of accuracy, clarity, euphony, and current English language usage."

The First Modern Black Bible
(KJVA 1993 A.D.)

This Bible Begins The Struggle To De-Colonize The So-Called Black Christian Churches, (mentally) And <u>Free</u> Them From <u>Eurocentric Lies; And (White Racist)</u> Mental Domination!

THE FIRST MODERN BLACK BIBLE
EVER PUBLISHED IN THE ENGLISH SPEAKING WORLD!

Our Bible | **Africentric**

28. The Original African Heritage Study Bible, AHB-KJVA (1993) – This Bible is basically an authorized KJV done from an Africentric point of view. This Bible sets out to tell the whole truth and correct all of the misinterpretations, mistranslations, and misrepresentations of all African-Edenic characters in the original KJV of 1611.

This Bible says that Africa-Eden was the Stage or Continent in which the Old Testament and Jesus Christ's Gospel took place and that all of the characters in this human drama of history were of African-Edenic descent. Meaning that from Abraham to Moses and all of the Prophets of the Old Testament to Jesus Christ and all of his <u>Original Disciples</u> were people of African-Edenic descent (<u>Black</u> or <u>Brown</u>). Egyptians, Ethiopians, Nubians, Hebrew Israelites, Babylonians, Canaanites, Phoenicians, etc.

After nearly a decade of hard work, research, cross-examinations, observations, analysis and deductions, this Bible was completed on July 30, 1993. It was published by James C. Winston Publishing Co. of Nashville, Tennessee. Rev. Dr. Cain Hope Felder, Ph.D. is the, General Editor and Dr. James W. Peebles, Ph.D. is the Publisher and Associate Editor. Some of the Historical Contributors to this Bible are as follows: Dr. Shaleak Ben Yehuda, Dean, Institute of Prophets, Jerusalem, Israel; Dr. Molefi Kete Asante, Ph.D., Dr. Cheikh Anta Diop, Ph.D., Dr. Yosef ben Jochannan, Ph.D., Dr. Ivan Van Sertima, Ph.D. and many other great scholars.

WHAT IS THE PURPOSE OF THE AFRICAN HERITAGE BIBLE? THE PURPOSE OF THIS BIBLE IS THREEFOLD!

1.   To replace (25) million Eurocentric (White Bibles) that are now in use in Black homes and So-Called Black Christian Churches. These White Bibles are mentally crippling and destroying our people, and has been for a very long time!

2.   To De-Colonize the So-Called Black Christian Churches (MENTALLY), by removing all White icons, images, frescoes, murals, pictures, paintings, stainglass, statues, etc. from them and replacing them with historically correct Black ones, or not replacing them at all!

3.   To stop all Black Preachers from teaching WHITE SUPREMACY to their BLACK CONGREGATIONS. They have pictures and paintings in their Churches of WHITE JESUS, and they teach Black people that JESUS IS GOD! This is WHITE SUPREMACY being taught indirectly, and this cripples Black children for life!! ENOCH, ABRAHAM, MOSES, JOSHUA, ELIJAH AND JESUS WERE BLACK HEBREWS! They were born, raised and died in Northeast Africa-Eden. History bears witness to this fact!

Index